History, Culture and the Indian City

Rajnarayan Chandavarkar's sudden death in 2006 was a massive blow to the study of the history of modern India, and the public tributes that have appeared since have confirmed an unusually sharp sense of loss. Dr Chandavarkar left behind a very subsantial collection of unpublished lectures, papers and articles, and these have now been assembled and edited by Jennifer Davis, Gordon Johnson and David Washbrook. The appearance of this collection will be widely welcomed by large numbers of scholars of Indian history, politics and society. The essays centre around three major themes: the city of Bombay, Indian politics and society, and Indian historiography. Each manifests Dr Chandavarkar's hallmark historical powers of imaginative empirical richness, analytic acuity and expository elegance, and the volume as a whole will make both a major contribution to the historiography of modern India, and a worthy memorial to a very considerable scholar.

History, Culture and the Indian City

Essays by

Rajnarayan Chandavarkar

CAMBRIDGE
UNIVERSITY PRESS

CAMBRIDGE UNIVERSITY PRESS
Cambridge, New York, Melbourne, Madrid, Cape Town, Singapore,
São Paulo, Delhi

Cambridge University Press
The Edinburgh Building, Cambridge CB2 8RU, UK

Published in the United States of America by Cambridge University Press,
New York

www.cambridge.org
Information on this title: www.cambridge.org/9780521768719

© Rajnarayan Chandavarkar 2009

First published 2009

Printed in the United Kingdom at the University Press, Cambridge

A catalogue record for this publication is available from the British Library

Library of Congress Cataloguing in Publication data
Chandavarkar, Rajnarayan.
History, culture and the Indian city : essays / by Rajnarayan Chandavarkar.
    p.   cm.
Includes bibliographical references and index.
ISBN 978-0-521-76871-9 (hardback)
1. India – History.   2. India – Social conditions.   3. Bombay (India) –
History.   4. Bombay (India) – Social conditions.   I. Title.
DS437.C484   2009
954 – dc22   2009019729

ISBN 978-0-521-76871-9 hardback

To Sumana Chandavarkar who gifted to Raj his intellectual curiosity, his warmth, his love of Bombay and so much else besides

Contents

Acknowledgements

A special debt of gratitude is owed to Gordon Johnson. It was Gordon's idea to produce this collection of essays, that are either unpublished or that deserve to be brought before a wider audience. And it was through Gordon's unstinting efforts that the project has come to fruition. Many others have made invaluable contributions to producing this volume. Steve Tolliday used his good judgement on the selection of the essays reproduced here. Kevin Greenbank gave unstintingly of his time and his intelligence to prepare the manuscript for Cambridge University Press. Doug Haynes commented on the manuscript. Richard Fisher at Cambridge University Press helped to smooth the path of this manuscript through to publication.

A number of individuals read and commented on the Introduction: Orlando Figes, Raj's dear friend and for a time his colleague at Trinity College; Eleanor Newbigin, Raj's graduate student, who is keeping Raj's legacy alive at Trinity; Andrew Larcombe, Raj's cricketing chum and one of the first friends he made upon his arrival in England; Susan Penny-backer who, together with a host of others, helped to make the period during which Raj wrote his PhD intellectually stimulating and who remained a pal ever since; Humeira Iqtidar who, together with Justin Jones, ensures that the Centre of South Asian Studies remains on the cutting edge of research into the subcontinent; again Justin, who with Kevin Greenbank organized a conference in 2007 which brought together many of Raj's graduate students from around the globe and demonstrated the scope of Raj's intellectual inheritance and the lasting respect of his students; Ornit Shani, another dear friend who was instrumental in securing the manuscripts which go to make up this volume; and Steve Tolliday, old friend and companion in undergraduate cricket and so much else.

Many other individuals have offered their support to this book, including Malhar and Janak Nabar and, of course, Sumana Chandavarkar. Thanks too should go to all Raj's graduate students, who kept him young and engaged even while costing him his hair and regularly driving him to distraction.

If this book will help ensure that Raj's invaluable contribution to historical study continues, so too will the work of all those he touched. Foremost among these are indeed his many graduate students, spread over the globe and producing important work of their own. Raj held his graduate students with deep affection and they him.

Finally, a special thanks must go to Anil Seal who drew Raj into the study of Indian history and steadfastly supported him throughout his academic career.

JENNIFER DAVIS
DAVE WASHBROOK

Publisher's note

With one exception, these essays were selected from a very substantial corpus of unpublished, semi-published and unfinished papers left by Dr Chandavarkar at the time of his death. The apparatus of each essay should be internally consistent, but no attempt has been made to impose any sort of uniform style or presentation, and there are inevitable substantive and bibliographic gaps. Each essay remains, we hope, true to the author's original intentions.

Introduction

The originality and the humanity of Rajnarayan Chandavarkar's work, which infuse the essays contained in this volume, may be traced in some measure to his own experience as an Indian in England as well as to the intellectual milieu in which he found himself during his formative undergraduate and postgraduate years in Cambridge. These essays also reflect his enduring love of storytelling.

By all accounts, not least his own, Raj had an idyllic, big-city childhood in Bombay in the 1950s and 1960s. In 1971, he won a British Council scholarship to study for two years at Lancing College. He claimed that, for him, the great attraction of Lancing was that it had a particularly impressive cricket field, was close to the Sussex County Cricket Ground and was in reachable distance of Lords.[1] After Lancing, he spent a further five years as a student at Cambridge University where he obtained a BA and then a PhD. He went on to research fellowships at Trinity College and the Centre for South Asian Studies and then to a lectureship in Indian History.

It was Raj's spirit of adventure (and his love of cricket) that sent him to England. And then the trajectory of a distinguished academic career which kept him there. To understand his work, it is first important to understand that he never intended to leave India for good; and that on his frequent trips to India and to his beloved Bombay he always saw himself as an exile, though by happenstance rather than by choice, coming home. It was this love of both the country and city of his birth which spurred Raj's research and which shines through much of his writing.

When it came to Bombay, Raj was neither selective in his affections, whether it be of workers in Bombay's mills, the fishermen of the Worli slum or the inhabitants of the gracious mansions on Malabar Hill, nor was he uncritical of the political and economic interests which were responsible for their existence or, in the case of the mill districts, their decline. Coming from a family which, both before and after Independence,

---

[1] Information from Andrew Larcombe, Lancing, 1968–73.

had a distinguished record of public service, Raj regretted the loss of the idealism which had inspired some of the best and brightest Indians to dedicate their lives to creating a secular and egalitarian state. But he was also intrigued by the effects of the liberalizing of India's economy which resulted in the great show of conspicuous consumption to be found today in the high-rises, the supermarkets, the clogged roads of Bombay and the society pages of *The Times of India*. And which exist alongside the enduring poverty of much of the city's inhabitants.

Raj's refusal in his work to employ fixed categories, such as class, caste, race and culture, to explain human action at both the individual and the social level also arose, in some measure, from his personal experience of such labelling. Although an Indian, he was hard put to identify any essential 'Indianness' which might unite the inhabitants of the subcontinent, let alone his own family or the millions of other inhabitants of Bombay. Conversely, neither did he recognize an essential 'Britishness' from which he might be forever excluded. Thus, he wrote in 1990, about the Empire builders in India:[2]

To suggest that the history of the sub-continent since the mid-18th century primarily consisted of a continuing clash between British values and Indian tradition is to flatten and distort the subject. At one level, the very notion that there was a single, consistent interpretation of British values is scarcely plausible and it is hard to imagine how some essence of Britishness might be identified or distilled. Moreover, its purveyors in India were usually unlikely agents. Many merchants, officers and even civil servants were drawn from marginal groups in British society, often from the Celtic fringe, sometimes from social and political outgroups seeking advancement through the Colonial Service, not infrequently from the ranks of adventurers and misfits who found outdoor relief, moral as well as material, in the Empire. They were out of step by a generation with the moods and fashions of the Mother Country and their disappointment with and alienation from a world which had changed utterly beyond their fond recall. On the other hand, the notion of an undifferentiated, unchanging Indian tradition in a land of innumerable languages, almost every faith known to man and every form of social organisation known to anthropology, from hunter-gatherers to urban working classes, from nomadic pastorialists to suave industrialists, ought to stupefy the imagination.

Indeed, if Raj loved but did not idealize India, the same might be said of his relationship with Britain. It is true that his description of British society as experienced by the increasing number of subcontinental

---

[2] 'India for the English', a review of Penderel Moon, *The British Conquest and Dominion of India* (London: Duckworth, 1983), Geeta Mehta, *Raj* (London: Cape, 1989) and Trevor Royle, *The Last Days of the Raj* (London: Joseph, 1989), *London Review of Books*; reprinted in *The Times of India Review of Books*, 1, 1, August/September 1990, 66–7.

visitors in the 1920s and 1930s as one characterized by 'lengthening dole queues and tawdry suburbs, its flying ducks and spotted dicks, its dreary pubs and weekly baths' might in some way mirror his own experience of fetching up at an English public school in the 1970s.[3] Nonetheless he also recognized and enjoyed the cosmopolitanism of its cities, the openness of its scholarship and the lack of any deadening sense of an essential Britishness which our present politicians are so anxious to revive (or, in truth, as Raj would have argued, invent).

Raj came to his studies in Cambridge at a time when 'social history' was accepted by many historians across the world as the most fruitful and engaging approach to an understanding of the past. Often termed 'history from below' because it eschewed the minutiae of high politics for descriptions of the quotidian experience of the 'common' people, it would be wrong to say, as some have argued, that it was history with the politics removed.[4] It is true that on its margins social history could lapse into antiquarianism by focusing simply on some aspect of popular culture divorced from the larger forces which might have shaped it.[5] However, the best social history, including that written by Raj himself, recognized not only the extent to which agencies of the state shaped social relations but also how at certain moments even the most marginal or powerless social groups might themselves circumscribe the actions of the state. Thus although Raj was sometimes described as a labour historian, that was no more an apt description of his work than if he were referred to as a historian of the state or indeed of capitalism, since in his view, to understand one, it was necessary to understand all.[6]

For those who like Raj came of age as historians in the 1970s and 1980s, Cambridge University provided a particularly rich seam of scholarship. On the one hand, the university boasted some of the best 'traditional' historians of their day, perhaps most notably Henry Pelling and Sir Geoffrey Elton, whose work, although divided by time and ideology, examined the links between political institutions and governance.[7] In the field of imperial history, the university also had a roster of influential

---

[3] *Ibid.*, 67.
[4] See, for example, Miles Taylor, 'The Beginnings of Modern British Social History?', *History Workshop Journal*, 43, Spring 1997, 155–76.
[5] Which might explain why, for some historians, the step from social history to cultural history was an easy one to take.
[6] Thus, Raj's first monograph was entitled *The Origins of Industrial Capitalism in India: Business Strategies and the Working Classes in Bombay* (Cambridge University Press: 1994).
[7] For Pelling, see *The Origin of the Labour Party, 1880 to 1900* (Oxford: Clarendon Press, 1954) and for Elton see *The Tudor Revolution in Government* (Cambridge University Press: 1953).

historians, including Eric Stokes,[8] Jack Gallagher[9] and Anil Seal, who supervised Raj's PhD.[10] In particular, Gallagher and Seal were credited with initiating a particular approach to Indian and indeed imperial history, which has come to be labelled as the 'Cambridge School'. A central assumption of the Cambridge School was that Indian nationalism was the product of elite Indians' reaction to shifts in colonial policy. Nationalist ideas and ideology were thus understood as little more than a facade for power struggles between colonial officials and wealthy and powerful Indians, but also within this group of Indian elites.[11] It is certainly possible to detect in Raj's work the influence of the Cambridge School. Thus, Raj took the view that colonial discourse and the discourse of Indian elites both before and after Independence did share a common concern. However, by contrast with the Cambridge School, Raj identified this concern as reaching beyond the mere question of who would handle the levers of state power. Instead he argued that the concern which the colonial state and its Indian successors shared in common was the need to discipline labour.[12] Hence, it should not be surprising, as Raj argued, that the Indian elites in the run-up to Independence and beyond characterized the working population much as it had been characterized by the colonial state, as marked by political volatility, indiscipline and sectionalism, and that they used key colonial institutions, most notably the police and the army, to discipline workers, often more brutally than had been the case under colonial rule.[13]

If the Cambridge School influenced to some extent Raj's characterization of the Indian state, he nonetheless took its assumptions in a wholly original direction. Indeed, to a great extent the originality of his work lay not simply in his willingness to reinterpret historical accounts of the Indian state in its transition from colonialism to independence, but also to reinterpret accounts of English industrialization, social relations and political discourse in light of his own discoveries from Indian history.

---

[8] Eric Stokes, *The English Utilitarians in India* (Oxford University Press: 1959).

[9] Alice Denny, Ronald Robinson and John Gallagher, *Africa and the Victorians* (London: Macmillan, 1961).

[10] Anil Seal, *The Emergence of Indian Nationalism: Competition and Collaboration in the Late Nineteenth Century* (Cambridge University Press: 1968).

[11] I am grateful to Dr Eleanor Newbigin for this description of the Cambridge School. Raj's critique of the school is dealt with later in this introduction.

[12] Rajnarayan Chandavarkar, *Imperial Power and Popular Politics: Class, Resistance and the State in India, 1850–1950* (Cambridge University Press: 1998), p. 23.

[13] *Ibid.*, p. 16. Chandavarkar further elaborated these ideas in his essay, 'Customs of Governance: Colonialism and Democracy in Twentieth Century India', *Modern Asian Studies*, 41, 3, 2007, 441–70. See below.

Raj's early work advanced three novel and significant arguments in the field of Indian history. The first was a rejection of a teleological approach to the emergence of socialism and trade unions, to be found in both Marxist and functionalist accounts of industrialization, and which were based on the belief that in the 'West', as Raj put it, 'economic development determined the character of labour, its social organization and its political consciousness'.[14] In Raj's view, such an assumption would of course fail to account for the political activism of Indian workers and the rise of the trade unions at a level of industrialization which had yet to 'evolve' to the stage at which such organizations had emerged in the West. Nor could it explain why, in Bombay, at least, the sectionalism of the workforce was exacerbated by the process of industrialization, when according to teleological accounts the reverse should have been the case.

Secondly, Raj eschewed cultural explanations, which were increasingly called in aid by historians, both of India and the West, to account for the actions of workers. In relation to India, such cultural explanations might take two forms. Indian industrial workers might be characterized as belonging to broad categories which would also be found in the West and which carried with them certain assumptions about the behaviour of those who belonged. Such categories might include 'the casual workers' who were deemed to lack the discipline of industrial workers and whose attributes included a propensity to violence and a lack of class-consciousness. Or, those employed in Indian industry might be described as 'peasants temporarily in proletarian garb' and hence characterized by a passivity in the face of exploitation and a disinclination to organize to protect their positions in the urban environment through collective action.[15] Furthermore, cultural explanations which applied specifically to the Indian working class might be used to explain these same characteristics. Hence, the sectionalism of the working class might be attributed to the importance of caste and religion to the self-identity of Indian workers and hence supply an explanation for the fact that industrial action was often short-lived. Interestingly, Raj pointed out that a number of these characteristics attributed to Indian workers by latter-day academics could be found in the discourses of the Indian ruling elites, both colonial and post-colonial. Thus, Raj rejected the essentialism which cultural explanations brought to the study of the Indian proletariat, much as he had rejected it for himself.

A third important thread running through Raj's early writing was his belief that the question to be answered in relation to India's workers was

---

[14] Chandavarkar, *Imperial Power*, pp. 6–8.
[15] Chandavarkar, *The Origins of Industrial Capitalism in India*, p. 166.

not why their political organization and their strikes were often short-lived but rather why these took place at all. Thus, he upended the usual assumption which both Marxist and cultural historians brought to their study of the subcontinent which was that the factionalism which characterized industrial relations and workers' politics was a function of the 'backwardness' of Indian workers in comparison with workers in the 'mature' industrial economies of the West. By contrast Raj argued that the political consciousness of Indian workers could not be read off from the level of industrialization in India but, rather, that

the political consciousness of the working classes appeared to be shaped crucially by their experience of, and their relationship with, the state. Their solidarities were not the natural outcome of popular culture or a reflex of the specific character of production relations, but, rather, they were politically constituted, and as such they were contingent, sometimes transient and even evanescent. The politics of the working classes had therefore to be situated in the wider context of the social and political alignments which shaped them.[16]

It followed from this, that to explain workers' politics and their relationship to the state it was necessary to know not only the material conditions in which the workers lived but also the power relations which were embedded in their neighbourhoods, since 'the social and political alignments of the working-class neighbourhoods reached out to wider arenas of politics, encompassing the colonial state and political organizations at various levels': a far cry indeed from the concern for elite politics of the Cambridge School. Indeed, in his later essay, 'Customs of Governance', Raj posited that, following Independence, the neighbourhood power brokers such as landlords, jobbers and local politicians owed their sway in working-class neighbourhoods to their ability to extract favours from the state, just as the state used these same power brokers to discipline labour.[17]

It is undoubtedly the case that inspiration for these arguments lay not primarily in previous studies of the Indian state, society or indeed of industrialization. Rather, Raj's understanding of the nature of the interaction between the state and the urban working class drew its inspiration primarily from writing in English social history: most notably from the work of E. P. Thompson and then Gareth Stedman Jones, who taught Raj as an undergraduate.

When Raj came to write his PhD dissertation in the late 1970s, E. P. Thompson was a commanding figure in the field of social history and

[16] Chandavarkar, *Imperial Power*, p. 9.
[17] Chandavarkar, 'Customs of Governance', 457.

his masterpiece was the book *The Making of the English Working Class.*[18] Although, as Raj noted, the book did not entirely escape the tendency to measure political consciousness against levels of industrialization,[19] nonetheless, 'The conceptual originality of *The Making* was, of course, to have represented class as a historical, rather than a structural fact, and the outcome of agency and struggle, experience and consciousness.'[20] He might have added that the breadth of Thompson's research which encompassed not only the material conditions of the working class and their politics but also the biographies of those individuals who played a role in forging the latter struck a chord with his own attraction to the telling of stories in the writing of history. In a coruscating essay on how historians involved in Subaltern Studies had adopted but misunderstood Thompson, Raj points out that Thompson, in his later work,[21] retreated from his teleological view of the link between class-consciousness and industrial development, which on its face would have precluded the idea that the Indian proletariat in the first half of the twentieth century might have joined trade unions and participated in political action. Rather Thompson elaborated on the idea of 'class struggle without class', which posited, as Raj put it, that: 'Since class consciousness was the product, not the prediction, of historical experience, class struggle preceded its emergence and indeed, facilitated its development.'[22]

The assumption that class-consciousness was an outcome of specific historical circumstances rather than a reflection of the level of industrialization in a given society of course played a major role in Raj's own work, including his first book, *The Origins of Industrial Capitalism*. But part of the originality of Raj's work was to show how the process of industrialization itself, the methods of labour recruitment and discipline, the links between the country and the city maintained by workers and the power structures of the Bombay mill districts might not only exacerbate

---

[18] E. P. Thompson, *The Making of the English Working Class* (London: Penguin, 1977, first published 1963).

[19] Most notably the Irish. Thompson described the Irish workers in much the same terms as had been employed by nineteenth-century observers, as 'unmoulded by the industrial work-discipline' and therefore useful to employers for jobs which did not require 'methodical application' but a 'spendthrift expense of sheer physical energy' married in Thompson's account 'to boisterous relaxation'. Thompson, *The Making of the English Working Class*, p. 473.

[20] Rajnarayan Chandavarkar, '"The Making of the Working Class": E. P. Thompson and Indian History', *History Workshop Journal*, 43, Spring 1997, 179.

[21] Edward Thompson, 'Eighteenth-Century English Society: Class Struggle Without Class?', *Social History*, 3, May 1978, 133–65; Edward Thompson, *Customs in Common* (London: Penguin, 1993, first published 1991), pp. 16–96.

[22] Chandavarkar, 'The Making of the Working Class', 180–1.

divisions in the workforce, based on caste and religion, but at other times facilitate and support united action against the employers and the state.

At the same time as Thompson was adopting a less deterministic view of the links between industrialization and class-consciousness, Gareth Stedman Jones published his own magisterial study of the relationship between poverty and politics in late nineteenth-century London, *Outcast London*.[23] This too had a profound influence on Raj's thought. In *Outcast London*, Stedman Jones discussed the issue of poverty and politics in three contexts. The first was a study of the casual poor, in late Victorian London, who made up a considerable proportion of London's workforce unlike in other areas of England which depended upon factory labour. The second was a consideration of how the housing question came to be seen, by the wealthy of London, as inextricably linked to the 'problem' of casual labour. The third was an account of how the ruling classes developed strategies for relieving the poverty of casual workers, which depended upon how they were perceived: as demoralized and lacking the attributes of foresight and discipline which were seen to characterize factory labour. In Raj's own work it is possible to detect the influence of *Outcast London*, but again it is possible to see how he developed these ideas further in the Indian context, perhaps most directly in his argument that ruling-class perceptions of casual workers, often shared by historians of Indian industry, bore no relationship to the actual genesis and attributes of this group. Indeed, he showed how maintaining a supply of casual labour was essential to the millowners' strategies, which depended upon the jobber system, and was therefore a product of industrialization in Bombay rather than the remnants of a pre-industrial economy. He also demonstrated that the terms in which casual labourers were described by capitalists and the state in India were eerily similar to those deployed by the wealthy of late nineteenth-century London and, as in London, they both fed ruling-class anxieties and legitimized the use of the police and the army to discipline them.

While Stedman Jones's *Outcast London* may have found echoes in Raj's first book, it was Stedman Jones's later work, *Languages of Class*,[24] and in particular the seminal essay 'Rethinking Chartism',[25] which were a key influence on Raj's subsequent analysis of working-class politics. According to Stedman Jones, Chartists saw themselves as part of a political movement. However, he goes on to argue that for both the

[23]   Gareth Stedman Jones, *Outcast London: A Study in the Relationship between the Classes in Victorian Society* (Oxford: Clarendon Press, 1971).

[24]   Gareth Stedman Jones, *Languages of Class: Studies in English Working Class History 1832– 1982* (Cambridge University Press: 1983).

[25]   Gareth Stedman Jones, 'Rethinking Chartism', in *Languages of Class*, pp. 90–179.

contemporary opponents of the Chartists and for later historians it was 'the movement's class character, social composition, or more simply the hunger and distress of which it was thought to be the manifestation, rather than its platform or programme which have formed the focal point of enquiry'.[26] By contrast, Stedman Jones argued for the importance of language in shaping political movements rather than the reverse. He writes,

We cannot therefore decode political language to reach a primal and material expression of interest since it is the discursive structure of political language which conceives and defines interest in the first place. What we must do therefore is to study the production of interest, identification, grievance and aspiration within political languages themselves.[27]

It followed from these assumptions that a particular political discourse may co-exist or conflict with others or replace earlier discourses, and thus one question it is necessary to ask is why at certain historic junctures this discourse will be successful in engaging a particular social group. As Stedman Jones writes in relation to Chartism,

A political movement is not simply a manifestation of distress and pain, its existence is distinguished by a shared conviction articulating a political solution to distress and a political diagnosis of its causes. To be successful, that is, to embed itself in the assumptions of masses of people, a particular political vocabulary must convey a practicable hope of a general alternative and a believable means of realizing it such that potential recruits can think within its terms.[28]

In other words, according to Stedman Jones, 'it was not consciousness (or ideology) that produced politics, but politics that produced consciousness'.[29]

Already at the time of undertaking his doctoral research, Raj had begun to question the essentialism which characterized so many studies of class, on the one hand, and Indian workers on the other, and which, at their not uncommon worst, combined the two. It was the work of Stedman Jones which helped him to formulate a theoretical framework with which to challenge essentialist accounts of the Indian working class and to go on to argue that workers' identities whether they be of class, caste or religion were historically contingent[30] and that power and politics at the level of the state, the province and the neighbourhood shaped these

---

[26] *Ibid.*, p. 93.   [27] Stedman Jones, 'Introduction', in *Languages of Class*, pp. 21–2.

[28] Stedman Jones, 'Rethinking Chartism', in *Languages of Class*, p. 96.

[29] Stedman Jones, 'Introduction', in *Languages of Class*, p. 19.

[30] A view he elaborated further in his account of nationalist politics in his essay, 'Indian Nationalism, 1914–1947: Ghandian Rhetoric, the Congress and the Working Classes', in Chandavarkar, *Imperial Power*, pp. 266–326.

identities rather than the reverse. It was also inherent in Stedman Jones's emphasis on the contingency of political language and hence of individual and group identity that it undermined those historical accounts which emphasized the exceptionalism of India's industrial development and the growth of class-consciousness in its industrial workforce. Thus, Raj extrapolated from Stedman Jones's accounts of workers' politics, which emphasized the particularity of the historical circumstances that gave rise to them, to argue that in a sense all political movements are exceptional, in that they arise in particular circumstances, whether it be in England or in India. Thus, as Raj, in the introduction to *Imperial Power and Popular Politics*, noted,

> The purposes of the colonial state would not have been served if they had not also been embedded in, and even influenced by, a wider political discourse in which diverse elements of Indian society shared. The process by which social groups were so defined and characterized in public discourse also created and developed political alignments and shaped social antagonisms which cut across class and caste, gender and community, religion and nation and sometimes reconstituted these old principles of social division.[31]

The originality of Raj's understanding of the process of industrialization and of workers' politics in India lay in some measure in his willingness to adopt concepts and arguments which had been framed by English historians, most notably E. P. Thompson and Gareth Stedman Jones, and to apply and develop them in an Indian context. Such an approach also owed something to the broader intellectual milieu which he inhabited during his period as a graduate student and research fellow in Cambridge. During the late seventies and the eighties, Cambridge boasted a cohort of young historians who identified themselves with a particular reading of social history very much in line with Raj's own. Perhaps remarkably, these historians whose subjects included a variety of countries and periods, from nineteenth-century London to twentieth-century Germany, from the rise of Nazism to the making of an English criminal class, understood themselves to be part of a shared project, and through seminars and less formal social gatherings exchanged ideas and developed arguments. It would be true to say that for those concerned, many of whom have themselves gone on to distinguished academic careers, their work was both enriched by and enriched Raj's own work on India and Bombay.

The essays gathered in this volume were written by Raj at various stages in what was to be his far-too-short career. Some represent interventions

---

[31] Chandavarkar, 'Introduction', in *Imperial Power*, p. 14.

in historical debates; some explorations of specific themes; some address issues of contemporary importance. But they all share the qualities for which he was so highly regarded: an incisive analytical intellect; a compendious knowledge of his beloved Bombay; and a compassion for the lives of his subjects, who were most usually of the 'humbler sort'. In essence, these essays, as collected here, reflect both the uniqueness and the importance of Raj's work.

Bombay's perennial modernities

From its inception, Bombay bore the markers of its modernity. Unlike most towns in India, perhaps anywhere, it did not develop at first out of its role as a seat of power or as a centre of administration. Nor did it emerge as a market, organically linked to its hinterland. Its origins lay in a tawdry settlement by a Europe poised on the cusp of modernity. In 1661, the Portuguese crown granted it to the British as part of Charles II's dowry when he married Catherine of Braganza. At the time, it consisted of a cluster of small islands, sparsely inhabited, if at all, off the west coast of India. It is doubtful whether the Mughals, pushing south in search of revenues, Shivaji seeking to improve his authority of the Deccan or any of the regional satraps of the subcontinent were aware of its existence. The gloss of modernity soon faded. The Crown quickly transferred its worthless possession to the East India Company. The Company over the next century duly considered abandoning it on several occasions. By the 1730s, the Company's factors, subordinated by Indian merchants in the trade of the much more prosperous port of Surat, recognized that they could use Bombay's natural harbour to build ships and deploy them to protect their consignments from 'pirates' in the Indian Ocean. In the late eighteenth century, it exported cotton and, later, opium to China, whose tea, sold in London, provided the Company with the only profitable part of its commercial operations. But it was not until Wellesley defeated the Marathas in the early 1800s that the Company was able to establish its hegemony in the region and secure its position in Bombay. By the mid-nineteenth century, Bombay had established itself as a major port and cotton market and had begun to acquire the shape of a major metropolitan centre. By 1860, Bombay had become, next to New York and Liverpool, the largest cotton market in the world. The opening of the Suez Canal benefited Bombay more than any other single port and reduced its distance from London by three-quarters. The construction of the railways from Bombay connected it to a wide hinterland, opening up the cotton and wheat tracts of central India, the rich agrarian hinterlands of Gujarat and Malwa and by the end of the century the fertile regions of the Punjab and the Ganges Valley. From the 1850s onwards, cotton mills began to proliferate in the city, mainly exporting yarn to the Chinese market, where it undercut Lancashire by the 1880s, and later producing coarse cloth for the domestic market. Bombay's emergence as a major commercial and industrial metropolis in the mid-nineteenth century was accompanied by its growing importance as an administrative and political centre. Its University was founded in 1857 and its High Court established in 1862.

In this light, it would appear that Bombay's growth was a product of its imperial connection and a function of modernity. Over the past two hundred years, it has often been characterized as India's gateway to the West and a doorway for the diffusion of modernity through its society. The multiple meanings of this proposition merit some scrutiny. Modernity, in this context, has been construed in at least two senses. First, it has denoted a set of characteristics and practices, deemed to have emerged in Europe after the Enlightenment, and to which Europe had privileged access: the rise of capitalism, science and rationality, secularism and liberalism. Modernity appears to be little more than the outcome of what functionalists in the 1960s described as 'modernization'. In the 1960s, modernization theory was built largely around the concept of 'industrialism'; in its more recent guise, its core appears to lie in a rather generic, loosely defined notion of 'culture'. Modernity, like industrialism, it would appear, is the culmination of a serial teleological process that those non-Western societies that adopt its logic might achieve. It implies passivity in the latter, and locates in the West the dynamic of history. By a circuitous and often scenic route, we have returned to the arid plains of Parsonian functionalism.

In its second variant, it is a colonial modernity that paraded into Bombay through the Gateway of India. The British asserted their legitimacy to rule in terms of the backwardness of Indian society. The historical process that yielded modernity also led to the colonization of India. In subjecting its people, colonial modernity denied them their identity and constructed them in terms of their backwardness. Rejecting in particular that the colonized were condemned to strive for the modern as a condition that they were doomed never to achieve, some scholars have sought to demonstrate that Indians came to a modernity of their own fashioning and in their own way. But this offer of an 'alternative modernity' does little more than return us to what must for historians remain a truism: that societies find their own route to their present and that they do so in their own ways, shaped by the particularities and constraints of their varied historical contexts. At the same time, the notion of 'alternate modernities' not only leaves the Eurocentric and teleological implications of the concept intact, but it also casts doubt on the utility of a concept that could signify so many different historical settings, phenomena and relationships. Moreover, it attributes to colonial rule the power, intent and ability to transform colonial societies. Notwithstanding the grounds on which the British asserted the legitimacy of their rule, they often acted to shore up Indian tradition and sometimes they invented it. In any case, their aim was to take resources out of India in order to deploy these in their global interests rather than to invest them in good governance. By operating on the basis of resources mobilized in India, the colonial state condemned itself to cheap government. The British in India lacked the means to attempt with any consistency to construct their few hundred million subjects in their image or to deploy greatly sophisticated systems of surveillance and control. Colonial rule relied upon the creation of domains in which the locally powerful could operate, relatively autonomously, as the arbiters of social exchange.

At a deeper level, the notion that colonial discourse, taken as a monolith, constructed India and its people, its social institutions, its body politic and its intellectual and cultural history, as the object of its knowledge and its power has narrowed the space within which Indians could make their own history. That space is derived in this view from incommensurability of colonial and indigenous knowledge. If the notion of incommensurability brings forward indigenous resistance to colonial modernity, it only does so within the constraints of cultural particularism. This assertion of difference, with its accompanying search for the true voice of the dispossessed (and not least their authentic representative within the academy), has often led to the reification of subaltern groups and their portrayal in essentialist terms. As a result, the critique of colonial modernity in Indian history has tended to reaffirm assumptions about the culturally specific, unique and exceptional character of Indian society and sometimes to restore some of the fondest shibboleths of colonial ideologues.

In a recent essay, Partha Chatterjee has considered the possibility that Indian cities, presumably thus far insufficiently modern, are at last 'becoming bourgeois'. His purpose is to illustrate the proposition that Indian society has followed its own route to its own alternative modernity. Until recently, he suggests, cities were characterized by mixed neighbourhoods, in which the poor existed in relationships of clientage with their rich patrons, in which 'the wealthy' provided 'social, cultural and moral leadership to the urban neighbourhood' and in which 'a dense network of neighbourhood institutions' created 'an active and participatory sense of urban community'. By the 1990s, cities became more segregated and their sense of community began to break down. Urban elites attempted to generate public spaces in keeping with their imaginary of global cities, while the poor have been swept out of the enclaves of the rich. The 'civil society' of the elites dealt with the state 'within a structure of constitutionally protected rights' while the 'political society' of the poor related to the state on the terrain of violence and on the margins of legality. Such an account of dominance and clientage in urban neighbourhoods or their relatively harmonious character, often adopted by colonial officials and Indian elites, can only be sustained in the face of the evidence.

Power relations in the urban neighbourhoods were characterized by reciprocity; they rarely flowed in a single direction. Patrons had to satisfy their clients or else lose them to their rivals. Their leadership, whether social or political, moral or cultural, was frequently rejected by their followers. Far from developing a natural sense of 'urban community', the social relations of the neighbourhood were constituted by tension and conflict, exploitation and violence. Nor was it the case that elites attempted to engineer the organization of public space in line with their dominance or their aspirations only at the end of the twentieth century. Town planning since the late eighteenth century signified periodic attempts by the British as well as by Indian elites to redefine urban space and its use in Bombay. Finally, it would be difficult to sustain a clear distinction between an elite political sphere constituted by legality and a popular political sphere constituted by violence, except perhaps in colonial representations of the social order. The social relations and political culture of Indian cities were shaped by the relationship, and the interplay, between different social classes and ethnic groups. In these interrelationships, there was nothing to suggest that either lawfulness or violence was a monopoly of a particular group.

This paper argues that Bombay's modernity was shaped largely by the relationship between various social groups that inhabited the city. Its growth, its social relations and political culture were influenced by the particular form of its relationship with the internal economy and not simply by the 'modernizing' forces of the West. Its commodity markets were linked to wider relations of production and exchange in its far-flung hinterland. Its cotton mills depended increasingly upon the penetration of domestic markets. Labour not only migrated from distant regions of the subcontinent but urban workers retained close ties with their villages and by remitting their earnings contributed to the reproduction of the rural economy. As late as 1921, 84 per cent of the city's residents had been born outside the city. Its specifically urban modernity was shaped by its interplay with a widening rural hinterland. The city's elites gained a considerable measure of autonomy in relation to the colonial state. From the early nineteenth century, they dominated local institutions and became entrenched in local and provincial government. Their shifting relationship with labouring groups within this domain of power shaped the changing character of the city's modernity. What characterized this modernity was its diversity and hybridity. By the late nineteenth century, a distinctive cosmopolitan and eclectic political culture had emerged in the city. Its public life was marked by its secularism, its equidistance from the particularisms of caste and religious community and often its transcendence of their differences. In the Indian imagination, the city had acquired from the late nineteenth century onwards an almost mythic significance as a major metropolis. Its inhabitants identified themselves with the modern and, however transitory their own claim on the city, they supposed that it set them apart from their country-folk. In the decades after independence, Bombay's residents saw themselves, and indeed the urban myth characterized them, as operating on a global stage. Sometimes frustrated by the constraints imposed upon them by state intervention and the deadweight of the traditional economy of the hinterland, sometimes resentful at their inability to take sufficient advantage of the opportunities created by state socialism, Bombay's residents took it for granted that they were a part of the vanguard that would pull India kicking and screaming into the modern world. By the end of the twentieth century, as the Indian state embraced the global, and cautiously dismantled its controls on the economy, so Bombay's dream of modernity disintegrated into its seemingly archaic fragments.

I

The emergence of this cosmopolitan and eclectic political culture in Bombay owed something to the degree of autonomy from colonial domination that the city's elites had been able to assert since the earliest days of the East India Company settlement. British power established itself late in western India and expanded slowly. The Company's political weakness and the relative poverty of its merchants increased its dependence on Indian merchants and dubashes. As a result, Bombay's elites had been able to appropriate considerable influence and wealth. Commercial partnership lent itself to political collaboration. Bombay's mercantile elites acquired a grip on important and lucrative areas of the city's economy, including, and indeed especially, the cotton textile industry. By marked contrast with Calcutta and Madras, the city's elites swiftly acquired a significant share of local power. From the 1830s onwards, they were firmly entrenched in local government. They were frequently consulted by colonial officials. They gained ready access to, and moved easily within, the Governor's court. Necessarily, they focused their attention on the city, where political power and influence was open to them, and ignored the hinterland over which they had little control. From this secure and significant base, they extended their influence over provincial affairs and by the 1890s began to exercise the determining influence within the Indian National Congress. As they battled for power within the Municipal Corporation, where they gained, by the 1880s, greater representation on a relatively wide franchise, they took particular pride in public standards in the city. This civic pride was manifested in rhetoric, philanthropy and in a measure of commitment to the working of the institutions of urban government. Of course, their benevolence was often selective, their rhetoric was often disciplined by their parsimony and their best intentions were qualified by harsher calculations of particular interests. Nonetheless, this civic ideology served to ensure a certain minimum in standards of governance and in public expectations about the city's institutions. From their application, most of the city's residents gained something.

The opportunities opened up by Bombay's growth brought people into the city from the whole Presidency and, indeed, further afield. It ensured that no single social group, whether defined by caste, language or religion, dominated its commercial or political life. Hindus, divided by caste and language, class and sectarian belief, made up about two-thirds of the city's population. But their strength of numbers did not ensure their social dominance. Parsis were among the largest property-owners in the city and among its leading merchants and entrepreneurs from the late eighteenth century. They played a prominent role in the city's public life and its municipal politics. But they formed only about 5 per cent of the population. About one-fifth of the city's inhabitants were Muslims, but they were no more homogeneous than the Hindus or Parsis and were divided by sect and caste, doctrine and language. In 1901, the census returned fourteen distinct communities of Muslims. The city's major Islamic communities – Bohras, Khojas and Memons – were largely converts from Hinduism and retained affinities with and adopted the ritual practices of their caste fellows. Religious or communal conflict was deemed alien to the city. In the nineteenth century, when the police or the press reported communal violence, they usually described conflicts between Parsis and particular groups of Muslim traders, not between Hindus and Muslims. In 1893, when a major communal riot occurred between Hindus and Muslims, colonial officials, the city's elites and the press concurred that it had arrived from the north. In the mid-1920s, as communal riots broke out across the north Indian plains and in Bengal, every affray in Bombay led its citizens to debate whether they had witnessed the city's first communal riot. No single linguistic group dominated the city's affairs. The proportion of Marathi speakers declined from about one-half in the late nineteenth century to about two-fifths in the mid-twentieth century. Gujarati speakers made up about one-fifth of the city's population, and as the flow of migrants from North India gathered pace, the proportion of Hindi speakers increased. By the 1960s, as migrants arrived from every corner of the subcontinent, a hybrid form of Hindi, immortalized by Bollywood, and occasionally celebrated in the poetry of Arun Kolhatkar, evolved as a means of communication, borrowing its vocabulary, declensions and sentence structure indiscriminately from Marathi, Gujarati or any other linguistic resource on offer. On the other hand, as migrants streamed into the city, they had every reason to keep their eye on its opportunities rather than dream wistfully of their rural homes. Bombay's history ensured that it never really became a city of its hinterland. It was neither simply a Gujarati nor a Maharashtrian city, until the reorganization of the old Bombay state took an awkward, if violent and decisive, step towards its definition in 1960. Indeed, it was precisely the diverse, hybrid, protean character of the city that led some to argue in the late 1950s that Bombay should be assigned neither to the state of Gujarat nor to Maharashtra but deemed a Union territory.

Indian elites who dominated Bombay's public life from the early nineteenth century had operated through political alliances that cut across communities. Class and wealth rather than caste or religion, race or community formed the basis of their politics. Neither their political dominance nor the development of a civic ideology in Bombay can obscure the fact that the city's modernity rested lightly over the appalling conditions in which its poorer residents were forced to live. Throughout its history, Bombay's urban growth has outstripped the sophistication of its infrastructure. The seven islands of Bombay were finally linked only in 1838, and by 1914, most of the city had until a few decades earlier been lying beneath the sea. For much of the nineteenth and early twentieth centuries, open drains, poor sanitation and a scarce, and often unhygienic, water supply characterized the urban environment. In 1925, when Bombay had more sewers than any other city in the East, the city's poorer quarters had none.

Inevitably, colonial officials and Indian elites made periodic attempts to reorder the city's social geography. In the early nineteenth century, following a major fire in 1803, a Town Repair Committee made the first sustained attempt to rationalize the use and distribution of space. Although merchants and travellers had observed the distinction between 'the English and the Black' towns in the mid-eighteenth century, it was after the fire of 1803 that concerted attempts were made to separate a 'native town' from the Fort and to relocate Indian merchants in its vicinity. Similar schemes had been effected in Calcutta and Madras in the early nineteenth century but racial segregation was far less crude in Bombay, where collaboration in business and politics continued to legitimize social fraternity.

In the mid-nineteenth century, with the expansion of Bombay's population, the native town crept northwards while Indian magnates began to move out of their wadis and mohallas to Malabar and Cumballa Hills, Breach Candy and Mahalaxmi, areas that had been occupied mostly by Europeans. While the Fort was characterized by 'its extraordinary salubrity' and stood in splendid isolation from the town, the poorer parts of the native town were increasingly overcrowded and unsanitary. At the same time, trades which 'caused offence to the public' – tanners, indigo-dyers and catgut makers – were removed from the Fort and relocated to the area north of the native town. From the 1850s, as cotton mills were floated, they too were situated to the north of the native town. Significantly, it was wealth rather than religion, caste or race that determined residential patterns. Social segregation in Bombay was always more fervently imagined than it was consistently practised. Thus, as one architect told a major town-planning committee in the 1880s, 'middle-class Europeans' live in middle-class areas of the city, while 'poor Europeans live in the same class of houses as poor natives'. The fact was, he elaborated, that 'the rich and the poor have always lived together – the former in the principal, the latter in the back streets – and always will'.

In a third phase, at the close of the nineteenth and early twentieth centuries, the social geography of the city crystallized more sharply along class lines. Cotton mills now proliferated to the north of the native town. Workers began to move out of the native town and into the vicinity of the mills. A distinctly working-class neighbourhood began to form in the city, known to its inhabitants as Girangaon or mill town. The common practice of casual hiring at the mill gates and variable working hours made it advantageous for job seekers to live near their place of work. In the 1880s, mills opened their gates at dawn. Since there were no public clocks in the area, and mills were prohibited from blowing their steam whistles at dawn, and it was impossible to tell when daylight would break, it was reported that workers slept on the approaches to the mill in order to present themselves as soon as the gates were opened and the jobbers arrived. By the 1920s, 90 per cent of the mill workers lived within fifteen minutes' walking distance of their place of work. The social organization of the workers, like the imperatives of factory discipline, integrated the spheres of workplace and neighbourhood.

At the same time, improvements in communication facilitated the dispersal of the city's population and encouraged the growth of new suburbs.

Moreover, the outbreak of the plague epidemic led officials to perceive social segregation as the solution to the city's problems. The Bombay Improvement Trust established in 1898 in the grim shadows of the plague epidemic to ameliorate the city's sanitary condition and to provide better housing for the poor conceptualized the city in terms of separate spaces for different social classes. As the threat of the plague to the city's elites receded, so did the Trust's enthusiasm for improvement. It demolished more houses than it constructed. Its principal achievement was to strengthen the commercial infrastructure of the city. By 1917–18, it had acquired about 11 per cent of the land area of the island, ostensibly for housing provision, but it had left two-thirds of this property undeveloped. The Improvement Trust had become another mechanism for transferring resources to the city's propertied elites and its millowners. The attempt to reconfigure the social geography of Bombay according to the lights of bourgeois modernity in the early twentieth century failed, rather like the previous schemes for applying the principles of colonial modernity to town planning. They failed for similar and structural reasons and not because of the recalcitrant customs and lifestyles of urban residents or their quest for an alternative or an indigenous modernity. In the 1920s, the Trust leased some of these lands to the cotton mills for a thousand years at a peppercorn rent. By the 1980s, the cotton mills were stripped for the value of their real estate, which is now being developed by the millowners to provide luxury apartments and shopping malls at a development profit conservatively estimated to amount to rupees 20,000 crores or about $5 billion. In other words, it facilitated the practice of what George Washington Plunkett had once famously described as 'honest graft', which had enabled him to buy up the swamp around what was soon to become the Brooklyn Bridge.

In the later twentieth century, the social geography of the city was transformed once more, under the pressure of the city's colossal expansion. Between 1941 and 1971, following a wartime influx and the migrations that followed the Partition of India, the city grew five-fold. A city of less than one and a half million in 1941 increased exponentially to about eighteen million today. In the late 1960s, the city's planners emerged with a bold and creative scheme for building a twin city on the mainland, across the harbour. Their proposal was to facilitate the dispersal of business activity from the area of the Fort in the south of the island. The Government of Maharashtra moved slowly and, while it deliberated, it allowed further land reclamation and property development for businesses in the south. In so doing, it subverted the proposals of the town planners and over the next few decades increased the concentration of activity, and the pressures on urban infrastructure, in the south.

At the same time, rent controls and tenancy laws introduced in the 1930s and tightened during the Second World War were further extended. It was now nearly impossible for landlords to evict tenants or raise their rents. Under conditions that were easily fabricated, protected tenancies could be inherited. Landlords now saw no reason to invest in the upkeep of their buildings. It was preferable to wait for the monsoon to take its toll. Disputes could not easily be resolved within an increasingly sclerotic judicial system. It is now estimated to take twenty-two years to process a civil suit through the courts in Bombay. Of course, landlords, or tenants, could hire muscle to protect their stake. Tenants who could not afford to invest in the maintenance of their buildings or to hire either muscle or lawyers could find themselves in the street. Landlords found their properties swallowed up by the arcane statutes of a rapidly growing Leviathan. In the 1960s, before tenancy laws were further extended, large business corporations and public sector undertakings appeared to be the most reliable tenants. They were unlikely to usurp the properties of the Bombay bourgeoisie. Since the 1970s, however, they have proved to be the most immune to both due process and the threat of violence. Far from protecting the poor, tenancy laws thus deemed that to those that hath, shall be given.

As the rental market shut down, property prices rose, and their rise was boosted by the concentration of business activity in the southern tip of the island. The scarcity of housing stock and overcrowding in the face of this massive urban expansion led to the proliferation of squatter settlements, largely on government lands. About 60 per cent of the city's population now lives in settlements of this kind. Slum residents often pay a substantial deposit to 'slumlords' to acquire a stake in the settlement, in addition to their weekly rents and other charges. Since these are squatter settlements, however, their investment is unsecured, even if the nexus of cash, muscle and power that is necessary to maintain them may provide some intermittent insurance. Indeed, the state government and the municipal authorities that often consent to provide basic services, like electricity and water, to these squatter settlements, periodically attempt to demolish them in the name of public hygiene, legality or the social order. Most recently, the state commissioned McKinsey's to produce a blueprint for Bombay's future. In February 2005, when the Bail Bazar slum was demolished in the wake of McKinsey's Vision Mumbai, one resident, Sultana Syed, declared that she had paid 40,000 rupees ($1,000) for her home and produced documents, including land titles, to support her claim. Having thus demonstrated to her own satisfaction that her legal rights had been violated by the police and the municipal bulldozers, she declared, 'We will vote out the people who did this.' The politicians whom Bail Bazar will thus vote into the place of those they eject will not be averse, however, to repeating the same action elsewhere. These recent attempts to reconfigure public space in Bombay have sometimes been inflected by imaginings of the global city. But they have not been undermined by the 'incommensurability' of popular culture. Rather, they have been ripped apart by a capitalism that remains proverbially red in tooth and claw, and whose operations have been advanced by (and whose dividends have often been shared with) politicians and officials, sometimes acting in the name of state socialism, sometimes, and with equal piety, in the name of the global free market.

II

Bombay's eclectic and cosmopolitan political culture derived in part from the purchase which its elites gained on local and municipal affairs. Having established a firm grip on the city's political institutions, they focused upon the urban and largely turned their back upon the hinterland. Their political programmes eschewed communal or sectarian issues and their alliances cut across caste and community. Their outlook was secular, liberal and, in relation to British rule, studiously moderate. Some of these public figures were willing to subject religious and caste orthodoxies to the most searching scrutiny. They had no wish, as Ranade observed in the 1880s, 'to break with the past and cease all connection to our society' but it was clear, at the same time, that 'we do not proceed on the religious basis exclusively'. This liberal, often progressive, political culture did not readily embrace the city's poor. Perhaps, their liberalism informed their reluctance to engage with broader constituencies and restricted the space that they allowed the city's workers in their political vision.

The Bombay millowners were integral to this political culture and the civic traditions which it yielded. They were especially ungenerous in their attitude towards labour. Since they regarded their workers as volatile and excitable, they were briskly dismissive of their demands. Since they assumed that migrant workers were inherently restless and difficult to pin down, they took it for granted that generous wage increases would induce them to return to their villages or initiate a spiral of unreasonable claims from which they would never escape. Consequently, employers tended to calculate rather harshly what they deemed to be the margin of fairness in the returns to, or conditions of, labour. Since they believed that workers would be impossible to discipline, they treated strikes as a breach of contract and dismissed those who participated. Since they claimed to be readily accessible to their employees and always receptive to their reasonable grievances, they insisted that workers' organizations were unnecessary and remained intolerant of, indeed, highly antipathetic towards, trade unions. Yet when strikes occurred, the employers were swift to identify a threat to the public order and to seek the intervention of the colonial state. This intolerance towards workers' demands combined with the repression of their organizations to give strikes a broader moral and political significance that wage disputes alone could not muster. The daily conflicts and minor disputes in the mills were repeatedly placed before the neighbourhoods of Girangaon and, in the process, acquired an explicitly political meaning. Workplace and neighbourhood were closely integrated not only by the prevailing practices of labour recruitment and discipline but also by the patterns of industrial action. There was clearly an important spatial dimension to the development of workers' politics in Bombay. The neighbourhood became an increasingly crucial arena in which the solidarities of the working-class politics were forged.

From the earliest days of the industry, Girangaon had witnessed extensive industrial action. Commentators observed the frequency of strikes since at least the 1880s. During the First World War, and in its immediate aftermath, strikes occurred with increasing frequency, both within the industry and outside, until the mill workers mounted and sustained industrial action on an unprecedented scale and for extensive periods in the general strikes of 1919 and 1920. By the 1920s, in the face of the hostility of the employers and repression by the state, a powerful labour movement had developed in the city. Between 1918 and 1940, eight general strikes occurred in Girangaon. None of them lasted for less than a month. The general strikes of 1928–9 lasted in effect for eighteen months. From the late 1920s onwards, especially during the general strike of 1928, the labour movement came to be dominated by a communist leadership. Around these general strikes in the 1920s and 1930s, there occurred over one thousand strikes in individual mills and departments. Not surprisingly, Girangaon sometimes came to be seen by the city's elites, especially in the late 1920s, as an insurrectionary centre.

In the 1920s and 1930s, the city's workers had declared their political presence. The maintenance of the city's civic tradition and cross-communal political culture, even in the face of communal riots of the 1930s, would not have been possible without the stake which the working classes had claimed within its history. The powerful public presence that the working classes had established in Bombay by the early twentieth century exerted a determining influence on the formation and reproduction of the city's distinctive urban character and civic tradition. Increasingly from the late 1960s onwards, the public presence and political influence of the working classes was progressively cut back. The marginalization of the working classes in the late twentieth century was accompanied by fundamental changes working their way through the city's political culture.

Nothing undermined the political culture of the city more seriously than the continuing failure of its cross-communal elite to accommodate the poor and manage labour more generously. This is reflected in part in their response to working-class discontents. The Bombay millowners, like most Indian employers, refused to tolerate the presence of trade unions and, when they came to be established, they sought as far as possible to weaken and marginalize their role in the industry. As working-class resistance gathered force, its public presence at times appeared menacing to the city's propertied elites, the employers and the state. Both before and after independence, working-class resistance intermittently evoked severe repression. Colonial rule had given Indian mercantile and landed elites the means to discipline and control labour more effectively.

With independence, they sought to extend and tighten their control. At the same time, the political solidarities of the working classes, welded together at least partially through the struggles of the 1920s and 1930s, began to fragment under the pressure of trade union rivalries and political competition by the 1950s. As trade unions became the instruments of political parties after independence, their quest for followers served further to fragment workers' organization, sometimes along the lines of caste, language and religion. Thus, the advent of democracy held out the promise of consolidating the political presence of the working class and the urban poor but in practice served to incorporate them into the political process on terms of such subordination that their political influence was considerably diluted.

Faced with working-class resistance on this scale, the employers and the state attempted to restructure the labour force and reorganize the framework of industrial relations. From the 1930s onwards, the textile industry differentiated with increasing clarity between 'permanent workers' and a sizeable 'informal sector' within the industry of dependent casual workers. The growing body of industrial legislation served to entrench this distinction and to extend it across the labour market. As these 'permanent' workers, whose employment rights were now better protected, drove up their wages or resisted efforts to alter work practices, employers and managers sought to assert their 'right to manage'. On the other hand, the informal sector continued to expand. Not only did workers here have few rights and poor returns, but employers, politicians and the state felt few obligations towards them. The closure of the textile industry, with the development of outsourcing to the power looms, and

deindustrialization in the city in general, can be seen as the logical extension of this strategy of 'informalization'.

Casual workers and those employed in the so-called informal sector
were often forced by their insecure conditions of work and low wages to
depend even more fully on contractors and intermediaries, patrons and
caste fellows, and assorted pedlars of influence, power and credit. By
the 1960s, therefore, as the fascist Shiv Sena emerged, the containment
and repression of working-class resistance had created the conditions for
exacerbating caste and communal differences.

These shifts in the structure of the labour force and the nature of the
labour market, accelerating since the 1960s, coincided with fundamental changes in the city's politics and together they pressed in the same
direction. In the 1930s, the communist Girni Kamgar Union had been
an effective agent in industrial relations but it had also created a wider
community of political sentiment around it in Girangaon. By the 1950s,
the communists were still a significant force in the labour movement
but they had begun to lose their position of dominance in Girangaon.
At the same time, the arbitrary and contingent nature of the Indian
Union was being exposed, not only by continuing disputes about its
borders with Pakistan and China, but also by arguments about the definition of its constituent units. Regional elites now sought to redraw the
boundaries of their states in the hope of consolidating their own positions within provincial politics. The Bombay state after independence
comprised diverse regions, joined, like most Indian states, by little more
than historical accident, the residue of colonial habits of administration
and the arbitrary nature of Partition. As the pressure for the linguistic
reorganization of the states gathered force, the political future of Bombay
city was thrown open to debate. This debate necessarily provided a stimulus for the city and its residents to define their identity. To some, this
suggested that the city could plausibly be deemed a Union territory and
administered from the centre. Significantly, there was a considerable and
widespread antipathy in Bombay to the alienation of the city to a central
administration. To others, it seemed that, if Gujarat were to be separated
from the state of Bombay, it might also have a large claim to the city by
virtue of long and close association. About two-fifths of the city spoke
Marathi as their mother tongue and some perceived, therefore, its spirit
to be quintessentially Maharashtrian. The movement to retain Bombay
within Maharashtra developed a popular base.

The communists now responded to the first signs of their decline in the
city in the 1950s, by perceiving the shape of a populist cause that might
enable them to regain their position of dominance. They jumped aboard
the Samyukta Maharashtra movement and hoped thereby to revive and

extend their political appeal. However, the argument that working-class culture was essentially Maharashtrian and that the workers' Bombay could only be safeguarded if it was integrated into the new state, served to reduce to a linguistic and communal base what had been a wider and culturally heterogeneous class movement. As a consequence, the communists surrendered ground to those, like the Shiv Sena, who made the 'nativist' argument with more force and who felt free to carry its implications further. As the Shiv Sena emerged from the interstices of the Samyukta Maharashtra coalition, employers began to see the advantage of inviting it to break up the base of the militant unions of the Left. To a large extent, they succeeded. Trade union rivalries, with a sharpening political edge, fragmented the solidarities of the labour movement further and opened it up to greater violence.

From the 1970s onwards, the public presence that the city's working classes had seized in the civic life of the city was increasingly nullified. Following the catastrophic general strike of 1982, the textile industry was closed down and the workers' claims to a stake in the city's social framework were swept aside. As the industry was dismantled, and the social organization of Girangaon began to disintegrate, workers sometimes sought protection in caste and communal affinities and the social connections built around them. With its active neighbourhood presence, its readiness to do favours for its clients, to find jobs for the boys, to confront authority and to terrorize the powerful on behalf of individual members, its spectacular displays of violence and its increasing access to state power, the Shiv Sena offered a kind of citizenship to workers, now seemingly disenfranchised and wholly subordinated, and created an arena in which they could at least fleetingly make a claim for dignity and equality. In the 1960s, the Shiv Sena had sought to fashion Bombay's image as a Maharashtrian city, primarily by attacking Tamils and South Indians, and its left-wing critics, especially the communists, both in the press and on the streets. By the 1980s, it set out to establish the primacy of the claims of Hindus to a stake in the nation, by making Muslims, whether Marathi-speaking or not, the object of their verbal and physical violence. In the 1980s, the Shiv Sena was reputed to be the party represented by the most candidates with a criminal record. When, in 1985, the Sena secured a majority for the first time in the Bombay Municipal Corporation – which commanded the revenues of a medium-sized Indian state – it gained access to vast resources and extensive webs of patronage. The powerful position that the Shiv Sena established in the city's politics concealed its much slower advance in the Maharashtrian countryside. Bombay city was now no more the city of its region than it had ever been. But its eclecticism had been broken down and its political temper was increasingly marked by the narrow, brutal sensibilities of a regional, Hindu nationalism. Bombay was now well on the way to being transformed into Mumbai.

At the same time, by the late 1960s and 1970s, the political economy of local dominance, and indeed the place of violence within it, had also begun to change. Local dominance had often depended upon the use of muscle. The workings of democracy created new opportunities for local bosses, including 'dadas' or neighbourhood toughs, looking for wider and more powerful and more lucrative connections. They began to penetrate the further reaches of the state. While politicians valued the dada's capacity to gather votes, the latter increasingly needed their connections with politicians in order to secure favours for their own clients and dependants. Their local prestige and influence could depend upon the efficacy of their connections. The insatiable appetite of politicians and political parties for cash, especially for their election campaigns, meant that their needs could only be met through the 'black' economy. In the 1930s, dadas collected subscriptions for Ganeshotsav or other religious festivals from local shopkeepers, who readily recognized that it was in their best interests to cough up. Thirty years later, Shiv Sainiks raised the money for their shakhas, to stand bail for their friends as well as to pay the costs of festivals and local events, not only from shopkeepers and graindealers but especially, during prohibition, from liquor and matka operators and racketeers. In the 1970s, with the end of prohibition, smuggling gold as well as high-value consumer goods that otherwise attracted high import duties became a lucrative cash-fuelled business and thus an important source of informal capital accumulation. However, as tariffs were lowered, smuggling lost its value and even gold lost some of its lustre. By the early 1980s, the heroin traffic from Afghanistan, stimulated by war, passed substantially through Bombay, but it quickly proved a high-risk specialism.

Increasingly, property development and construction became the focus of attention for what were now being described as 'mafia' networks. Catastrophic urban planning, archaic tenancy laws and land ceiling legislation served to push up property prices swiftly while the construction industry offered high returns within the informal economy. Now local bosses could claim generous subventions for their political campaigns. Property developers eyed the lands on which slums and squatter settlements had been built. Indeed, some squatter settlements had over the years improved and reclaimed the land on which they stood and thus made them yet more valuable for builders. When these external pressures on slums mounted, it also created opportunities for profiteering and protection rackets within them. In the 1920s and 1930s, dadas were in some measure constrained by the demands and expectations of the neighbourhood. The nexus of cash, muscle and political power that had taken shape in the city by the 1970s and 1980s placed them beyond the reach and influence of those they had once, at least intermittently, served. No longer could the residents of Girangaon impose, to any great effect, the constraints and obligations of reciprocity upon their patrons.

In the 1990s, in the age of 'globalization', Bombay seemingly came into its own. The city's ethos had always been dominated by its commerce. It had always looked upon its hinterland as a deadweight upon its modernity and regarded the meddling of the colonial, and later, the national, state as a fetter upon its enterprise. Now it would seem it was poised to fulfil its historical role and drag India into the twenty-first century. At this point, the millowners began to close down the textile industry. Faced with rising land prices, sustained industrial action, severe competitive pressure and a hostile fiscal regime, the millowners diversified, outsourced and withdrew from the industry. The real estate on which the mills stood appeared to be worth more than the industry could realize. In the powerloom industry, by contrast, the threat of labour was easier to contain, fixed costs were low and greater flexibility afforded in responding to market fluctuations. The closure of the industry created both problems and opportunities for the city. Some 200,000 workers lost their jobs. Of course, the millowners had to pay the workers their dues and entitlements. The millowners were reluctant to meet their obligations to the workers. At the same time, having closed their mills in order to develop the properties on which they stood, they encountered planning restrictions. In the early 1990s, the government relaxed some of the planning restrictions in order to allow the millowners to develop some of the mill lands and thus pay off the workers. The new rules allowed the millowners to develop one-third of the land, provided the other two-thirds were set aside for urban amenities and for public housing. Many workers still did not receive their dues. The zoning rules were now revised yet again to allow the proprietors to develop the whole of their estates and left little for public housing, urban amenities or job creation. On these terms, proprietors rushed to demolish the mills and build luxury apartments, shopping malls and expensive playgrounds for the rich around the collapsing tenements in which some of the unemployed continued to live. As this frenzy of construction got under way, the investigation of the leases under which the mill lands had been used suggested another complexity. The millowners had leased their lands from the city, some for a hundred years from the municipal authorities, in the late nineteenth century, some for a thousand years from the Improvement Trust in the 1920s. The leases on some of the lands would appear to have expired, while all of them were subject to restrictions on use. Lands that were not used for industrial purposes had under the old terms to be returned to the city. It is probable then that some of the proprietors and property developers taking a share in the expected development profits of $5 billion may not have clear title to their lands. Once their numbers are added to the illegal squatters on government lands who pay deposits for rights they do not have and the tenants whose legal right to the properties they acquire under rent control, which are based on nothing more lawful than possession, it would appear that a vast proportion of the city's booming economy is driven on transactions in assets by those who do not legally own them.

Significantly, it was in this age of globalization that Bombay came to be characterized, in Suketu Mehta's phrase, as 'the maximum city'. While for the visitor, or the travel writer, it might have offered even more recognizably than before a sensory maximization, its social relations and political culture suggested that its modernity was being dissipated into archaic divisions. When the British claimed their right to rule India on the grounds of their modernity, they pointed to communal differences and antagonisms as the defining features of their colony's backwardness. If, at the end of the twentieth century, Bombay and its inhabitants had found their own way of becoming bourgeois, it was a rather modern route to an archaic political sensibility. Moreover, as the citizens of Bombay found their route to unique forms of violence in the 1980s and 1990s, they erased rather forcefully any distinction between an elite civil society that operated by means of legal negotiation and a mass political society which was governed by violence. On the contrary, violence became the central motor for the accumulation of capital and the acquisition of property rights. The interplay and interconnections between the city's elites and its poorer residents had, throughout the nineteenth and twentieth centuries, influenced its civic traditions and its changing political culture. The city's elites had shown no propensity to treat its poor with generosity. The failure to accommodate the city's workers undermined the eclectic, cross-communal and cosmopolitan political culture that had developed since the 1830s.

At the same time, as the cosmopolitan and eclectic ethos of the city was increasingly consumed by communal antagonisms, and indeed was blown apart in the anti-Muslim pogroms of 1984 in Bhiwandi and of 1992–3 in the city itself, there were other fundamental and general processes at work. It may be argued that the propensity of a democratic state to protect human rights and civic freedoms, including freedom from want, that is the civility of its practices of governance, will be determined largely by the attitude to the poor entertained by politically and socially dominant groups. Deindustrialization, the diversification of investment and the stripping of the textile mills to capitalize on the value of land, was in part the outcome of political choices. They did not disclose a generous attitude towards labour or its stake in the city. Indeed, the formation of a new nexus of cash, muscle and office by the 1980s, operating on a larger scale of wealth and power, was facilitated by the workings of democratic politics, but also suggested a certain degradation of governance. Local bosses were now no longer simply the arbiters of social exchange within their own domain. Their reach had extended deep into, and at times apparently hollowed out, parts of the structure of the state. While the civic traditions and political culture of Bombay until the 1960s, characterized by its apparent secularism and its transcendence of caste and communal difference, was inconceivable without the assertion of the public presence of the working classes, the degradation of governance was a necessary precondition for the pogrom against Muslims in Bombay in 1992–3 or indeed in Ahmedabad and Gujarat in 2002. The future of the city as a peaceful, habitable and successful metropolis will turn on the stake that its poorest residents, including the former mill workers and their progeny among them, are allowed within its society. In this respect, as in many others, axioms that apply to Bombay city also apply to the workings of the nation as a whole.

Sewers

I

The fashion of 'urban history' in the 1970s directed attention to the development of transport systems and suburbanization, local government and municipal polities, rural migration and labour markets, commodity trades and industrialization, law-breaking and law enforcement. But it passed by without delving into the question of drains and sewers. Yet to a large extent such simple and underlying issues set limits upon urbanization and the shape of social relations.

This paper seeks to examine more closely the process by which an infrastructure was put together for what was to become one of the world's largest metropolitan centres in the twentieth century: Bombay.

Bombay's beginnings were humble. In 1661, this cluster of seven islands off the west coast of India were acquired by the British as part of Charles II's dowry in his marriage with Catherine of Braganza, and as every chronicler of Bombay's growth has since recorded, there were many who presumed at the time that Britain's new possession lay somewhere in the vicinity of Brazil.

For a century and a half Bombay remained 'the Cinderella of the English settlements in India: the poorest, unhealthiest and most despised'. For the penurious Company traders who operated from this base, fortunes were less easy to come by than alcoholic fevers and venereal diseases.

Bombay's growth was in its role as the major port for the China trade in cotton and later opium, which, by enabling the Company to pay for its purchases of tea, facilitated the only profitable part of the Company's operations. The China trade not only allowed Bombay to establish strong connections with the hinterland, it also integrated it more firmly into the imperial economy. While Bombay replaced Surat as the chief port and commercial capital of the west coast, the expansion of British power

Table 1. *Population of Bombay city 1780–1981*

1780	100,000	1911	979,445
1814–1815	180,000	1921	1,175,914
1846	566,119	1931	1,161,383
1864	816,562	1941	1,489,883
1872	644,405	1951	2,994,444
1881	773,196	1961	4,152,006
1891	821,764	1971	5,970,575
1901	776,006	1981	8,243,405

at the expense of the Monathas enabled it to usurp Pune's role as the major administrative and political centre in western India. The most important changes in the structure and character of trade (domestic as well as, and, indeed, equally, international) acted positively in Bombay's favour: the American civil war boom, the opening of the Suez canal, the depreciation of silver and the growth of Indian exports, a larger proportion of which was now routed through Bombay. In the 1850s the first cotton mills were built in Bombay. The textile industry expanded rapidly with a vigorous spirit of mill-building in the 1870s and 1880s, and by the early 1890s there were nearly seventy mills in the city employing on a daily average about 70,000 workers. Although mill construction thereafter was to slow down, the size of the workforce was to double itself over the following three decades. Until the turn of the nineteenth century, it had seemed doubtful that Bombay would become a significant commercial centre. By the end of the century, this inhospitable fishing hamlet, where Englishmen did not expect to survive two monsoons, had become a modern industrial city.

This transformation was accompanied by rapid population growth as rural migrants from an increasingly wider hinterland came to Bombay to seek work. In the 1780s, the islands' population was estimated at 100,000. By 1864, its size, inflated by the frenetic economic activity associated with the American civil war boom, had increased to 816,562. Although the city's population had declined by a fifth by 1872, when the boom collapsed, it continued to grow until the end of the century, when its increase was checked by an outbreak of plague in the late 1890s. Between 1901 and 1941, Bombay's population doubled (despite suffering a slight decline in the late 1920s and early 1930s) and multiplied nearly six-fold by 1981.

Perhaps the most significant factor in this process of urban growth was that it had virtually no base upon which to build. Until 1838, this cluster of seven marshy islands had not even been linked. Subsequently, its rate of growth rapidly outpaced the sophistication of the town's infrastructure, and this has remained a persistent theme of its development to the present day. The case of Bombay city provides a rare opportunity to examine the process by which a major city was put together brick-by-brick.

But there are other reasons to look at the history of Bombay's development. Its commercial and industrial growth imposed severe pressures upon its physical structure. The construction of an infrastructure to serve its growing needs required sustained and directed social policy. Incomplete remedies for urban problems only made their solution more complex, and more imperative. But social policy is rarely a matter of a body of just and wise men identifying given problems and setting briskly about overcoming them. In Bombay, the specific circumstances created by poverty and limitations of the Indian economy, the particular interests of the colonial state and the perceptions of colonial rulers, and the absence of any significant precursory urban structure, made social policy a particularly savage arena in which social relations were played out. Social policy became an expression of the meshing of financial and factional interests, class and ethnic divisions, nowhere more clearly than in the attempts by Bombay's rulers to deal with the town's appalling sanitary condition.

The formulation of social policy for an urban complex which was expanding rapidly was not only governed by selfish, material interests, but also by perceptions of how the poor live, the habits and customs of the 'natives' and what might constitute an acceptable minimum standard of living conditions. Such perceptions carried implications for the determination of wage levels and the enforcement of labour discipline, and thus impinged on a variety of social issues, beyond the simple matters of drains and sewers. Thus, in a sense, in the formation of a social policy for Bombay's urban problems, ruling attitudes towards labour received their practical manifestation.

Finally, it is hoped that an investigation of the historical development of Bombay's urban problems, and attempts to deal with them, will provide some perspective upon more recent approaches to urban planning in the city.[1]

II   Social geography and residential patterns

From the second quarter of the nineteenth century, the commercial development of Bombay increasingly outpaced the sophistication of its

---

[1] For an account of the current situation, albeit somewhat dated, see N. Harris, *Economic Development, Cities and Planning: The Case of Bombay* (Bombay, 1978).

urban environment. As Bombay was pulled into the imperial orbit and more firmly integrated into the world economy, it became clear that the full realization of its commercial potential demanded that its physical structure be swiftly developed and adapted to its expanding needs. The seven islands of Bombay had to be linked and roads built to connect them. Internal transport had to be developed to facilitate the movement of goods and people. A rapidly growing population required a whole range of services, from housing for the living to cremation and burial grounds for the dead. As the rate of migration to the city quickened, so sanitation and sewerage, water supply and land availability became pressing problems. The magnitude of this task can scarcely be exaggerated. The whole infrastructure of a modern commercial and industrial city and an international port had to be constructed even as its size multiplied, its population became more concentrated, its streets and neighbourhoods more congested and its economic activity more hectic.

The agenda before Bombay's rulers in the early days of its growth was rarely acknowledged or consistently articulated and it was never to be completed. Since the late eighteenth century, improvement and development of a healthy urban environment have always lagged behind the demand imposed upon it by economic activity and population growth. In what is largely a story of failure, it is as well to begin with an appreciation of the constraints upon achieving success.

Bombay's physical geography was less than ideal for the creation of a healthy urban environment. The seven islands which made up Bombay were not linked until 1838 – for the most part – and were covered by pestilential swamps which had to be drained and which generally provided a breeding ground for malaria and other endemics. Moreover, Bombay was so low-lying that 'the bulk of the island was originally below the mean level of the sea'. To provide an adequate system of sewers and drains under these conditions, when gravitation into the sea was impossible, not only had the effect of 'considerably enhancing the cost of drainage-operations' but also placed enormous demands upon engineering ingenuity. Even in the early twentieth century, 'after a large portion of the interior has been filled up and reclaimed, the elevation of the land is too slight to admit of gravitation into the sea at a distant point of outfall'.[2] These geographical preconditions of Bombay's urban growth imposed powerful constraints upon the efficacy of social policy.

The magnitude of the task of fashioning a relatively healthy and hygienic urban environment in Bombay was matched by the stringency of resources required to execute it. Municipal 'improvement', as it was

[2] *Gazetteer*, III, 42.

called at the time, was expensive, whereas *laissez-faire* had the enormous advantage of cheapness. To pay for these improvements through taxation, the British would have to lean heavily upon their most favoured collaborators: the city's sheikhs, merchant princes and millowners. In principle, the British were averse to taxing those whose political support counted for most. And, these men were, as Lytton informed Queen Victoria, 'the best of your Majesty's subjects . . . they are all fat, rich and happy . . . and loyal to the power that protects their purse'.[3] Again, taxation and expenditure required a more systematic municipal administration and the devolution of political power to those who were being taxed. From 1815, a tax had been levied on houses in Bombay. By 1845, a municipal fund had been established to pay for police as well as civic expenses. Despite the willingness to tax and to systematize municipal finances, the delicate complexities of local politics distorted any sustained social policy.[4]

At a more immediate level, financing civic improvement through taxation was liable to engender intense conflict over how these revenues might be paid and which programmes might take priority. If tax burdens were to be placed on the city's business elites, then it followed that the improvements which it paid for could best be justified in terms of commercial use. Roads, then, were to be preferred to drains or houses. Roads, moreover, were to be built from dock to warehouse, from the cotton fields to the cotton green, and drains were to be more conveniently placed in the army cantonment at Colaba and the more salubrious suburbs of Parel or Malabar Hill, rather than in the overcrowded slums of the working classes.

In addition, such pressures were accentuated and such constraints accentuated by the fact that land was both scarce and valuable in Bombay, an island substantially comprising swamp and marsh. The supply and price of land also influenced the manner in which the city grew and determined where the rich and the poor might live. This coincidence of geographical and social divisions was not present at Bombay's making;

---

[3] Cited by Seal.

[4] This was why finance remained a constant source of friction between the Government of Bombay and the Bench of Justices in the city as both attempted to define their proper sphere of activity and mark their areas of jurisdiction. For instance, in Bombay (unlike Calcutta and Madras) the municipal fund had to meet police expenditure. This remained the case until 1907. See H. P. Mody, *Pherozeshah Mehta: A Political Biography* (Bombay, 1963), pp. 318–21. After the Municipal Act of 1888, expenditure on primary education was to be shared. But, as Bombay's notables complained, the government, which had done as little as possible as long as primary education lay under its care, goaded the municipality into action once the liability was partly removed. H. P. Mody, *Mehta*, pp. 148–53.

with the dramatic expansion of its wealth in the nineteenth century, they became increasingly and starkly clarified.

III

European travellers in the seventeenth century found Bombay noxious and pestilential, as it remained for many of its inhabitants – especially the poorer ones – in the twentieth century. In the mid-nineteenth century, when Bombay's urban growth and commercial expansion had already begun, conditions of hygiene and sanitary provision remained extremely rudimentary. The needs of Bombay's inhabitants were served by one 'main' drain built at the end of the eighteenth century, which began as an open nala leading into the sea at the Great Breach. Between 1824 and 1856 it was gradually covered from the Esplanade northwards to Pydhuri and Bellasis Road. 'Open drains, or rather receptacles of filth, abound in the Native Town of Bombay to an extent I believe to be unparalleled elsewhere,' reported Coneybeare in 1852. These drains could 'only be considered in the light of continuous open cesspools, extending along on both sides of the whole length of nearly every street in the Native Town, and rendered (irrespective of their greater extent) more objectionable than ordinary cesspools, by the circumstance of their being in actual contact with, and soaking into the foundations of, the whole street-frontage of each house'. In contrast, he remarked upon the 'extraordinary salubrity' of the Fort. 'All round the Island of Bombay', wrote one observer in 1855, 'was one foul cesspool, sewers discharging on the sand, rocks only used for the purposes of nature. To ride home to Malabar Hill along the sands of Back Bay was to encounter sights and odours too horrible to describe . . . To travel by rail from Bori Bunder to Byculla, or to go into Mody Bay, was to see in the foreshore the latrine of the whole population of the Native Town.'[5] The sewers in the town, even in the army cantonments, covered only with rough hewn slabs with perforated stones to let in the rainwater, collected grit and filth from the road. Since they were irregularly cleaned out, 'many were found to be choked and did not pass on the sewage they received, and some were from repletion refusing to admit more so that filthy pools were forming on the road'.[6] In the absence of adequate sewers[7] the 'night soil' had to be 'conveyanced'

---

[5] S. M. Edwardes, *The Rise of Bombay* (Bombay, 1902), pp. 279–80.

[6] Report on the Sanitary State of the Army in India, p. 39.

[7] There were in 1855 less than 14 miles of sewerage for 442,031 people in Bombay, inclusive of the well-supplied Fort. London, on the other hand, boasted 700 miles for 1,873,000 people. H. Coneybeare, *Report on the Sanitary State and Requirements of Bombay*, Selections from the records of the Bombay Government, new series, vol. XI (Bombay, 1855), pp. 16–17, 21, 27.

away. In order to achieve this, houses were built slightly apart leaving a gully running between them. This was meant to act as a drain for the slops and waste water from the houses, and more crucially to provide access to halalkhores ('scavengers').

During the 1854 cholera epidemic, the death rate in the Fort was 9.9 per mille; in the Native Town, including its less insalubrious streets, it was 60 per mille.[8] At least 'one half (or about 8,000) of the deaths that annually occur in Bombay are due to various removable causes, and the drainage of undrained streets would of itself and irrespective of all other sanitary improvements reduce our annual death rate by at least 20 per cent or 3,000 souls per year'.[9]

The inadequacy of drainage and sewers was matched by an insufficiency of water supply. At times of scarcity, for instance in 1854, water had to be brought to Bombay by rail and country boats. By the late 1850s, a project to draw water supplies from the Vehar nala had been effected. But the influx of migrants to the island in the 1860s made an increased supply imperative. In the 1870s, the water of the river Tasso was diverted into the Vehar lake and a covered reservoir constructed at Malabar Hill, increasing the supply by 4.5 million gallons per day. In 1884, the Bhandarwada reservoir, to accept water from both the Tulsi and Vehar lakes, was completed. But with the expansion of the textile industry in the 1880s, the supplies of the Tausa lake had also to be harnessed. But even in the early twentieth century, the city's water supply depended upon a 'regularly recurring monsoon' and, in addition, it was unevenly and selectively distributed to the town – first to commercial needs and to serve best the residential areas of the city's elites. Most people continued to rely upon wells and tanks, although the contents of 'nearly every one ought to be pronounced unfit for drinking purposes'. When water supplies dried up, the inhabitants of the poorer quarters were sometimes 'compelled to drink the water of those filth-sodden wells and tanks'.[10]

The 'pitiable sight' which the Health Officer observed, 'of men, women and children awaiting around a pipe eagerly and quarrelling for the miserable dribble from it',[11] had not by any means become a thing of the past by the twentieth century.

Similarly, fears about illness and the spread of epidemics inspired attempts by the municipality to organize the retail trade. Attempts to

---

[8] Coneybeare, *The Sanitary State*, p. 13.   [9] Coneybeare, *The Sanitary State*, p. 2.
[10] Report of the Health Officer for Bombay Town and Island, for the 3rd Quarter of 1871 (Bombay, 1872), p. 24.
[11] *Ibid.*

regulate the meat trade more strictly, and especially the prosecution of two butchers for bringing diseased animals for slaughter, led to a strike by the town's butchers in 1865.[12] Nonetheless, descriptions of Bombay's fruit, meat and vegetable markets suggest a considerable need for close supervision. Most markets in the nineteenth century were concentrated in the overcrowded and largely unsanitary Native Town.

The Duncan market in Shaikh Memon Street consisted of 'ranges of low tiled open sheds, badly paved and undrained'. The Boribunder mutton and fish market was in the same yard as the slaughterhouse, while a private market in Abdul Rehman Street was said to be 'of a most insanitary character'.[13] The condition of the slaughterhouses and the quality of the meat sold excited the most attention. The slaughterhouses, situated until the mid-1860s in Mandvi and at Bori Bunder, were, 'if possible, less sanitary than the markets... one of them being a mere shed built on stakes, below high water-mark, from which the blood and offal streamed on to the mud of the foreshore, where it was left to putrify for several hours'.[14]

No more considerable light is shed upon the standards and conditions of living (and dying) in the mid-nineteenth century than the clumsy attempts to deal with 'the nuisance occasioned by the burial of low caste hindoos, cattle etc on the beach in Back Bay'.[15] Since Back Bay lay to the windward side of the Native Town, the graveyards produced a 'stench which is most disgusting, and overpoweringly offensive'. Such 'unwholesome emanations', it was believed, 'could contribute to exceptionally high mortality rates during epidemics'.[16]

When the Board of Conservancy submitted plans for new burial grounds 'for the internment of cattle and low caste Hindoos',[17] it was hindered not only by its own parsimonious, cost-paring approach to the problem, but also by a genuine lack of finance. In January 1848, consideration was given to dispensing with the enclosure around the burial ground, but it had to be set aside in view of the likelihood that the 'carcasses would be disinterred by the great number of jackals and pariah

---

[12] *Ibid.*   [13] *Gazetteer*, III, 54–5.   [14] *Gazetteer*, III, 54–5.
[15] G. Hancock, Clerk to the Board of Conservancy to J. G. Lumsden, Secretary to Government, Letter No. 134 of 1852, 15 June 1852, in *Correspondence Relating to the Prohibition of Burials in the Back Bay Sands, and to Dr Leith's Mortuary Report for 1854* (Bombay, 1855), p. 1.
[16] Dr A. H. Leith, *Mortuary Report for 1854*, para. 11, in *Correspondence Relating to the Prohibition of Burials*, p. 11.
[17] G. Hancock to J. G. Lumsden, Letter No. 134 of 1852, 15 June 1852, in *Correspondence Relating to the Prohibition of Burials*, p. 1.

dogs which would resort to the spot'.[18] These schemes were shelved because of an uncertainty that 'the experiment [was not] so certainly calculated to secure the desired object as would justify so large an outlay'.

By 1855, however, 'the horrible and dangerous condition of the burial ground' was recognized as requiring swift and immediate action.[19] The unwillingness of the colonial state to spend was matched by its hesitancy to intrude, least of all 'to interfere with arrangements which the inhabitants may make for the disposal of the dead'.[20] But the burial conditions were so appalling as to pose a considerable threat to the health of the living.

The Mortuary Report for 1854 recorded that the burial ground at Joonapur cemetery was too small for the 4,649 bodies which had to be buried each year. If the number of corpses for each year were 'laid at the same time, shoulder close to shoulder, without intervening space, they would not only cover the whole area, but they would have to be laid in two tiers, the second equally closely packed as the first and there would still be more to form part of a third tier of corpses'.[21] This situation, it was argued, was mitigated by 'the rapidity with which the bodies decompose' so that after only eight days an old grave could be reopened for a new burial.[22] Among other disadvantages was the fact that, at high tide during the monsoon, people observed 'surf washing the newly interred from the graves'.[23] Although the new burial grounds were completed by 1853, the beach at Back Bay was still being used to bury low-caste Hindus and cattle in March 1854.[24] Moreover, the new grounds at the Flats were

[18] G. Hancock to J. G. Lumsden, Letter No. 134 of 1852, 15 June 1852, in *Correspondence Relating to the Prohibition of Burials*, p. 3. As a compromise, it was suggested that, if not the burial ground for cattle, then at least that for 'the lower caste of Natives' be enclosed.

[19] G. Hancock to J. G. Lumsden, Letter No. 134 of 1852, 15 June 1852, in *Correspondence Relating to the Prohibition of Burials*, pp. 5, 7, 9.

[20] G. Hancock, Acting Clerk to the Board of Conservancy, to W. Hart, Secretary to Government, Letter No. 269 of 1853, 25 August 1855, in *Correspondence Relating to the Prohibition of Burials*, pp. 14–15.

[21] Dr A. H. Leith, Mortuary Report for 1854, para. 10, quoted by W. Hart, Secretary to Government to the Acting Clerk of the Peace, 7 July 1855, in *Correspondence Relating to the Prohibition of Burials*, p. 10.

[22] The learned doctor pondered this phenomenon: 'were decomposition in this sandy soil not so rapid, it would of course be impossible that so many dead could be deposited there; yet as in putrefaction the soft solids of the body are changed with poisonous gases, the greater rapidity of the process does but the more intensely pollute the air, by giving a layer quantity of those gases in a given time'.

[23] W. Hart, Secretary to Government to the Acting Clerk of the Peace, 7 July 1855, in *Correspondence Relating to the Prohibition of Burials*, pp. 10–11.

[24] It was ingeniously suggested, too, that it was 'highly desirable that the graves for cattle should, if possible, be separated by a wide interval from the graves for human bodies'. G. Hancock, Acting Clerk to the Board of Conservancy, to W. Hart, Secretary to

not devoid of hindrance. There was no road which allowed access to the graves, and water was often encountered at the depth of a mere 6 feet. During the monsoon, there was but 'three foot on the raised portion clear of water, while the unraised portion is flooded to the extent of one foot'.[25]

By this stage the government, having spent some money, was less interested in the results. Government concluded (conveniently, if a touch fantastically) that there was 'sufficient evidence that the cemetery . . . will be suited for its purpose throughout the year'.[26] The burial of cattle and animal carcasses on the Back Bay sands was now prohibited. The new burial grounds had scarcely resolved the overcrowding of the dead. As late as 1867, moves were still afoot to forbid burials at Girgaum and Sonapur as soon as new cemeteries were opened.[27] In the next few decades, burial grounds were built and improved, and new sites were acquired in the outlying northern villages at Matunga and Dewn. If the problem of the overcrowding of the living was never to be properly confronted, some efforts were being made to serve the needs of the dead. But the needs of the living could not entirely be ignored.

Of course, various attempts were made to ameliorate social conditions in Bombay. But they generally offered too little far too late. The town's water supply, like its burial facilities, was improved. The municipal authorities sought to regulate more closely the retail trade in foodstuffs and vegetables and especially in meat. From 1865, these trades had to be licensed, and in 1872, licensing was directed specifically at 'dangerous and offensive trades', construed broadly as those 'dangerous to life, health or property, or likely to create a nuisance'.[28] The slaughterhouse was moved out of Bombay to Bandra from where special meat trains were run to maintain the city's supplies.[29] Various schemes were projected for extending and improving the systems of drains and sewers, but until the 1880s, 'a definite plan of operations, acceptable to all, was however still a desideratum' and the history of drainage was 'one of delay and of destructive rather than constructive energy' as successive plans

---

Government, Letter No. 269 of 1855, 25 August 1855, in *Correspondence Relating to the Prohibition of Burials*, p. 17.

[25] The Senior Magistrate of Police was 'unwilling' to say 'whether the parties using the burial-grounds would dig their graves two feet below the surface of the water'. W. Crawford, Senior Magistrate of Police, Bombay, to W. Hart, Secretary to Government, Letter No. 382 of 1855, 22 September 1855, in *Correspondence Relating to the Prohibition of Burials*, pp. 26–7.

[26] Government Resolution, 5 October 1855, in *Correspondence Relating to the Prohibition of Burials*, pp. 28–9.

[27] *Proceedings of the Sanitary Commissioner*, Bombay, January 1867, p. 18.

[28] *Gazetteer*, III, 48.   [29] *Ibid.*

were rejected faster than they were made. Between 1878 and 1909 the municipality spent Rs 125 lakhs on drainage works.[30]

Large parts of the city, however, had virtually no sewers as late as the 1920s.[31] Waste continued to be deposited in the gullies in the narrow spaces between houses and tenements and a number of neighbourhoods relied upon the municipal halalkhores and scavengers to carry it away in baskets.

IV

This piecemeal social engineering did not produce any effective or lasting results. The conditions in which the city's poor were compelled to live reflected on how limited programmes of 'improvement' had been. Invariably these represented attempts to mediate large structural problems with immediate and impermanent solutions. However, as the city grew, the proliferation of social conflict, the demands of expanding commerce and the consolidation of local interests forced the confrontation of these problems. The task of improving social conditions could not simply be subordinated to the provision of an infrastructure for the city's commerce. Rather, the consequences of neglect in one sphere could play back upon the other, hindering, for instance, the full realization of the city's economic potential. Moreover, poverty and disease were a threat to the immediate political and physical safety of Bombay elites. Epidemics which were bred in the unsanitary hovels of the poor could not simply be stopped at the gates of the rich. This was not a mere matter of municipal politics; it could not be dismissed as lightly as spending on paving stones or street lighting. It exercised the imagination, it threatened the very existence of shetias and shorffs, of millowners and civil servants, of Indians and Europeans alike.

The city's rulers did not doubt the wisdom of improving social conditions. But they approached the problem strictly within the parameters of dominant class interests and the prism of their specific perceptions of how the poor might or ought to live.

In the mid-nineteenth century, Coneybeare, a pioneering architect of Bombay's urban structure, observed that expenditure on sanitation was measured directly in terms of commercial results or even assessed in human lives. In 1858, for instance, municipal improvements were deemed to be justified only if they were likely to reduce the death rate by

---

[30] *Gazetteer*, III, 42ff.
[31] A. R. Burnett-Hurst, *Labour and Housing in Bombay: A Study in the Economic Conditions of the Wage-Earning Classes in Bombay* (1925), p. 21.

20 per cent.[32] Faced with this calculus of profit and loss, life and death, Coneybeare strongly challenged 'the general impression' that 'a defective police is a greater municipal evil than a defective sanitary condition'. With the persuasive economic rationality borne out of mid-Victorian capitalism, Coneybeare drew attention to 'the loss of property . . . [which is] attendant on a high rate of mortality'. He pointed out that 'a high rate of mortality can only be occasioned by premature death', and for every premature death, he calculated there were fourteen cases of protracted illness. During these protracted periods of sickness, 'the patient is not only unproductive himself, but is a burden to the productive labour of others, and that, in fact, premature deaths presuppose unhealthy and unproductive lives'. Moreover, he argued, *sanitary reform is in itself a police improvement*', for 'crime, dirt and a high rate of mortality are found co-extensive' and, in any event, sanitary advances 'would occasion annually a preventable loss of life and productive labour greater than that occasioned by riots and disturbances of the last thirty years'.[33] These were powerful arguments. They linked the health of the labourer to his efficiency as a factor of production. Carrying the resonances, even perhaps drawing upon the ideas and knowledge of the sanitary commissions and health enquiries of Britain in the 1840s, their message was clear: the full realization of the potential capital was incompatible with the neglect of social conditions or the wastage of human lives.

More immediately, what motivated British administrations and Indian magnates was neither commercial nor humanitarian, nor even necrogenic, concern, but the fear of epidemics.

The question of sanitation and hygiene became acute in the wake of an increasing concern in the 1860s with the health of soldiers in their encampment at Colaba. Each soldier, it was reported in 1863, cost the Government of India a sum of £97 annually, while £388,000 per annum was spent upon illness.[34] The death rate in the cantonment at Bombay was higher than every other town in the Presidency, apart from Surat.[35] It was noted that there were in Colaba only a few wells and these contained 'very indifferent water'. Water for the troops was brought from the well on the Esplanade, by pukhalie bullocks at first, later by iron pipes, and it was not until the mid-1860s that a seven-inch main was brought from the Vehar lake supply across Colaba causeway to supply the troops.[36]

[32] Coneybeare, *The Sanitary State*, p. 1.   [33] Coneybeare, *The Sanitary State*, pp. 22–3.
[34] *Report of the Commissioners Appointed to Inquire into Sanitary State of the Army in India*, with précis of evidence, p. 33.
[35] *Report of the Sanitary Commissioner for Bombay*, 1866 (Bombay, 1867), p. 83.
[36] *Report of the Sanitary Commissioner for Bombay*, 1867, Inspection Report No. 1, p. 10.

The sewers presented no better prospect for standards of hygiene. Frequently choked and overflowing, they were receptacles for the excreta and waste and rainwater which they collected and held.

The municipality's attempts to deal with these problems through 'active conservancy' remained painfully insufficient and the construction of sewers and their discharge into the foreshore 'must in great measure render unavailing all measures for improvement far short of reconstruction'.[37] Meanwhile, the barracks had to flush their 'badly constructed slab drains . . . by means of hogshead casks, with valves below, to discharge at once a large body of water into the trapped openings of the drain'. The Regimental latrines, too, were 'very offensive'. Raised on pillars, it was 'expected that the tidal water would carry away the excrement that fell on the foreshore', but instead, 'the filth has been found to accumulate'. The construction of new latrines and the disposal of night-soil at Chinch Bandar, where it was carried by cart – deodorized, en route, by means of Macdougall's powder, no less – provided some amelioration. The village of Cavelpoor, 'consisting of many wretched hovels' – with its thatched huts and unmetalled roads – contained 'cesspits with foul water' and was 'occupied by camp followers and prostitutes'. Similarly, the Regimental bazaar, although it faced St John's Church, was 'a nest of prostitutes, the close vicinage of whom has had deplorable results, and has been the subject of frequent complaint by those interested in the well-being of our soldiery'. That the foreshore on both sides of Colaba 'was the constant resort of the poorer native inhabitants, who had no necessaries either public or private', posed an additional threat. The sanitary question was conceived less as a social than an administrative problem, concerned in the first place with the health of European troops, and with the safety and well-being of British and Indian elites.[38] ('Public opinion' stood to gain.) The fact that the issue of sanitary conditions had first attracted attention in relation to the health of the troops is at least one important indication of the direction of policy. It received prominence once again following the growth of the cotton mill industry in the 1870s and 1880s. It was revived by the nightmare of the plague of 1896–1900 which combined most dramatically the dual threat to both the wealth and the health of magnates which the multiplication of appalling conditions represented. In the aftermath of the 1918–19 influenza epidemic and the growing stridency of popular protest in politics, the Governor of Bombay,

---

[37] *Report on the Sanitary State of the Army in India*, p. 39; *Report of the Sanitary Commissioner for Bombay*, 1867, Inspection Report No. 1, p. 11.

[38] *Report of the Sanitary Commissioner for Bombay*, 1867, Inspection Report No. 1, pp. 10–12.

Sir George Lloyd, became the moral conscience of the rulers from the safety of Government House, Walkeshwar. But, throughout these years, when the drama of crises propelled the authorities into action and forced the powerful vested interests in local politics to acquiesce, improvements were made selectively, directed at improving the condition of the rich and muscling the poor into their segregated enclaves.

Thus, as early as 1848, the Girgaum and Kalbaderee roads, 'the two principal thoroughfares of the Native Town, and those most frequented by Europeans', were the first to have the side gutters covered. 'Owing to the deficiency of funds', however, 'very little progress' had been made 'in the back streets of the Native Town'. Over the next decade, covered drains snaked their way to these districts; but drains and sewers remained overused and inadequate in the poorer back streets.[39] As late as 1925, Burnett-Hurst pointed out that, although Bombay had more sewers than any city in the East, its 'poorer quarters' often had none.[40]

Water supply had always been a major problem. Until the 1860s, the troops in Colaba received their water transported by 'pukhalie bullocks' from wells in the Esplanade. This was the first area of the island to receive a main connection for water from the Vehar lake in the 1860s, which albeit 'by gradually diminished channels affords a moderate supply to all the inhabitants to the extremity of the Peninsula'.[41] The improved supply of Vehar water was in the 1870s celebrated for its expected effect in reducing cholera rather than for its availability for consumption. This revealed eminent sense. The availability of water could not be celebrated simply because it was not as yet widely available. In 1871, Vehar connections supplied no more than every eleven families on shore and, accounting for the harbour population, it served every eighty-six persons on the island. However, this facility was so thinly spread that 'the number of connections seriously interferes with the general service by taking off pressure, so that no water reaches the outlying districts until a late hour of the day. House occupiers get disgusted at having to wait for sufficient water to supply their domestic wants, and it is a pitiable sight to see men, women and children awaiting around a pipe eagerly watching and quarrelling for the miserable dribble from it.'[42] There were 56,866 people comprising 7,120 families in 1,967 houses in Khetwadi, Chaupati and Girgaum. In these districts, 300 cesspools and 754 tanks and wells were 'the only sources of water supply'. The Health Officer commented:

---

[39] Coneybeare, *The Sanitary State*, p. 17.

[40] Burnett-Hurst, *Labour and Housing in Bombay*, p. 21.

[41] *Report of the Sanitary Commissioner for Bombay*, 1867, Inspection Report No. 1, Colaba, p. 10.

[42] Bombay Health Officer's Report for the 3rd quarter of 1871, Bombay, 1871, p. 24.

the poor people living in these districts have access to but two dipping wells and three public foundations . . . I am certain that the water in nearly every one [of the wells and foundations] ought to be pronounced unfit for drinking purposes. My anxiety is therefore great, as at all events there is room to fear that the inhabitants of these sections may, in the course of the next few months, be compelled to drink the water of these filth-sodden wells and tanks.[43]

When scarce rain placed the city's supply on rationed quantities, it was true as late as 1925 that 'the poor quarters of the city suffer the most'.[44]

Land reclamation was a particularly spectacular example of the selective operation of social policy. Land reclamation was essential primarily for the linking of the seven islands which comprised Bombay. It was necessary, too, for the construction of markets, houses and even drains. Without the filling up of old tanks and the reclamation of swamps, it was futile to attempt to confront the virulence and frequency of malarial epidemics. However, in keeping with the general pattern, effective and far-reaching schemes for reclamation were directed at commercial improvement and the housing of the rich. Some of this reclamation was directed primarily at building bundars and docks to improve the facilities of the port. Between 1873 and 1909, the Port Trust reclaimed 165 acres in the improvement of Bombay's docks. The Mazagaon-Sewri reclamation begun in 1907 remained, until the Back Bay reclamations of the 1920s, the most impressive. Its reclamations added nearly 5 per cent to the land area of the island, it provided a wharf frontage over 2.5 miles long and cost about Rs 157 lakhs. As the *Gazetteer* noted, 'The chief benefit arising from the project when completed will be the transfer from Colaba to Mazagaon of the Cotton Gren, which will occupy 330,000 square yards of land against 180,000 occupied at Colaba.' It was in addition to be supported by the provision of improved railway facilities. By contrast, the Back Bay reclamations were intended to provide residential land. This project 'proved so lucrative that the desirability of reclaiming further areas in Back Bay has already become a subject for serious debate'.[45]

The improvement of social conditions was advanced only slowly and it proceeded very selectively. That it advanced at all was due to the fear of disease and discontent. The appalling conditions in which most of the island's inhabitants were compelled to live threatened also, at times, to bring its commerce to a standstill. The magnitude of the task which faced Bombay's rulers required it to devise an essential infrastructure for a rapidly growing city, imposed limitless demands upon limited

---

[43] Bombay Health Officer's Report for the 3rd quarter of 1871, p. 24.
[44] Burnett-Hurst, *Labour and Housing in Bombay*, p. 24.   [45] *Gazetteer*, I, 69–70.

Table 2. *Examples of rise of property values in Bombay 1860–1910*

Vacant land	1863	Rs 1,700
	1874	Rs 2,600
	1888	Rs 2,550
	1906	Rs 20,903
Vacant land and small bungalow	1816	Rs 1,200
	1860	Rs 12,000
	1907	Rs 155,000

Source: *Gazetteer*, I, 329. These examples suggest no more than the trend of rising prices.

finances and upon an administrative psychology already and conveniently partial to the predatory instincts of *laissez-faire*. Operating under these inescapable constraints, it is not surprising that municipal programmes tended to be highly selective in their implementation favouring those concerns which were most relevant to the large economic interests and the more immediate material needs of the dominant classes.

At every stage in its history, land appeared to be scarce in Bombay. Once the seven islands were connected, more swamps drained and land 'reclaimed' from the sea, the available space by the mid-nineteenth century increased, but the population of the island grew even more rapidly. From the 1850s, it was said, rents were 'exorbitant even with the most wretched accommodation'.[46] If land was scarce and valuable, this encouraged investment and speculation in property, whose effect was to push prices up rapidly. Rising land prices could devastate programmes of urban development and drain municipal funds. On the other hand, the municipal revenue yielded by Bombay, in proportion to the level of expenditure it ought to have borne, was calculated by Coneybeare in the 1850s to be lower than any town in a comparable situation.[47]

Scarce resources and high costs combined to pose more sharply the choice in social policy between roads and houses, between welfare and utility, between commercial interest and social conditions. The high price of land may have discouraged administrative intervention, provided a spurt to speculation, and increased the temptation to put it to commercial use. Certainly, financial stringency forced the construction of strict priorities in municipal policy. The development of an infrastructure for trade had to be set against expenditure on improving hygiene, housing and health. But it should not be supposed that the price of land alone

[46] *Gazetteer*, I, 324.   [47] Coneybeare, *The Sanitary State*, p. 24.

Table 3. *Average price of land per square yard paid for by Bombay Municipality for setbacks in different wards 1871–1906*

Ward A	Rs 15–50	Ward E	Rs 8–20
Ward B	Rs 20–75	Ward F	< Rs 1–10
Ward C	Rs 20–70	Ward G	< Rs 1–3
Ward D	Rs 8–20		

Source: Gazetteer, I, 328.

retarded the implementation of policies to ameliorate social conditions in Bombay. Land was cheapest, of course, in the predominantly working-class wards of D, E, F and G (see Table 3), and more expensive in the European centre of the city, while parts of wards B and C, which comprised the heart of the old Native Town and the stronghold of its merchants, was the most expensive of all.

Yet improvements in the systems of drains and sewers and water supply went furthest in precisely those areas where land was most expensive and inhabited by the wealthier classes, both Indian and, especially, European. In the context of a social ethos, which combined the morality of profit-seeking with hostility to administrative intervention, the scarcity and high value of land helped to create conditions in which social problems generated by rapid urban growth were dealt with only when they were catapulted dramatically to the forefront of the city's social, economic or political concerns, and were handled pragmatically as they arose in a manner devoid of any general strategy of amelioration. Whereas the development of an infrastructure most conducive to profit maximization received the most sustained attention.

This bias was facilitated by the way in which, within Bombay's munic-ipal institutions, the shifting, wayward and always tense alliance between the city's dominant classes deflected the direction of policy to suit their specific interests. From the mid-nineteenth century, Bombay's elites were afforded a considerable degree of control over the city's municipal affairs. To a large extent, municipal politics, especially as it impinged upon the creation of a habitable urban environment, hinged upon the abil-ity of various social groups to shift the burden of taxation onto others while deploying these revenues to suit their own commercial interests. Of course, these social groups and commercial interests, so active in municipal politics, frequently overlapped with each other. The 'shetias' of Bombay who dominated its trade as well as its politics began in the early nineteenth century to invest in land. Thus, Dadabhai Pestonji Wadia was said to own a quarter of the island in 1851.[48] The high price and considerable shortage of land provided the basis for a long and enduring relationship between landlords, commercial enterprise and local power, which served to obstruct attempts to deal even remotely adequately with the urban needs of housing and health, sanitation and sewerage. On the other hand, the main thrust of municipal policy was to develop the commercial possibilities of the city, which in turn was a product of the alliance between the millowners, large landlords and merchant princes who dominated Bombay's politics.

While the city's employers, landlords and administrators were certain that something should be done to improve conditions in Bombay, their material interests restricted action and favoured postponement. On the other hand, the threat of disease and discontent remained at the forefront of elite perceptions. The result of this impasse was despair. Socially, as will be discussed, it was manifested in the flight of the 'better classes' to the new suburbs and the more salubrious quarters. Ideologically, the failure of social policy was attributed to dirty, native habits, overlooking the fact that the conditions in which the poor lived were the product not the cause of ineffective policy. However, the ingrained habits of the peasant were believed to contribute to the deterioration of the new environment into which he crowded. Coneybeare argued that 'many bad smells' which were attributed to the cesspools, the sluices and the open drains of the town, were in reality 'due to other causes not so readily removable' such as 'the low caste and filthy habits of the inhabitants of a neighbourhood'. Coneybeare, like many successors, did not find it difficult to discover a sociological argument which nailed his class prejudice firmly to the mast of universal truth. 'It could not be expected', he wrote, 'that any town containing half a million people can be without a dirty quarter, and this is particularly the case in India where the connection of caste has a tendency to concentrate sweepers and others of low caste in one locality. Municipal improvements can only provide the means of cleanliness to those who are willing to avail themselves of them, and the inhabitants of Cammattee Porra are not so.'[49]

In 1851, after all, 'Captain Parr and a number of other gentlemen who were in the habit of riding on the Back Bay sands' were appalled 'by disgusting spectacles, which it was impossible to describe'. Coneybeare found the same complaint 'is made, and with equal reason by the

---

[48] H. D. Darukhanawalla, *Parsi Lustre on Indian Soil* (Bombay, 1939), pp. 87–91; Wadia, p. 116; Dobbui, *Urban Leadership*, p. 12.

[49] H. Coneybeare, *A Comparison between Different Methods of Conveyancing and Ultimately Disposing of Night Soil*, p. 28. Printed as Appendix H to his *The Sanitary State*.

inhabitants of every street in the Native Town and the Fort', and added vehemently, 'I believe there is no place in the world where so disgraceful a disregard of decency prevails as at Bombay. It is idle to attempt to keep the town clean, or to teach the inhabitants the value of cleanliness and decency, while they are permitted to indulge in this disgusting offence with impunity, in broad day and in the public streets (often too, in the immediate vicinity of the police *chowkies*, and under the eyes of individual policemen).'[50]

These were the frustrations of administrators who could conveniently wear the garb of didacts and pedagogues. Dirty native habits could be cleanly disconnected from the objectively horrendous state of the town's sanitation. Thus Coneybeare inveighed against so 'disgraceful a disregard of decency' as prevailed at Back Bay and yet urged in the same report that, 'Public necessaries are in my opinion indispensable at Bombay because a large proportion of our labouring population inhabit lodging houses too densely crowded to admit of private accommodation to the requisite extent.' Defecation in the streets, he believed, could be prevented by employing two mounted policemen armed with hunting crops to keep a close eye on miscreants and by a stricter enforcement of Regulation III of 1815, 'yet', he recognized, 'it would be a hardship to enforce this Regulation strictly without first providing such accommodation as would enable the poorer classes to observe it'.[51] Indeed, one contemporary observer commented in 1855 that, 'To travel by rail from Bori Bunder to Byculla, or to go into Mody Bay, was to see in the foreshore the latrine of the whole population of the Native Town.'[52]

Such descriptions did not cease with the 'improvements' of the late nineteenth and early twentieth centuries, but if they attracted the attention of the traveller they pertained to more specific localities and more isolated enclaves. Similar arguments about their cause were not confined to the mid-nineteenth century; they too were repeated into the twentieth century. These arguments did, however, become more sophisticated. Dirty native habits provided the subject for saloon humour or indignant club conversation. But administrative reports, journalistic articles and academic observations became permeated with the sophisticated terminology which discussed the problem in terms of the adaptation of the peasant to city life. The low-caste native unwilling to learn habits of cleanliness from the municipal commissioner was the paradigm of the

---

[50] Coneybeare, *Different Methods of Conveyancing*, p. 15.
[51] Coneybeare, *Different Methods of Conveyancing*, p. 28. It remains difficult to reconcile the relentless logic of this wisdom with its dissociation from characterizations of native scatology.
[52] Quoted in Edwardes, *The Rise of Bombay*, pp. 279–80.

1850s, the ignorance and unsanitary habits of simple country-folk provided the explanation of the 1920s. 'All sense of cleanliness appears to be absent,' wrote Burnett-Hurst, '. . . it is no exaggeration to say that the masses are utterly unacquainted with even elementary ideas of hygiene and sanitation, and little improvement can take place until they have been educated to a different standard of living.'[53] Already, the native character provided the determination of the more general failure of social policy. Nothing could be done, ran the argument, to develop India socially and economically until the native character itself was altered. More crucially, by the 1920s, the old argument was used in a new and more general context. It was suggested that the transformation of the Indian economy would have to wait upon the transformation of the Indian character. In Bombay, this meant raising the moral as well as productive standards of the Indian labourer. Sir Stanley Reed carried Burnett-Hurst's argument to a more explicit conclusion when he linked even the question of hygiene to the backwardness of the Indian economy. 'The whole future of India,' he wrote, 'based as it must be on an efficient and contented labour force, is bound up with an improvement in the hygienic conditions in the great industrial centres.'[54]

These perceptions were governed by real problems of control. Faced with the growing clamour of nationalist criticism, which occasionally posed some awkward questions in Britain, the colonial state used these arguments partly to secure the legitimacy and justice of its rule against such criticism. That the colonial state functioned according to generally accepted notions of social justice was necessary to affirm its moral right to rule India, even though in the last instance the potency of its physical force might provide sufficient sanction. For its critics 'at home', imperial administrators and ideologues developed images of India which suggested that its society was peculiarly different and hence demanded peculiar policies.

It was from just such a wide ideological terrain that these connections between standards of civic hygiene and economic development could be drawn. Beyond these connections lay the fear of disease which dogged the psychology of British administrators and some of their Indian collaborators. Imperial ideology threw up an armoury of myths with which to confront its critics in metropolis and colony alike, but it also believed the fantasies it generated. Thus, as explanations of the appalling social conditions of Bombay developed and became more sophisticated, they did not change in content. When Burnett-Hurst urged that Indians must

[53] Burnett-Hurst, *Labour and Housing in Bombay*, p. 27.
[54] Sir Stanley Reed, Foreword to Burnett-Hurst, *Labour and Housing in Bombay*, p. vi.

be 'educated to a higher standard of living', he echoed the mystification which cloaked Ovington's fantasy that in Bombay it rained frogs from heaven during the monsoons. Ovington's amazement at the mysterious ways of the Orient is easily understood in the light of the contemporary fear that exposure to the dark rites and the magical customs of heathens could have consequences as 'direful' on their morals as the tropical climate and stagnant air would have on their health. The obsessions of Luther were visited upon the rulers of India. The persistence of these fears, at a more general level, suggests how the British presence existed on its nerve-ends, watchful, weary and forever wary, always conscious of the 'thin red line', and the need to defend itself individually against moral and physical sickness, collectively against intrigue and conspiracy. As their position as rulers grew more entrenched, their fantasies about India grew more abstract. At the same time, they bemoaned increasingly the difficulties of the burdens they carried. Hardships and hazards, like heat and dust, provided the essence of the imperial romance. But they posed very real threats, as well. This was where some of the pressure to ameliorate the sanitary and hygienic conditions in Bombay was generated.

V   The plague: despair and solutions of despair

Epidemics, so deeply feared by the colonial rulers, were no rare occurrence in Bombay. Outbreaks of influenza and cholera, typhoid and malaria took their toll throughout the period. Despite the sanitary state of the city, it was said repeatedly that the most significant source of epidemics were the large numbers of people – export traders, migrant labourers, devout pilgrims – who passed through Bombay. Sanitary commissioners, health officers and municipal authorities often urged greater control by the railway companies to prevent cholera-ridden people from entering the city, the exclusion of travellers from infected districts and rules of guidance for village patels in preventing the sick from travel. Pilgrims, whether they came from Mecca or Pandharpur,[55] were said to be a major source of the 'importation of cholera poison'.[56] The Municipal Commissioner even suggested in July 1867 that the Pandharpur jatra, the major centre of pilgrimage in the Deccan, should be forbidden in certain years, because cholera 'has always raged in Bombay immediately after the return of pilgrims from Pandharpur'.[57] Occasionally, the threat of

---

[55] *Proceedings of the Sanitary Commissioner*, Bombay, March 1866, p. 69.
[56] *Proceedings of the Sanitary Commissioner*, Bombay, June 1868, p. 215.
[57] *Proceedings of the Sanitary Commissioner*, Bombay, July 1867.

Table 4. *The highest rates of mortality per week reached (1897–8 to 1909–10)*

1897–1898	2,250	1904–1905	1,785
1898–1899	2,450	1905–1906	1,812
1899–1900	2,820	1906–1907	2,180
1900–1901	2,620	1907–1908	1,340
1902–1903	2,594	1908–1909	1,250
1902–1903	1,902	1909–1910	1,152
1903–1904	2,604		

Source: Gazetteer, I, 175.

epidemics prompted talk about sanitary cordons.[58] Just as sanitary cordons were thought necessary to protect the lives of European soldiers, so they might stop epidemic diseases from polluting the city. As late as the 1920s, one observer commented, in the metaphor of sanitary cordons, that Bombay was 'the gateway of India' not merely for trade but for disease as well.[59] Sanitary cordons represented the most far-fetched solution conceived to deal with Bombay's urban problems, a counsel of despair.

The outbreak of bubonic plague in the 1890s was the product, not only the cause, of such despair. It remained the most dramatic and destructive manifestation of municipal failure in the nineteenth century. 'The terrible fate of Mandvi and similar localities', wrote one contemporary, 'must have sunk deep into the minds of those in whose charge lies the welfare of the island.'[60] During the 1890s, Bombay's population was reduced by more than 45,000. Flight and outmigration accounted in part for this reduction. But mortality rates were dramatically high and remained at over 1,000 per week for over a decade.

The outbreak of the plague in 1896 also led to 'the flight of the rich and better class population to healthier, outlying localities and in evacuation of the city to all save those whose daily work obliges them to live there'.[61] This coincided with a far more brief, if still massive, exodus of Bombay's working classes which led to an acute shortage of labour in 1897[62] and to 'open bidding for labour at the street corners and the shattering of the tie hitherto binding the employer and the employed'.[63] The millowners

---

[58] *Proceedings of the Sanitary Commissioner*, Bombay, July 1867, pp. 234–5.
[59] Burnett-Hurst, *Labour and Housing in Bombay*, p. 5.
[60] Edwardes, *The Rise of Bombay*, p. 333.   [61] *Gazetteer*, I, 197.
[62] *Report of the Municipal Commissioner on the Plague in Bombay*, 1898–9.
[63] Edwardes, *The Rise of Bombay*, p. 330.

made some attempts to recruit labour from North India,[64] although by late 1897, workers had begun to return.

Coinciding with a trade depression in the textile industry, creating a labour shortage and disrupting the stability of labour supply, the immediate effect of the plague was to increase the bargaining power of the workers who remained in the city and to demonstrate the power of collective action, in 1897 when there was 'open bidding' for labour in the streets, in 1899 during the plague riots against official intervention, whose severity was matched by its desperation, and more especially during the mill strikes of 1900–1. These manifestations of working-class power combined with the vital threat of disease to invite more serious attention from both the city's elite and the government. It also drove the city's business classes, concerned about efficiency at work, low wages and contentment in the streets, into a closer dependence upon the state. The plague became the focus of this alliance; it also became the focus of workers' antipathy towards both.

The plague left an indelible impression on the social experience of the city. As late as 1925, Burnett-Hurst believed that it 'still retains its hold on the city'.[65] More materially, it had forced the crystallization of class antagonism and class identity. The plague as a consequence of the abysmal sanitary conditions of the town had combined as a social moment the disruption of the city's commerce, the subversion of its political order, as represented by the 1898 riots, and the threat of fatal disease even to that part of the city's elite which lived in relatively antiseptic surroundings.[66] It showed then that the contrast between the strategies of development which sought to develop the commercial possibilities of the island, and those which attempted to alleviate its material and physical conditions, represented an essentially false dichotomy.

The horrors of the plague prompted the most sustained period of state intervention in the affairs of the city. The Government of Bombay, sensitized to the problem of sanitary and social conditions in its Presidency capital, grew increasingly critical of the achievements of the Bombay Municipal Corporation. In 1898, it formed the City of Bombay Improvement Trust in response to and as a condemnation of the failure of the municipal authorities to deal satisfactorily with the city's problems. The Trust, moreover, was placed firmly outside the control of the municipal

---

[64] *Bombay Millowners' Association (BMOA) Annual Report*, 1896, pp. 149–50, 150–6; *BMOA Annual Report*, 1897, pp. 4–6; *The Indian Textile Journal (ITJ)*, 7, 81, June 1897, 207–8; *ITJ*, 9, 99, December 1898, 65.

[65] Burnett-Hurst, *Labour and Housing in Bombay*, p. 5.

[66] Some of the wealthier families migrated to their country refuges. See M. R. Jayakar, *The Story of My Life*, vol. I (Bombay, 1958).

corporation. Its brief was not only to improve the sanitary state of the city and the standard of housing for the poor, but also to build and widen roads, embark on land reclamations and strengthen the essential facilities of transport and communications which served the city's commerce.

The Improvement Trust set about its tasks with breathless energy, enthusiasm and radical purpose. Unsanitary dwellings were simply to be demolished, and replaced with new and healthier buildings for the working classes. Roads were to be widened and arterial thoroughfares, relieving congestion and facilitating easy access and movement, were to be pushed through the town. The city itself was to be restructured, the contours of its social geography to be redrawn. The Improvement Trust spelt out its strategy in 1907: 'It seems, for example, probable', recorded the *Gazetteer*, 'that the middle classes will eventually find more suitable accommodation in the northern sections of the island . . . ; the upper classes, particularly the Europeans will perhaps find relief in the reclamation of the western foreshore of the island; while the whole of the central belt of the island between Grant Road and Jaigaon Cross Road will thus be reserved for the industrial and lower classes.'[67]

The Bombay Development Committee, which reported in 1914 largely on the basis of the evidence of the city's merchants, millowners and property magnates, not only accepted this general plan of segregation but even exaggerated its implications. Thus it argued that mills should be concentrated in the north-east of the island and the workers should continue to live near their place of work. Indeed, it was 'of obvious importance' to preserve Bombay's 'attractive western frontage' for residential purposes and 'to avoid the location, along the western belt, of industries or trades of an offensive or defacing character'.[68]

To enable the western shore of the island with its cooling breezes and attractive frontage to be preserved for the accommodation of the upper classes, the report strongly supported schemes for reclamation, especially of the Back Bay, in the west. At the same time, improvements in transport and congestion in the centre pushed the middle classes towards the north. In the central portions of the island, there remained the city's labouring classes. Reclamation of new land had been the traditional solution for the decaying conditions of the town. Selective and partial improvement had been fortified by old precedents.

Yet once again in their turn such sweeping measures were themselves swept away and ambitious plans foundered on scarce resources and long legal battles. The Bombay Improvement Trust ran out of money and

---

[67] *Gazetteer*, I, 20; Annual Reports of BCIT.
[68] *Report of the Bombay Development Committee*, 1914, p. v.

got drawn into lengthy disputes over the proper compensation for the properties they acquired. By 1917–18, more than two-thirds of the land which it had acquired in the pursuit of its schemes – an area which covered 11 per cent of the land area of the island – remained undeveloped.[69]

It had constructed 21,387 new tenements between 1898 and 1920 but it had also demolished a further 24,428 tenements to achieve this.[70] Like the agency it had replaced, its energies were channelled into the widening and improving of roads and main thoroughfares. The problems of overcrowding and unsanitary housing, which the Trust had been set up to remedy in the brutal aftermath of the bubonic plague, persisted while the widening of roads and the construction of thoroughfares through congested areas of the city only served to exacerbate the degree of overcrowding and the pressures upon standards of housing and sanitation.

Throughout this period, in the two decades following the plague, the Municipal Corporation proved to be no more committed to the amelioration of living conditions in Bombay than it had been in the later nineteenth century.

Between 1900 and 1915, its expenditure on public health increased by 14 per cent, while its outlay on public works (such as road widening and pavement construction) increased by 88 per cent. Sir George Lloyd (of impeccably imperialist credentials), who came to Bombay as Governor in 1918 during a nostalgic revival of the imperial high noon in Britain, wrote to Montagu: 'Had I not been a long time in the East I should have been almost moved by the generous sentiments that characterised the Municipality's interest in the poor of Bombay . . . But in fact what have they done? They are responsible and unashamed for a system of housing and insanitation which would have caused the worst of Abdul Hamed's valis to blush crimson.'[71]

The last years of the First World War and its immediate aftermath witnessed considerable labour and nationalist unrest in the city and a vast influx of migrant workers, as a boom in the Bombay textile industry coincided with scarcity and famine in the countryside.

In this turbulent context came the influenza epidemic of 1918, which revived memories of the plague and showed that the continued neglect of housing and sanitation could well lead to another catastrophe.

Sir George Lloyd determined to launch another, yet more grandiose, scheme for attacking Bombay's urban problems, and to this end he

---

[69] *Annual Admin. Report for the Bombay Presidency*, 1917–18, p. vi.
[70] Burnett-Hurst, *Labour and Housing in Bombay*, p. 32.
[71] Sir George Lloyd to E. S. Montagu, 28 February 1919, Montague Papers, Mss EUR D 523(24), IOR.

established a separate government department, autonomous of both the Municipal Corporation and the Improvement Trust, to initiate and supervise a programme of development. This programme included the construction of 50,000 tenements to house nearly 250,000 labourers. It offered the possibility of middle-class housing in Jalsette and of reviving the old scheme for the reclamation of the Back Bay. This expansive programme was to be financed by a fund-raising scheme and especially through a town duty of one rupee levied on each bale of cotton which entered the city. The logic of this scheme was to make the millowners contribute to the housing of labour. For the most part, most millowners were willing to accept this in 1919. First, the town duty fell most directly upon cotton merchants, who thus had to share with the millowners the burden of housing industrial labour. Second, the industry was making unprecedented profits and the millowners in an expansive mood were not unwilling to make social provision in order to avoid political discontent. Third, in 1919–20, the millowners had accepted a self-denying ordinance which restricted them to single-shift working in the midst of a boom. No doubt the decision was based upon a reading of future market trends and the fear of overproduction. Of course, it divided the millowners and led to bitter conflict within the Bombay Millowners' Association, when members appear to have regularly reported others to its committee for working two shifts. But one reason underlying the majority acceptance of this limitation was that double-shift working would massively increase the flow of migrants to Bombay. This, they feared, constituted a 'serious menace and danger to the city' because neither the available housing nor the sanitary conditions could bear such an influx.[72]

However, over the next five years, the situation changed dramatically. The Back Bay scheme soaked up most of the Development Department's finances. By 1924–5, it had received Rs 4.68 crores out of the total expenditure of Rs 7.22 crores. At the same time, the scheme was hampered by numerous problems. The Back Bay reclamation was begun during the post-war boom when a high return was expected, but it had to be continued when prices were falling drastically. Technical incompetence, the massive increase in municipal expenditure in general and especially the pressure this exercised on the incidence of taxation, and above all the effects of the slump placed enormous constraints upon its accomplishment.

As boom gave way to slump, the millowners became less generous in their willingness to subsidize urban development. The increased burden of taxes, which such schemes necessitated, was increasingly resented.

[72] *BMOA Annual Report*, 1921, pp. 39–43.

Legislation affecting hours of work, workmen's compensation and trade unions was felt to raise their transactional costs. At a time when they were being undersold by Japanese importers as well as up-country mills, Bombay's millowners resented the Government's refusal to abolish the excise duty and resistance to any policy of effective tariff protection. The amounts which the cotton mills paid in municipal taxes rose rapidly from Rs 742,815 in 1914–15 to over Rs 2 million in 1924–5, which amounted to about 6.5 per cent of the total municipal revenue.[73] The 'enormous burden on the trade' arising from these financial pressures could in 1923 'hardly be borne without serious injury to the industry in the present state of trade'.[74] Social improvement now slid down their list of priorities. When the Municipal Commissioner warned the Bombay Millowners' Association that he would cover their water tanks as they bred malaria, the millowners replied indignantly that 'malaria was in fact the result of insanitary conditions and poor water supply fostered by municipal neglect'.[75]

If they had responded to Lloyd's original scheme in 1919 with some enthusiasm, the millowners were sullen, resentful and sometimes highly critical by 1925. Indeed, the Bombay Development Department projects had in execution exceeded the original estimates by 90 per cent, and constructions they felt should have been stopped well before this 'huge waste of public money'.[76]

By the mid-1920s the Development Department, faced with mounting costs, had streamlined their ambitious project, reducing the number of tenements they intended to build from 50,000 to less than 17,000. In 1925, nearly three-quarters of the completed tenements remained unoccupied. This was partly because the rental was too high, pitched at Rs 5 to recover an 'economic rent' in terms of the outlay on construction, and partly because some of the tenements (such as the chawls at Worli) were situated too far away from the cotton mills, so that workers could not, in the absence of satisfactory public transport, reach them easily on foot.[77]

In 1926, the Back Bay scheme was shrouded in scandal, in the celebrated Harvey-Narimen case. It was with reason that the millowners protested that this ineffective policy had been financed by 'the cotton trade of India' which had borne a town duty of a rupee on every bale of cotton to enter the city since 1920 in a largely futile cause.

Since the early nineteenth century, commercial, industrial and landlord interests had shaped the formulation and implementation of a social

[73] Rutnagur, p. 351.   [74] *BMOA Annual Report*, 1923, p. 103.
[75] *BMOA Annual Report*, 1924, p. 155.   [76] *BMOA Annual Report*, 1925, p. 73.
[77] *BMOA Annual Report*, 1925; TLIC; *TOI*, 25 December 1925.

policy for Bombay city. In keeping with the perceptions and preferences of British officials, such 'improvements' that were implemented proceeded selectively favouring the rich and the powerful at the expense of the poor. Even the hectic activity which followed the plague subsided into the old familiar pattern of selective but limited improvement aimed largely at developing the facilities and infrastructure for commerce. Neither the Municipal Corporation, nor even the Development Department, were able to make a significant intellectual or practical contribution to the amelioration of social conditions. They failed to evolve any long-term strategy for the creation of a generally hygienic urban environment. They could not overcome their own institutional inertia or the massive complacence of the city's elites.

The formulation of a sustained and effective policy was complicated by the delicate balances which the colonial state and its local manifestations sought to maintain between conflicting needs: the need to fight epidemics, the need to attract labour, the need to minimize political discontent, the need to respect the old maxim of political control, and light taxation. The political context of 'improvement' had served to produce the deliberate geographical and social restructuring of the city. The same process which had served to obstruct the real confrontation of the city's civic problems provided a spur to the development of its social geography, already being determined by the pattern of its economic change.

Peasants and proletarians in Bombay city in the late nineteenth and early twentieth centuries

To a remarkable extent, historians and sociologists of widely differing intellectual traditions appear to have converged upon broadly similar approaches to the study of a migrant working class. Modernization theorists, neoclassical economists and sociologists of development have been preoccupied with the adaptation of a rural workforce to an urban and industrial setting and have tended to portray protest largely as a response to this process of adaptation. The form and content of labour protest in this view is determined by the extent of industrial development. Thus, while labour protest in the initial stages of industrialization is characterized by spontaneity and violence, the organization of trade unions and skills of negotiation and formal collective bargaining are said to be the achievement of a working class in a more advanced stage of its formation. Within the Marxist tradition, such teleology stems not from the rational allocation of resources, and in the case of migrant labour its most efficient deployment and control, but from the ontological role of the working class, in its full proletarian maturity, as the agent of transition to socialism. In either case, and of course there are several varieties of each, the migrant character of the workforce has symbolized a transitional phase in the making of the working class between its original peasant status and its fully developed proletarian character. Many of the existing approaches to the subject offer a teleological rather than a contextual perspective; and to that extent tend towards the ahistorical. Moreover, they often indicate a typology of working-class politics which is closely related to its structural characteristics. However, the problem with the explanation of political action as the function of the dislocation caused by industrial development is that it leaves no room for the effect of politics itself, and of political choice and agency in the explanation of political behaviour.

Many of these frameworks of analysis are particularly inadequate when applied to the case of Bombay. Here, migration was no transitional phase in the formation of the labour force. In 1921, 84 per cent of the city's population had been born outside Bombay. In the 1960s, according to one study of the city's labour market, Bombay's working population 'consists overwhelmingly of migrants'. Moreover, the political behaviour of the working class does not fit easily with postulates of the political response of migrants displaced by industrialization, apparently characterized by spontaneity, violence and an inability to organize. Between 1919 and 1940, there were eight general strikes in Bombay, each lasting longer than a month, while the strikes of 1928–9 were sustained for at least twelve months out of a period of eighteen.

Problems of definition as much as ambiguities of conceptualization have complicated the assessment of the nature, and even the strength, of the rural connections of Bombay's workers. Migrant labour was a term which could apply in the vocabulary of contemporary social comment as much to workers who were entirely dependent upon the city for their livelihood but who retained strong rural connections as to workers who migrated seasonally. Local labour could mean as little as an indication of the workers' place of birth and this in any case was an unreliable guide to residence since most families preferred to return to their villages for the birth of their children. On this accounting, workers who could count among the second- and third-generation factory workers would by virtue of having been born outside the city still be counted as migrants. Since the status of migrant labour was so ambiguous it is hardly surprising that few of the characterizations based upon it have yielded much clarity. Even attempts to calculate the distribution of mill workers by district of origin is, as Morris pointed out long ago, riddled with insuperable problems.

The bulk of Bombay's population in the nineteenth century came to the city from the Konkan and the Desh. From the early decades of the twentieth century, it attracted an increasing number of migrants from the United Provinces and from North India generally. A similar dispersal can be observed in the composition of the city's textile workers. Migrants from Ratnagiri were among the first to entrench themselves in the city's cotton mills. By the 1930s, their proportion of mill workers had probably fallen slightly, while workers from the UP formed about 10 per cent of the workforce, and Satara and Poona contributed about 7 per cent.

The general pattern was for males, usually the younger sons, to leave for the city in their adolescence or in their late teens, having spent their childhood predominantly in the village. Few men emigrated with their families, and when they did, they usually returned to the village to have their children. Throughout their working lives they maintained close connections with the village. They returned to the village to help with the harvest or the sowing or to participate in village and family celebrations so that observers often spoke about the 'annual exodus' from Bombay in

April and May. Some workers also remitted money to their near-relatives to supplement their income or liquidate their debts.

If workers migrated without their families, they did so within the structure of their kinship connections. If migration was meant to boost the rural resources of the family, urban workers also sought its support in numberless ways. When they moved to the city, they lodged with their relatives and found work with their assistance. In sickness and retirement and sometimes in unemployment, they returned to the village. They were not merely providers for the village economy; they were also dependent upon its use as the basis for material provision. The village base was integral to the family economy of the Bombay working class. It is in terms of the operation of the family economy, rather than the slippery nature of migrant or permanent labour or the smooth transition from peasant to proletarian, that the rural connection of the Bombay working class is perhaps more fruitfully examined.

People returned to their villages, for instance, in the event of major illness when medical attention was often unobtainable and, at the very least, expensive. Despite this, the working-class districts registered the highest rates of mortality. 'Respiratory diseases constitute the determining factor', wrote the Bombay medical officer in 1921, 'in rendering the death rate of a working class district notably higher than that of a good residential district and in rendering that of a poor slum higher still.' Those who survived these conditions returned to their villages to recover. Most women who migrated returned to their villages to have their children. In Bombay, more than half the number of births occurred in one-room tenements. It was also in one-room tenements that 83 per cent of infant deaths took place. Bombay's workers returned to their villages in periods of unemployment and more certainly in retirement. The Bombay Port Trust noted that the average working life of a dock labourer amounted to about ten years. This spell of heavy labour made men too old and infirm to work so that 'the majority retire to their village holdings giving way to younger men to take their places'. Kinship and village connections constituted an indispensable instrument of material protection against these perilous margins of survival.

The official memorandum to the Royal Commission on Labour in India described the manner in which this family economy operated:

Only a few members of a family migrate to the towns. The family itself remains domiciled in the mofussil and the centre of the family life is there, so that women folk return to it to bear their children; the men folk when age and disability comes to them, or when death causes a vacancy in the agricultural worker of the family. So far as the Bombay textile workers are concerned it may be said that although they maintain a very close and living contact with their villages, the bulk of them are not merely birds of passage but continue to work in the industry for a considerable period of time once they join it.[1]

So if migration was induced by rural distress, it was also facilitated by the structure of the family economy, which enabled some workers to leave their dependants behind and yet obtain crucial support from the village base while living in the city. It is the integrative operation of this family economy which explains why workers could be both permanent in their dependence upon the city and yet maintain 'a very close and living contact outside it'.

Necessarily, in this context, kinship was very generously interpreted. It could, indeed, reach beyond the extended family to include affinities of caste and village and even loosely those who were known to kinsmen. To be materially effective in conditions of considerable poverty, both rural and urban, the 'joint-family' had to be extensive rather than exclusive in its operations. As industrial workers attempted to build up networks of welfare provision, they were well advised to base them as widely as possible. This explains why workers whose stake in the village had long ceased to be based in land or whose share in the crop was minute, could construct, maintain and utilize these village connections. It explains, too, why they returned periodically to attend village ceremonies, marriages or celebrate festivals. The notion of such an integrative family economy is not intended to convey a picture of rural harmony; rather it serves to demonstrate how the rural connection could, and often was required to, endure the 'proletarianization' of the working class.

Indeed, only those for whom, as one official report observed, 'conditions were so bad in their villages that they had no option' migrated as whole families to settle permanently in Bombay, and consequently weakened, sometimes ruptured, their connections with the village. The famines of 1918–19 brought streams of family migrations from Ahmednagar and Nasik, largely consisting of Mahars into Bombay city. Even mill workers with permanent jobs, albeit under conditions of only relative security, sometimes supported their immediate families in the city but nevertheless retained close ties with the village. The severing of village connections was more often the product of hopeless distress than abnormal success or even relative prosperity.

Perhaps the most remarkable feature of this pattern of migration is its endurance. In the mid-1920s, two-thirds of the males in Ratnagiri between the ages of 14 and 45 years were working in Bombay. Kunj

---

[1] *RCLI, Evidence taken in the Bombay Presidency*, Government of Bombay, vol. I, part i, p. 8.

Patel's survey of Ratnagiri district conducted in the early 1960s reported, 'It is very difficult to find a young male who is between 18 and 25 years in the village. A young man stays there [in the village] if he has [not] yet got a job in the city... Most of those remaining in the villages are either retired or unfit for industrial employment in the city.' Patel estimated that 88 per cent of the families in her sample had a relative working in Bombay. Similarly, the Joshis found not only that the 'overwhelming majority' of the city's working population were migrants but that the majority of migrants had been in the city 'for a considerable length of time'. In other words, they followed the old practice of living in the city for the major part of their working lives and returning to the village in retirement. Although the districts which fed the streams of migration to Bombay were among the poorest regions of the country, their long connections with the largest industrial centre in India did not bring them riches. Forces of capitalist development which were powerful enough to dislodge men on the margins of peasant society failed to provide for their absorption into the industrial economy. If migration was the product of distress, it did not follow that industrialization provided for its relief. This point may be generalized: areas like Ratnagiri, Chota Nagpur, parts of Bihar and east UP, major suppliers of labour to various industries and various centres, remained among the poorest and most backward regions in the country.

Beneath these powerful continuities, of course, some changes are discernible. There have been differing and unreliable estimates of the extent of landholding among mill workers and of the proportion of workers who were born in the city or of those who lived in the city with their families. The tendency may have been for the proportion to rise. It is likely that increasing pressure on the land and the effects of the slump on relationships of debt and labour rendered the rural base of migrant workers less effective. On Morris's interpretation of the census figures, the proportion of mill workers who were born in Bombay increased from 11 per cent in 1911 to 19 per cent in 1921 and had a decade later reached nearly a quarter of the workforce. Dr Nair in his minute of dissent to the Factory Labour Commission estimated that only 20 per cent of mill labour in India possessed any land. In the early 1930s, one mill manager estimated that about 40 per cent of the mill workers had nothing to do with agriculture, and of the rest, a substantial number 'have made Bombay their home and though they retained their connections with their native towns, most of them have ceased to be agriculturists themselves'. In 1946, the Labour Investigation Committee reported that 45.1 per cent of the workers whom it interviewed claimed an interest in land, but it was being worked by relatives or sublessors, while the remainder were largely landless. Few of these estimates are unproblematic; clearly, all of them vary wildly; some, such as that of the mill manager, were rather extreme. Even at their most accurate, figures of landholding are not strictly comparable. For the methods of investigation as well as the definitions upon which they were based varied considerably. To be landless was perfectly compatible with owning a share in the crop. To have nothing to do with agriculture did not mean that their relatives did not cultivate the land, let alone that they had no stake in the village. Often, the village base was modest, even perhaps largely symbolic: a house or a small strip of land, maintained by earnings from field labour or remittances from the city.

The stability of the village connection within the family economy of the working class should not conceal the struggle which was waged by urban workers to maintain it. This determination is reflected in the Konkan, for instance, by an official statement in 1923 on the fragmentation of land-holdings and proposals to check its progression, which reported 'cases in the coastal talukas of Ratnagiri and Kanara where a single coconut tree is a hiss and is moreover jointly owned by several persons'.[2] As Kunj Patel observed forty years later, property 'serves as an invaluable security in times of unemployment, severe economic distress, old age, disabled condition, illness in the family and the like'. Even a small house or a plot 'becomes the last resort for him [the migrant worker] and his family in difficult times. He comes to Bombay to earn but keeps his sheet-anchor in the village.'[3]

Considerations of status also influenced the desire to retain a foothold in the village. Even if its direct economic utility was diminishing, to surrender all claims upon a village base often amounted, for most urban workers, to the weakening of their position within networks of material provision, which were vital in the urban and industrial setting. 'The man who has land in the village', the Collector of West Khandesh told the Royal Commission on Agriculture in the mid-1920s, 'is in every way more respected than a mere tenant. If a man gets into trouble and he wants to prove he is respectable, the first thing he tells you is that he had land of his own in his village.'[4] For untouchable and low-caste migrants, it was even more important to secure their base in village society. But this was matched only by the fact that it was facilitated only by their cash earnings. The Mahar labourers of the Deccan, wrote Harold Mann, 'will

---

[2] Bombay Land Revenue Proceedings, February 1922/3, A, vol. 11330, p. 65: Note by Deputy Secretary, GOB, Revenue, 'Proposals to check excessive sub-division and fragmentation of holdings'. OIOC.

[3] M. Kunj Patel, *Rural Labour in Industrial Bombay* (Bombay, 1963), p. 37.

[4] *Royal Commission on Agriculture in India, Evidence, Bombay Presidency*, H. F. Knight, Collector of West Khandesh, vol. II, part 1, para. 630.

rarely, if ever, think of sacrificing their connections with the village where they hold vatan rights. To do this would make them landless outcasts and hence they return – many of them very frequently, but almost all at intervals – to the old home of the family.'[5] Of course, it is not intended to suggest, by these indications of the determination of migrant workers to retain their holdings, that they invariably achieved their objective. As Charlesworth has shown, the pressures of commercialization, population growth and the fragmentation and subdivision of landholdings became very severe for the poorer peasantry of the Bombay countryside in the early twentieth century.

Clearly, however, migrant workers considered it as important to hold on to their village base in the 1960s as in the 1920s. It is less clear how these continuities may be explained. For factory commissioners and civil servants, millowners and labour leaders, indeed even for some recent writers, this is to be explained by the rural mentalities of industrial workers. Some tended to assume that migration signified betterment and in time modernization; others that peasants came to the city primarily to raid its wealth before returning to the land; most of them assumed that, in the course of time, village connections would be dissolved. It is also clear that these assumptions are not borne out by the evidence from Bombay.

The beginnings of a more plausible explanation lie in the character of industrial development. The initial development of the cotton textile industry was based on the export of yarn to China. Its major competitive advantage lay in its cheap labour costs, especially in relation to Lancashire. By the early twentieth century, when the Chinese demand for its goods had declined, the Bombay mills were forced to turn their attention to the domestic markets. Here, in the 1920s, they faced increasingly stiff competition from cheap Japanese imports, from the inland centres of production and from the continued, if declining, Lancashire presence. In other words, if in the initial phase of development it was essential to hold labour costs down in order to penetrate export markets, this became necessary in the interwar period simply to compete in the domestic market.

The question of cheap labour can be related to a wider structural problem in Indian economic development. The uneven development of industrial capitalism was characterized by the virtual absence of a capital goods sector. Thus, it was only on the eve of the Second World War that the first serious attempts were made to initiate the production of textile machinery and it was not until 1946 that Birla's Textile Machinery

[5] H. H. Mann, 'The Mahars of a Deccan Village', in *Social Framework of Indian Agriculture* (Bombay, 1967).

Corporation produced its first complete ring frame. The heavy reliance of Indian mills on machinery supplies from Britain meant that some of the gains of industrial development were leaked back to the metropolis. Similarly, only 316 machine tools were produced in India as late as 1942. While this imbalance in the economy contributed to the conditions of low effective demand in the domestic market, which acted as a constraint upon industrial expansion and investment, it also signified the high cost of capital goods. Not only were low labour costs the major competitive advantage of Indian industry, but industrial development was predicated on the intensive use of labour. The need to maintain the cheapness of labour provided the structural determinant of industrial relations; it also shaped the character and operation of the family economy.

Between the 1890s and at least the mid-1930s, the cotton textile industry in Bombay maintained a reserve supply of labour – employed casually and irregularly – which fluctuated around one-third of the total work-force. This force of casual labour, of course, helped to cheapen wage costs, but it also strengthened the existing structure of labour discipline which was centred on the jobber, without whom it would probably have been impossible to manage such a flexible supply of labour. The industry was characterized by considerable fluctuations in the volume and types of goods produced. Conditions varied from mill to mill. The labour requirements of each mill were determined not only by absenteeism, but also by the short-term fluctuations of the market, which in turn varied with the price of raw cotton, the shifting demand for particular varieties of yarn and cloth and the accumulation of stocks in the mill itself. Most mills produced cloth which had already been sold in the forward markets two or three months earlier. As T. V. Baddeley, Chairman of the Bombay Millowners' Association, explained in 1939, 'there are many mills which either through their financial position or for reasons of general policy do not make heavily to stock. They do not subordinate their selling to their production. They make what they sell.' The composition of output determined the degree to which a mill followed this policy and therefore its impact upon the demand for labour. Mills which produced a substantial volume of fancy goods could not afford to risk making seasonal goods, which might remain unsold, or vary their output at short notice, and would tend therefore to regulate production according to the quality of forward sales more heavily than in the case of plain grey goods.

From the mid-1930s, the Millowners' Association introduced various kinds of decasualization schemes. The badli control scheme of 1935 stipulated that each mill would maintain a register of its own badli or casual workers, who would have first claim on temporary employment. When permanent vacancies arose, casual workers who had appeared at the mill gates most regularly were employed. Its effect was to tie casual workers into the particular mills with which they were registered. At the same time, labour mobility into the industry was reduced and a large number of casual workers were forced out of the industry on the periphery of which they had previously existed. The problem of unemployment was overcome by the simple expedient of transferring it out of the industry. Further, for the registered badlis themselves, it is not clear that the recruitment of labour was so considerably systematized as to be consistently beneficial. By making decisive inroads into the domain of the jobber, who had previously exerted much greater control over the hiring and firing of workers, it helped to modify the more arbitrary aspects of recruitment; however, jobbers and other supervisory personnel continued to remain influential. Indeed, the general tendency was that, as industrial relations legislation offered permanent workers greater security of tenure and protection against unfair dismissal, casual workers held their badli status for much longer periods, not because fewer vacancies arose, but because employers were reluctant to confirm casual workers in permanent jobs. The problem of casual labour and its enforced dependence upon the countryside persisted; but with one major difference. Since their elevation to permanent status depended upon the regularity with which they appeared at the mill gates, the badli control scheme restricted the casual labourer's option of returning to the village in periods of unemployment while at the same time, by lengthening his spell as a casual worker, increasing his dependence on his village connections.

Both before and, to a lesser extent, after the introduction of the scheme, badlis returned to their villages more frequently than permanent workers, especially when their labour was most urgently needed by the family during the harvest. This period coincided with the general exodus of mill workers from Bombay in April and May, when the casually employed might most easily secure a foothold in permanent employment. That they could be drawn away to the village when their chances of longer spells of employment and perhaps promotion into the permanent workforce were greatest reveals the importance of the village connection. By the twentieth century, it is perhaps more valid to speak in terms of seasonal migration out of Bombay into the countryside rather than the reverse.

Casual and irregular employment was the predominant condition in the Bombay labour market. The Bombay Port Trust offered its permanent workers various leave and pension privileges. But workers qualified for this permanent status only after a three-year period of continuous employment, allowing for fourteen days' leave each year. Many workers returned to their villages 'during or before the monsoon to attend to the cultivation of their fields or repairs to their homes in their native villages and rejoin afresh on their return to Bombay after an absence of two or three months'. This period of absence constituted a break in their record of continuous employment. Thus, only those who could break their village ties, or those who had none, stood any chance of admission to the ranks of the permanently employed. Similarly, in its maintenance workshops, labour was taken on 'according to the amount of work in hand'. Among general dock workers, 80 per cent were casually employed on the basis of 'daily engagements as required'. Moreover, only 70 per cent of the labourers who appeared at the gates received work; the rest were forced 'to pick up stray work from individual consignees or merchants or take up day labour in the cities'. The Bombay Electric Supply and Tramways Company was another important employer of labour; its personnel policies were among the most progressive in Bombay. Since its operations were not directly concerned with production, its need to employ casual labour was less and it was confined largely to the mains department, which hired workers daily to lay electric cables. But it was the unskilled employees who 'usually take leave, prior to, or at the beginning of the monsoon, chiefly to repair their houses in their native country or to make agricultural preparations'. The bulk of municipal labour was untouchable, largely recruited locally and on a temporary basis. Although the Municipal Corporation claimed that there was no turnover in their permanent staff, they also said that 'the men on the temporary staff do not always continue in employment throughout the year. They generally go to their native places before the rains for tilling the fields and return at the end of the monsoon after gathering the harvest.' The case of the municipal workers further emphasizes the inadequacy of the distinction between local or permanent labour and migrant or casual labour.

The distinction, at any rate, cannot be grounded on intent: upon assumptions about the persistence of rural mentalities among industrial workers. This long-standing division of the family economy of the working class between city and countryside was rather the product of intolerable social conditions, the uncertainty of employment and the complete absence of welfare provision. As the Social Service League pointed out, 'the most important reason' for the separation of families was 'the inadequacy of wages in the case of a large number of workers'.

Related to the question of low wages and irregular employment were the problems posed by living conditions in the city. Among other reasons for the fact that the families of working-class migrants remained in their villages, the Social Service League began its list with 'the bad effect of continued residence in Bombay on health'. Even the relatives of the mill workers came to the city for brief periods, rarely longer than a year.

The cost of living in the city was too high and rents, in particular, too expensive to permit most workers to support their families in Bombay. The Indian Seamen's Union spelled out a condition which applied to most sections of Bombay's labouring classes:

The housing accommodation in Bombay is so expensive that seamen who are not born and bred in Bombay very rarely live with their families. They generally keep their families in their native villages and pay them such visits as they can afford from time to time. This state of affairs brings out very prominently the question of adequate wages. Indian seamen are so poorly paid that they cannot afford to live with their families, and have to live under the most revolting conditions. It is hardly necessary to say that these conditions are not conducive to their moral or physical welfare.[6]

Nor should it be necessary to add that their moral character received more sustained, indeed meticulous, attention from the city's ruling elite than the more mundane problems of survival.

The policies of employers and, in a wider sense, the development of production relations, enforced working-class dependence on its rural resources, which were in any case being subjected to increasing demographic and economic pressures. If migrants came to Bombay temporarily to raid its wealth, they often found that they could not afford to stay permanently and for their pains they rarely returned with their pockets, let alone their stomachs, full. Obviously those migrant workers whose rural base was more substantial than a part share in a coconut palm were better able to draw upon its resources, while workers in permanent and relatively well-paid jobs could sometimes augment the rural resources of the family. Obviously, too, the relative importance and utility of the family economy varied with each particular case. On the whole, however, the bulk of the evidence suggests that a substantial portion of the cost of the reproduction of labour power was borne in the countryside. Casual workers, even if barely able to support themselves in Bombay, relieved by their own departure the pressures on the family's rural resources; on the other hand, if they could not afford to maintain their families in the city, it was in the village that their subsistence costs were at least partially met.

To some extent, remittances contributed to rural subsistence. In a recent article, Gail Omvedt has strongly argued that remittances were not substantial. However, some of the figures which she cites in support of her case cannot be so easily discounted. For instance, the six districts of North Bihar, according to Omvedt, received about Rs 107 million in

[6] *RCLI, Evidence, Bombay Presidency,* The Indian Seamen's Union, vol. I, part i, p. 291.

remittances from Bengal between 1915 and 1920. According to Peter Musgrave, the remittances to Gorakhpur district in the 1890s exceeded the land-revenue demand. In Bombay in the early 1920s more than a quarter of average industrial earnings were estimated to have been remitted. Another estimate for 1921 calculated that 306,000 money-orders to the value of Rs 71 lakhs were dispatched from thirteen post offices in the mill district. Moreover, in an attempt to keep workers as far as possible at their machines on pay day, the Bombay Millowners' Association attempted to come to an agreement with the postal authorities so that remittances could be made directly from the mill premises. Between July 1937 and July 1939, nearly 100,000 money-orders worth over Rs 16 million were sent from the post offices of the predominantly working-class areas of Bombay. Of course, such figures are very crude. They do not tell us where the money-orders went, let alone who sent them. Moreover, the post office destroys its records of money-orders every two years and such figures as exist are insufficient grounds for conclusions about the volume of remittances or their long-term fluctuations. Indeed, it is likely that the working classes used the postal system rather less than other groups to transfer funds, preferring to send cash home with friends and relatives or carry it back with them. In any case, such figures underestimate the amount of money which flowed out of the city; at the same time they probably tell us less about workers' remittances than they appear to. Moreover, these post offices did not handle money-orders sent exclusively by workers while those that were sent by workers probably emanated disproportionately from the better-paid among them.

This may, however, be put into some perspective. In Ratnagiri, it was by no means uncommon in the late nineteenth century for a man to mortgage his labour while contracting for credit. In the 1880s, an able-bodied labourer, it was said, was valued at Rs 10 per year in liquidation of his or his ancestors' debts. In one case, reported in 1880, an 8-year-old boy served his creditor for twelve years in preference to paying off a debt of Rs 20 at 12 per cent interest. The problems of obtaining credit and the monumental difficulties of repaying loans made remittances indispensable to the family economy in its rural base, so that even a trivial sum might enable the workers' kin to purchase seed or even a few years' freedom from debt-bondage.

The implications which stem from the question of remittances have sometimes been stretched too far. Omvedt, for instance, has argued that such remittances usually took the form of cash advances made by labour contractors to release the rural poor from the debts that bonded them to their landlords and in effect to transfer their bondage to the labour contractor. Thus, concludes Omvedt, much of the reverse flow went to what she calls 'the feudal sections' of rural society. While such cash advances were made in the recruitment of plantation workers and coal miners, they were certainly not ubiquitous. Moreover the labour contractor in the tea gardens and coal mines was a very different figure from the jobber in the cotton mills. Mill workers could scarcely be considered the wage-slaves of the jobbers who recruited them. Recently, completely opposite conclusions have also been drawn from the same evidence. It has been suggested that remittances may have cheapened the cost of agricultural labour in contrast to the old view that village connections enabled employers to hold factory wages down. Although remittances were vital to the subsistence of some rural families of the working class, it is doubtful whether they were of such magnitude as to bear the brunt of the cost of reproduction of agricultural labour. They certainly did not appear to have facilitated any fundamental agrarian transformation. Moreover, there is some evidence from the Konkan to suggest that agricultural wages were rising in the first three decades of the twentieth century.

This argument receives some impetus from the recent work of Mazumdar on labour supply to the Bombay textile industry. Mazumdar postulated that there was an enormous disparity between wages for agricultural labour and cotton mill workers. This disparity was maintained despite an excess supply of labour to the mills. Moreover, the extensive use of casual labour in the mills which was both undisciplined and inefficient did not drag down the wages of permanent workers. Mazumdar's explanation for this paradox lay in the existence of a dual labour market in which a higher supply price was paid to stable or permanent family labour in contrast to the lone migrant who worked for a lesser wage. However, Mazumdar's problematic, however elegant and interesting in itself, is based on important misconceptions. For instance, his wage data is derived from sources which recorded the rates paid in certain, selected occupations which were highly paid. His own analysis did not allow for the differentials which existed even between various permanent occupations in the cotton mills with the result that it exaggerated the disparities between the earnings for some industrial work and for field labour in general. It was also based upon a misreading of some of the evidence. Mazumdar's argument rests on a survey of working-class budgets conducted by the Labour Office in 1921. Not only was their sample unabashedly random since the criterion for selection was to take evidence only from those who willingly gave information, but also they were interested primarily in family budgets. Therefore, they collected four times as many family budgets as those of single men and considered only those families with an income of over Rs 30 per month. More crucially, their results showed that the average income of a family was only marginally greater than that of a single man. Furthermore, the fact that the average monthly income of permanent two-loom weavers was among the highest in the cotton mills, does not lend much credence to the assumption that only single men worked as badlis. Finally, his notion of a dual labour market is grounded on the assumption that workers who came to Bombay with their families constituted a permanent labour force while single men in the city were temporary migrants. But this cannot be taken for granted. Whether workers' families lived in the city was more usually determined either by their rural destitution or by their considerable urban affluence. In any case, the implication of Mazumdar's formulation that some sections of industrial labour had to be induced to come to the city stands in flat contradiction to the considerable body of evidence which indicates that Bombay's workers, if paid considerably more than agricultural field labour, themselves lived on the margins of subsistence.

Remittances from industrial earnings were insufficient to offer the rural poor social mobility and economic advance. But these did help them resist the growing pressures of impoverishment. While the Gazetteer of Ratnagiri district stated in the 1880s (which several subsequent official reports plagiarized), 'the teeming population of Ratnagiri has been one of the chief factors in the development of Bombay city', it would probably have been more accurately said that it was the development of Bombay which enabled their survival. For some families, cash earnings and urban remittances helped them to augment and strengthen their rural base; others received little from those who upon migrating to the city found themselves dawdling in the nether regions of the labour market. For most, it was probably the case that remittances helped them simply to hold on to their position in the village. In one respect, Kunj Patel's findings for the 1960s after several generations of remittances are instructive. 'Villages do not derive any appreciable benefit from urban employment,' she observed, 'since migrants are unable to render any substantial financial help to their kinsfolk in the district.' However, she concluded 'that those who have relatives working in Bombay are slightly better off than those who do not have any members of their family working in the city'.[7] The decisive advantage of a relative in Bombay was not his sizeable savings but his easier access to credit. By facilitating borrowing, migration locked some families into a circuit of credit which enabled them to stand still.

[7] Patel, pp. 21–2.

Beneath the old recurring patterns of migration, therefore, were deeper, underlying layers of stagnation.

Significantly, migration appears to have been largely a matter for men. Women, along with the very old and the very young, the insane and the infirm, remained in the village. The general tendency has been to take this for granted and few explanations have been forthcoming for the entirely male character of migration. Gail Omvedt, among the most radical and prolific of feminist writers, has recently put forward what can only be described as the patriarchal case. She assumes, or at least accepts without challenge, the privatization of women's social and economic life. Migration, she argues, entailed 'a sexual division of labour between the sectors in which women and families remain in the village, while men... migrate to become workers'.[8] Curiously, for Omvedt, a 'holistic' discussion of the Indian working class must make a distinction between 'workers' and 'the working-class family' and must focus upon 'the role of women, who have usually maintained the strongest connection with agrarian society'. The assumption that the role of women lay in maintaining and servicing their domestic connections provides a highly suspect explanation for their confinement to this role. Nor is there much to be gained by distinguishing and therefore isolating the working-class family from the context of work.

For Morris D. Morris, on the other hand, the male character of migration is to be explained in terms of the culturally specific: the joint family system, the early age of marriage and childbearing. Yet the difficulty with this explanation is that it succeeds only in reformulating the problem: the conditions under which these institutions were framed and social conditions and traditions reconstituted. Later in his book, Morris suggested that 'the responsibilities of family life... probably made women an unreliable sort of labour', but added with grace that 'this explanation... is not completely satisfying'.[9] While social attitudes to women's work and their status acted as a constraint upon female migration, it is also important to recall that women played a central role in field labour. So this line of analysis would have to be supplemented with the investigation of rural attitudes to and images of the city, perceptions of the opportunities for work and of the uncertainties of urban life, especially in the initial phases of migration. For these must have combined with socially determined predispositions to have created a preference for families to send away

---

[8] Gail Omvedt, p. 186. 'To a certain extent,' she admits, 'adult working women' did migrate to the cities.

[9] Morris D. Morris, *The Emergence of an Industrial Labour Force in India: A Study of the Bombay Cotton Mills, 1854–1947* (Bombay, 1965), pp. 68–9.

only their men. Later this exclusion was probably consolidated by the employers' reluctance to take on women, especially as their conditions of work came to be governed more and more closely by legislation which in the 1890s restricted their hours of work, by the 1920s introduced compulsory maternity benefits and by the later 1930s prevented women from being employed on night shifts. Significantly, industries which fell outside the purview of the Factories Act employed a relatively larger proportion of women and children. While only 8 per cent of the work-force in perennial factories were women, the proportion in rural seasonal industries approached a quarter. This was epitomized in the bidi indus-try which largely employed women and children, and whose wages and working conditions were said even by the Census Commissioner 'to con-stitute an evil'.

If the employment of women on an extensive scale was any more than a hypothetical possibility in the 1920s and 1930s, it would probably have met with even more fierce resistance from male workers, for instance in the cotton textile industry, fearing the erosion of their skill and wage dif-ferentials. By the interwar period, the proportion of female migrants, or the concentration of women in the villages, was not determined simply by the fact that employers sought male labour but more generally by the fact that a different set of options had emerged at this time. The vital importance of these village connections to the family economy of the working class was now more starkly juxtaposed with the lack of adequate or, for some at least, suitable work in the city. In fact, a large propor-tion of women did remain in the village; but this was neither inscribed in the nature of things as Omvedt seemed to suggest, nor was it, as Morris has argued, culturally determined. It was rather the outcome of a social, indeed ideological, process which has not been adequately investigated.

Yet, if given these limited sets of choices, rural women sometimes exer-cised a preference to stay in the village, this was by no means universal. Observers also noted among women who had already migrated to the city a reluctance to return permanently to the land. In the 1930s, the pro-portion of women employed in the Bombay cotton mills declined from about 22 per cent in 1929 to about 15 per cent in 1939. This decline was accounted for almost entirely by the expansion of night shifts on which only men could be employed. For in absolute terms their num-ber declined marginally from 25,000 in 1929 to 22,000 in 1939. Yet throughout this period, women's jobs had come under increasing pres-sure. If they could not be employed on night shifts, some millowners preferred to replace them with men. Otherwise, the change-over of shifts would entail chaos; alternatively, they would have to ensure that the volume of output on the day shift in those departments in which women predominated was sufficient to supply the night shift.

Moreover, women were concentrated in the reeling and winding departments of the cotton mills. Since the First World War there had been a considerable reduction in the amount of reeling in the Bombay industry. Yarn used to be reeled to facilitate its bundling and baling for export to the Chinese markets. As mills used an increasing proportion of this yarn in their own weaving sheds they took it unreeled, while such yarn as had to be reeled for dyeing was increasingly transferred to reeling machines. This was expected by the millowners to constitute the most painless changes in work practices. But technology was not always the determinant. In the winding department, drum winding, which was used only for coloured yarn, had become obsolete and mills now ran their grey and coloureds together, and in any case the old drums were being replaced by the vertical spindle machine on which yarn could be directly fed on the bobbin rotating the spindles. But here women's jobs were not as severely threatened. For one thing, women winders were believed to be 'skilled'; but they were to be paid less than 'the coolies' or the unskilled labourers in the winding department in the new efficiency schemes which the millowners were in the process of introducing. This was because, as Fred Stones, the millowners' spokesman, told the Fawcett Committee, 'the one is a man, and the other is a woman'. Despite these pressures, however, women winders and reelers resisted their redundancy, in part through work-sharing schemes, and in part through industrial action, notably in the Bitiya Mill strike of 1939, when winders and reelers surrounded the millowner in the manager's office for over twenty-four hours and thus invented 'the gherao'. Their informal attempts at work-sharing resulted in increasing complaints from the millowners about the inefficiency of reelers and winders. S. D. Saklatvala complained that women in the winding and reeling departments brought their relatives to work and insisted on sharing their work. Their logic, he complained whimsically, 'is beyond man's wit'. But the owners who attempted to cut wages, he went on, were faced with vigorous complaints about low wages and 'yet are compelled to employ a larger number than necessary'. The millowners tolerated this state of affairs partly because they had not been able to invest sufficiently in the 1930s in the reorganization of work to either dispense with reeling or marginalize winding, and partly because as the industry began to recover from the slump so too did the Girni Kamgar Union from the repression of the early 1930s, and the millowners were reluctant to force further industrial conflict before their fortunes were restored. Such evidence scarcely indicates women's shyness of industrial work.

The widows of mill workers often preferred to stay on in the city and work in the mills rather than return to the village because they believed they would thereby retain some degree of independence. The Royal Commission on Labour suggested in 1931 that some workers left their villages 'to escape from family conditions that have become intolerable'. In general, however, the family, as the fulcrum on which the vital village connections turned, was not seriously breached. However much other caste-based practices were modified, marriage endured. It continued to be endogamous and to be arranged. But marriage practices, too, were beginning to witness the play of delicate, almost imperceptible changes. The daughters of mill workers 'brought up in Bombay', one observer noted, 'would never willingly marry an agriculturist in Ratnagiri' and their marriages were mainly arranged with men 'who work in the same or adjoining mills and reside in the same neighbourhood'.

Village connections formed an important base for social provision and material protection in the city, but it could not be the only one. As Bombay's workers organized themselves to find jobs, accommodation and credit, they entered into a social nexus which possessed its own autonomy and momentum, which transformed the perceptions of migrant workers, defined their interests and clarified their conflicts. This autonomy is witnessed in the changing relationships of dominance and discipline at the workplace, the different rhythms of production and the altered possibilities of consumption which confronted rural migrants in the industrial setting. It was also manifested in the social institutions of the neighbourhood and in the political and cultural arena of the street. Its focus was Girangaon, the mill district of Bombay, landscaped by over-crowded, jerry-built chawls in which, as the Rent Enquiry Committee observed, every sixth person lived in 'conditions which are prohibited even by the existing antiquated law'. Its momentum and its conflicts were derived from the tamasha players and public religious observances, from liquor shops and gymnasiums. These institutions and practices were not specific to the working-class districts alone. What underpinned them here was their use as a platform from which workers could organize to meet their urban needs.

The most convenient way to find work was through relatives or village contacts. The more established residents in the city helped their caste-fellows, co-villagers and relatives to find work either through jobbers they knew or through their own influence. The Divisional Commissioner at Poona, for instance, observed that among migrants from Satara 'a considerable number . . . have practically established themselves in different labour centres. The annual migrants go to these men who form a sort of nuclei around which the others congregate.'[10] The more established workers had much to gain from extending their patronage to newer workers. It created a relationship in which the demands imposed would be reciprocal. It created goodwill within the wider kinship structure which even the best-placed workers could not afford to ignore. More immediately, the new migrants might lodge with their relatives in the city. This was another incentive for the older residents to help the newly arrived to find work. Once they secured employment, they could contribute to the household's income. In any event, most working-class families needed boarders in order to pay the rent even for their one-room tenements.

The importance of these kinship and village connections was reinforced by existing recruitment practices. Most trades recruited through jobbers, usually experienced workers who combined the roles of supervisor, pacemaker and in some cases paymaster. Several observers noted that jobbers attempted to recruit workers from their neighbourhood. Appropriately, jobbers were appointed less for their village connections and more for their prestige and power in the neighbourhood and their influence among their peers. It was said of the building trade, but it would apply to most sections of the labour market, that the jobber preferred 'to secure the necessary labour from amongst his friends. He finds this course preferable as the men in the market are not only inferior workmen, but also resort to "bargaining", particularly if special rates have to be fixed or a large number of workers secured.'[11] This suggested, first, that although employers often made the hopeful and convenient assumption that their maistries and mukadams, their jobbers and serangs enjoyed complete mastery over the men, this was rarely the case. The relationship between jobbers and workers was characterized by reciprocity. The power of the jobber depended upon the position he occupied relative to other jobbers and with his own patrons. In addition, to make certain of his control, the jobber had to lean on social connections outside the workplace such as kinship and neighbourhood. The more diffuse the basis of his control the more difficult it would be to maintain it. This was why the jobber or the maistry preferred to employ his 'friends'. These 'friends' were generally connected with the jobber outside the workplace, most frequently through links established by kinship or based in the village. While these

[10] *RCLI, Evidence, Bombay Presidency*, Mr J. Ghosal, I.C.S., Commissioner, Central Division, Poona, vol. I, part i, p. 205.

[11] A. R. Burnett-Hurst, *Labour and Housing in Bombay: A Study in the Economic Conditions of the Wage-Earning Classes in Bombay* (1925), p. 87.

connections established channels for seeking work and gave the jobber greater informal control over his men, they also clarified the means by which workers could circumscribe that control.

The jobber system formed one, albeit crucial, part of a wider range of connections through which workers found jobs. In addition workers pressed their jobbers to act as a channel for the expression of their grievances and demands to their employers. At times, the jobber system could be used to protect wage differentials. This system of recruitment, like the various uses of kinship as a basis for social provision, gave rise to the formation of occupational clusters by caste, language and region. Thus, Muslims from the Konkan, but especially from the UP along with Marathas from Ratnagiri, made up some three-quarters of the weavers in the industry; North Indian Hindus were commonly employed in the preparatory processes; while about half the dalit workers were employed in ring spinning. Sometimes these clusters were encouraged by employers seeking to insure against working-class solidarity. For instance, the Bombay millowners appear to have switched from employing local to migrant labour in the 1870s. By the 1890s, they were attempting to co-ordinate the recruitment of North Indian labour avowedly to hedge against the threat of combination and high wages. After the 1929 strike, they came to an agreement with Ambedkar to introduce a large number of Mahar workers, particularly to the weaving shed. The Hindu–Muslim riots of 1929 followed attempts by the oil refineries in the city to recruit Pathan workers to replace Hindu strikers and a few weeks later by the millowners to employ Pathan and Muslim workers to break up a general strike in the mills. However, these occupational clusters were also the product of 'restrictive' practices. In the weaving shed, in particular, the Marathas sustained a remarkably effective closed shop against dalits.

If it was through these connections that men sought work; it was also through them that they sought protection against distress and unemployment. For one thing, work-sharing practices were widespread. In the cotton mills, there is some evidence of groups of badlis, dependent on the same jobber, sharing work between them. In the maintenance workshops of the Bombay Port Trust, the introduction of a scheme allowing compulsory periods of leave maintained a circulating force of surplus labour. Among seamen, too, arrangements were made for rotation of employment, although if union complaints about their misuse by serangs are to be believed, they were not very successful.

It would not be unreasonable to believe that migrant workers, alienated from the city and pining for the open fields, would return to the village in periods of unemployment. Although this clearly did occur, workers often revealed considerable persistence with industrial work, remaining in the city or even moving to other cities in search of work, rather than returning to the land. The Social Service League stated that the unemployed spent prolonged periods in the city in search of work. Similarly, the Indian Seamen's Union probably spoke for more than its constituents when it 'pointed out that even though during recent years there has been continuous unemployment among a considerable section of the men, it is ascertained that seamen scarcely migrate back to their village and prefer to tide over their difficulties by taking some temporary work on shore'. However, it was imperative to organize more firmly for periods of unemployment. Perhaps the most explicit and formalized of such organizations were 'village clubs', where workers could live in return for a regular subscription. Some clubs even provided for sickness and death; all provided for unemployment. Although every member was entitled to live in these clubs, those who were unemployed were given preference. Non-resident members were also required to pay their dues to aid their unemployed fellows. Conditions were rudimentary. 'Each man', it was reported about one such 'club' in 1931, 'had to use his own box containing his belongings as his cot' and in some clubs it was said more than twenty people lived in each room.[12] Similarly, the khanavalis of the mill districts were boarding houses to which groups subscribed in return for their meals; here, too, it was customary to allow extensive credit. These constituted necessary responses to a widely experienced set of conditions. Casual labour and periodic unemployment were conditions in which most workers shared and participated. Whatever the heterogeneity fostered by the rural connections, the 'muluk' or the village had an indispensable place within the fabric of working-class life. Whatever the depth of their connections with the countryside, Bombay's workers were forced to organize and act within the urban social context.

Of course, while their rural connections formed an important part of the common experience of Bombay's workers, their use also registered differences between them. The utility of these rural connections varied with their place in both rural and urban society. North Indian workers in Bombay were often constrained in collective action by the distance which separated them from their own rural base and were often considered the most vulnerable element in a strike. Muslim weavers were increasingly alienated from the mainstream of the labour movement by the growing communal tension in the city, which stemmed from the accelerated decline of the city's handloom weaving factories, the challenge posed especially by Ratnagiri Marathas to their skilled status and wage differentials, the impact of urban planners upon the delicate social

---

[12] *RCLI, Evidence, Bombay Presidency*, The Bombay Seamen's Union, vol. I, part i, p. 293.

and political balances, and sometimes the cultural symbols, of the neighbourhood and the increasing bitterness which the constitutional changes received in Bombay's mohollas. On the other hand, those who could fall back upon their village connections were the most resilient in industrial action.

The survival of these village connections has frequently been associated with political backwardness. Thus, Richard Newman has dwelt upon 'the millhands' emotional attachment to the village' in the 1920s which ensured that 'he bore long hours and poor conditions with more equanimity than a worker with no escape from the urban environment'. Yet such sanguine sentiments about working-class politics in Bombay in the 1920s fit uneasily with the fact that six general strikes occurred between 1918 and 1929, another two followed in the 1930s and, in the face of a repressive state, a significant communist presence came to be established in the labour movement. David Arnold has inverted the old myth of peasant passivity, asserted their inherent predisposition to violence and argued that this was simply brought over by migrants into the workplace, while Dipesh Chakrabarty has discerned 'the immigrant mind at work' in the Hindu–Muslim riots among jute workers in Calcutta in the 1890s. The prevailing consensus appears to be that rural values were transmitted to the industrial setting and decisively shaped the form and content of working-class action. What is left unexplained, however, is how. Few attempts to resolve this problem have gone beyond the assumption that it was effected simply by the rural poor going to work in the factories.

These assumptions are so widely made that they deserve closer scrutiny. Obviously, rural migrants did not abdicate their own social and political experience when they entered the city. No doubt this experience conditioned their responses to the new environment. But this experience did not produce for migrant workers a set of immutable characteristics, whose integrity survived intact its interrogation by any further experience. For what such an argument ignores is that rural migrants encountered in the industrial and urban setting a social nexus with its own momentum, autonomous of the countryside, even as it was continuously interacting with it.

Indeed, underlying the argument that rural characteristics were transferable, like so many commodities, to urban society lies the assumption that the 'rural' and the 'urban' form generic social entities, with modes of political action and types of social consciousness specific to themselves. The notion that the character of social action can be understood in terms of its 'culture', as being for instance essentially rural, is not proved and need not be assumed. In any event, it exaggerates the uniformity of these societies as well as the forms of action associated with them. Consequently, it becomes possible to hypostatize the rural poor or industrial workers, to overlook the important differences between them and to underplay the choices and decisions, the tensions and contradictions, the advances and setbacks that characterized the constitution of political action.

Rather than any simple 'transference' of political culture from the rural to the industrial setting, the operation of the family economy enabled the working class to draw upon their rural resources in industrial action. As early as the 1890s, Bombay's textile workers appeared to the millowners to be increasingly capable of manipulating the labour market to their own advantage, and official observers noted that any attempt to reduce wages was likely to lead to stubborn resistance. Between the wars, industrial action brought these rural connections into play more readily. One mill manager explained in 1931 that it was upon workers who had lost all connections with the land that 'the millowners generally depend to break the strike as these people have no home to return to and hence they are the worst sufferers at such times'. Indeed, contemporary observers used to assess the mood of the strikers in Bombay by whether or not they had begun to leave for their villages. On the eve of the 1928 general strike in Bombay, which lasted for six months and ended in a short-lived triumph for the workers, the police authorities observed that 'the strikers [are] determined not to work the new system and are gradually leaving for their native places by the coastal steamers and trains after receiving their wages'. Workers with the closest connections with their villages often revealed the most sophisticated political consciousness. Their actions were not limited by a violent tradition supposedly imported from the countryside. On the contrary, their rural connections impinged directly upon labour relations at the point of production, upon bargaining and negotiation in the workplace and thereby on the possibilities of labour politics itself.

Clearly, the intersection of village, caste and kinship connections injected important tensions into the development of workers' politics in India, but it is also possible that these associations of caste, kinship and village created political opportunities for important sections of the working class where the labour market was overstocked and where conditions of employment were casual and impermanent. It is probable that industrialization, far from dissolving caste, strengthened its bonds. At the same time, as caste constituted another source of tension embedded within class relations, it could also be mobilized in class struggle.

The relationship between caste and working-class politics may be approached in a different way. There were few permanent jobs in Indian industry; conditions of employment were always insecure. It was among the sizeable sections of industrial workers who were employed on a largely casual basis or who existed on the margins of the industrial economy that ties based on kinship and village, caste, jobber gangs or neighbourhoods played a critical role in the organization of their work and lives. Their political weakness stemmed from their tenuous hold over employment. In this sense, their position was comparable to what has often been called 'the casual poor'. Their most striking political characteristic has usually been assumed to be their rootless volatility; they lacked, it is said, a history of combination or struggle; their past appeared to be changeless; their future punctuated by aims and needs which were as short-term as they had always seemed to be. In this case, it is possible to argue that their sense of belonging and of history was rooted in the ties of caste, kinship and village. These connections were the material foundations upon which their lives were organized; the manner in which they operated, for instance changes in the generosity and utility of their patrons and providers, shaped their social consciousness and influenced their political perceptions. The coherence which such connections imparted to social groups may have informed the tensions underlying political action, but they also injected solidarities into the labour movement. It is this factor which may explain why Bombay's workers were able to mount such a sustained defence of their interests in the face of an overstocked labour market, powerful employers and a repressive state.

The nature of the rural connections of the working class, observed the Royal Commission, 'is a variable quantity; with some the contact is close and constant, with others it is slender and spasmodic, and with a few it is more an inspiration than a reality'.[13] The inspiration of the village as an ideal but distant 'home', could in comparison with the urban environment serve to radicalize workers' perceptions. To some extent, the 'village' fulfilled a utopian function within working-class culture. Conditions of life and work in the city make their antipathy to its environment perfectly comprehensible. But we need not conclude thereby that this hostility was expressed purely in retreat. Indeed the strategic use of their rural connections revealed for Bombay's workers, for instance, a shrewd appreciation of their own position within the urban social nexus. Political consciousness and political action were rooted in an experience which integrated both town and country. In any event, it did not in the early twentieth century wait upon the dissolution of caste, kinship and village connections, while proletarianization was not accompanied by a significant weakening of rural ties.

[13] *RCLI Report*, p. 13.

State and society in colonial India

In Marx's famous phrase, the capitalist state was 'the executive committee for the management of the common affairs of the whole bourgeoisie'.
But it is by no means self-evident whose affairs were managed by the
colonial state. The colonial state in India was neither the political crystallization of the social power of the dominant classes in India nor simply
the instrument of metropolitan capitalists. Rather, its role throughout
the colonial period rested upon the mediation of the infinite demands of
metropolitan society and the political, social and economic constraints
upon their realization in India. Ideally, therefore, an adequate history of
the colonial state would have to integrate the changing imperatives of
imperialism and the shifting interests of the metropolitan ruling classes,
on the one hand, and the processes of social and political development
in India, on the other. This paper pays homage to this ideal but it cannot
aspire to its realization.

Whether British rule thwarted or fostered Indian economic development has been the subject of a long, largely inconclusive and generally
sterile debate which has raged since the early nineteenth century between
the proponents of British imperialism and their enemies. Nationalists
placed the blame for the impoverishment of India squarely on the effects
of British rule. Imperial proconsuls, on the other hand, claimed to have
rescued India from primeval Asiatic stagnation. Ironically, both sets of
arguments shared one common assumption: that the British constituted
the only active element in Indian society, whether their weight was exerted
to plunder or to mobilize India's resources. In so doing they overlooked
the dynamism of Indian society, the indigenous forces making for change,

This essay owes a large debt to the work of a number of historians. It has been influenced, in
particular, by the following works: Eric Stokes, *The Peasant and the Raj: Studies in Agrarian
Society and Peasant Rebellion in Colonial India* (Cambridge, 1978); David Washbrook, 'Law,
State and Agrarian Society in Colonial India', *Modern Asian Studies*, 15, 3 (1981); C. J.
Baker, *An Indian Rural Economy 1880–1955: The Tamilnad Countryside* (Oxford, 1984);
and C. A. Bayly, *Rulers, Townsmen and Bazaars: North Indian Society in the Age of British
Expansion, 1770–1870* (Cambridge, 1983).

which in their turn acted upon and shaped the imperial impact. Historians have long invited us to choose between the Indian social structure and colonial rule as the main cause of economic backwardness. We may do better by declining this choice and by exploring more fully the interplay between them.

There are three general propositions about the interplay between state and society in colonial India upon which this essay builds. First, contrary to the notion of some recent ameliorist historians, I shall be arguing that the colonial state was not development-minded. It was concerned from the very early days of the East India Company to take resources out of India, not to invest their own in the subcontinent. Second, the logic of maintaining the Indian Empire was grounded largely on how far India could serve Britain's metropolitan needs and more especially its international system of profit and power. At the same time, what the British could achieve in India was constrained by the internal political and class structure. They could not always bend Indian society to their will, to give effect to their intentions or to simply achieve what they chose. Third, the nationalist argument that the effect of British rule was uniform and progressive impoverishment flies in the face of the facts. Indians were rarely passive or willing victims. Elements within Indian society were at times able to bend the colonial state to their advantage, to harness its institutions and ride them in their own interests. Some were able to take advantage – of course, strictly at the expense of others – of the growing commercial opportunities created by India's closer integration into the international economy. It now looks as if national income probably increased in the late nineteenth century, although it began to decline again in the 1920s. Some social groups, some regions, some industries were able to prosper, flourish or expand at specific periods of time. But these fitful spasms or geographical enclaves of growth did not generate any structural transformation of the economy.

The role of the colonial state in India was conditioned by several factors. First, its role in India was guided by Britain's changing imperial aims, not only in terms of how its Indian empire may fit its metropolitan needs, but also how it might serve Britain's economic and political position in the world. Second, the fulfilment of these aims was conditioned by the processes of social and economic change within India. Third, it was also determined by the way in which the colonial power fitted into the internal political structure of India and how efficiently its systems of collaboration worked for its larger imperial purposes. Their interplay may be conveniently examined within three distinctive phases in the development of the relationship between Britain and India: what Gallagher and Robinson called the mercantilist phase in the first century of British rule; the period between the 1850s and the First World War, when India began to fit more conveniently into Britain's imperial system; and the years between 1914 and 1947 when metropolitan decline, international crises, imperial rivalries and internal political developments imposed new demands upon the colonial state, forcing it to intervene more closely in Indian society and deploy its Indian base to meet unprecedented imperial needs, at the very moment when Indian forces were liable to resist such use most strongly.

Necessarily, periodization of this kind reflects verisimilitude rather than accuracy. In one sense, it is possible to detect the dissolution of the Company's mercantilism and the dawn of free trade imperialism as early as 1833 with the passage of the Charter Act. From another perspective, the colonial state continued to use the power of dominion to Britain's economic advantage in the later nineteenth century, to build railways at guaranteed rates of interest, to facilitate the extraction of raw materials and the imports of metropolitan manufactures, to knock down internal barriers to trade and to keep the Indian market open to British imports. In the age of free trade imperialism, the British scarcely operated a *laissez-faire* regime in India. By the 1940s, the colonial state appeared to return to the mercantilist form when its intervention in the retail trades of essential commodities and introduction of rationing recreated what was virtually a state monopoly in grain and cloth.

I

The expansion of British power in India was a slow and insidious process. For most of the first century of British rule, the Company state remained essentially militaristic, engaged in conquest and always liable to embark upon expensive military campaigns. Britain laboriously swung the heavy hammer of political force in order to open up the Indian economy and reshape it in its own image. This factor determined the nature of the state and conditioned its role in early nineteenth-century India.

Looking back over the accomplished fact of British expansion, it is easy to exaggerate the drama, even the completeness, of military conquest. The facts are somewhat different. There were very few sustained military confrontations in the history of the Company's expansion and the Company's redcoats inflicted few outright defeats on Indian rulers – none outside Bengal, for instance, until as late as 1799. When they confronted the strongest Indian military powers, in the Marathas or Tipu Sultan, the Company's armies suffered heavy losses and their military victories were narrow indeed. Once the Company became a territorial power, its advance was both gradual and selective. Large parts of the north and west were annexed only in the 1840s and Awadh was finally brought under British rule only in 1856, a full century after Plassey. In fact, the Company's advance was so gradual and selective that it left nearly one-third of the subcontinent under the rule of various Indian princes.

Territorial expansion in the eighteenth century opened up differences within the state: in London, concerned for the purity of the British constitution, vulnerable to corruption by the loot of India; among the Company's directors, anxious about its costs; and in view of the general wisdom that an Indian empire would be difficult and expensive to maintain. Nevertheless, much of this expansion occurred in the wake of private traders seeking to ensure supplies of raw materials, such as cotton in Gujarat, or to profit from political power, for instance through the sale of trading privileges in Bengal, and dragging the redcoats in behind them. These controversies laid bare the several levels at which the colonial state would operate as well as the tensions which were liable to manifest themselves at each.

There were, however, firm limits within which these differences of opinion and conflicts of interest would manifest themselves. Whatever the disputes over territorial commitments, it is also clear that the Company was at no stage interested in renouncing its acquisitions. It was precisely these limits which Clive expressed in the initial stages of the process when he declared that 'nothing but extreme necessity ought to induce us to extend our idea of territorial acquisitions' but added the rider that there could be no contemplation of any reduction 'to our ancient state of merchants'. Underlying this rough consensus lay the fact that a wider range of increasingly substantial interests was coming to rest upon India. As time wore on, these interests were to become ever more substantial.

It is instructive to recall what the Indian connection was worth to Britain in the late eighteenth and early nineteenth centuries, not only directly, but also in underwriting Britain's global interests. In 1757, the trade with India commanded 2.2 per cent of British shipping, 13 per cent of British imports and 5.5 per cent of British exports. The export of raw cotton and opium from India from the 1780s onwards enabled the Company to pay for its consignments of Chinese tea, the demand for which was now rapidly increasing in Britain. Between 1793 and 1813, the China trade yielded the Company profits of £18 million. The China trade not only saved the Company from bankruptcy but constituted the most important and the only profitable part of the Company's operations. In roughly the same period, the Company's activities generated nearly £40 million in duties for the British treasury. To all this, as the Select

Committee pointed out in 1813, must be added the 'Fortunes known to have been made in a variety of shapes, from India to England, through extraneous and circuitous channels, to an amount which there is no possibility of tracing with accuracy'. The large Indian revenues brought further advantages to the Company and to Britain, as their territorial control was tightened. In 1765, the Bengal revenues, worth £3 million, subsidized the trading losses of the Company and subsequently financed the conquest of India. By 1818, the Indian land revenues yielded £22 million. This sum covered Britain's balance of trade deficits with India and China. It was an important channel for remitting the Home Charges and the salaries and fortunes of private traders and Company officials to Britain. It helped to maintain the Company's credit and to attract investments in Company bonds from up-country merchants and magnates. In turn, this served, by swelling the supply of capital, to keep interest rates low, a fact greatly appreciated by the European private traders. Land revenues also financed the large and expensive armies of the Company which began to be deployed throughout Asia to protect Britain's commercial interests outside India: in Java in 1808–12, in the Malaysian campaigns of 1822–4, in Burma and Afghanistan, in Persia in 1856 and in China in 1839, 1856 and 1859. Finally from the 1820s onwards, Lancashire's cotton manufactures began to flood into the Indian market, creating the promise of fresh opportunities for the metropolitan economy in its crucial phase of industrialization. Thus between 1815 and 1834, Indian imports of British cotton goods increased ten-fold. It is easy to understand Dundas's sentiment in the decade following the American War of Independence that 'the East is our last stake'.

The Company's military commitments and the revenues needed to finance them interacted to promote territorial expansion and combined to shape the character of the Company's regime. On the one hand, territorial acquisition and military power enabled revenues to be collected more efficiently. More informal arrangements involving the farming of revenues or the levying of subsidies invariably dragged the Company into closer administrative control. On the other hand, revenues had often to be collected through coercion while the territories which yielded them could not be secured through goodwill. As military technology became more sophisticated, it also became more expensive. As the Company's possessions swelled, its armies had to be vastly expanded. Clive in the 1760s, Wellesley in the 1800s, Dalhousie in the 1850s, each emerged from their conquests to announce that their new acquisitions had made the Company's revenues safe. In each case, they had vastly extended its debts. During Wellesley's period of office, the Company's debts trebled. Between 1834 and 1852, gross revenues increased by 55 per cent and total debt by 40 per cent but the administrative costs of annexation tipped the Company's revenues into virtually perennial deficit.

It was clear at the same time that revenues raised almost entirely from the land would also have to be shored up. In the first half of the nineteenth century, the land revenue soaked up nearly 50 per cent of the value of the agrarian produce. If its revenue administration largely inherited existing institutions of the pre-colonial state, it was also the case that the Company state made them somewhat more efficient. The Mughal state had also been known to absorb a high proportion of the agrarian produce. But for the most part, as the Dutch factor Pelsaert had observed of Jahangir, the king who 'possesses the largest area of all the kingdoms of the world . . . is to be regarded as king of the plains or the open roads only'. However sophisticated the mansabdari bureaucracy, the burden of revenue had fallen unevenly on the land. While over 90 per cent of the villages had been measured and assessed for revenue in the Mughal heartland between Allahabad and Lahore during the reign of Aurangzeb, less than 2 per cent of the villages in the Bengal had received such attention and the average for the rest of the Empire was slightly under half. The Permanent Settlement was more systematic and remained for generations more burdensome as well. Between 1793 and 1815, more than a third of all titles to land were transferred in Bengal while Cohn found that in Banaras almost half the land suffered the same fate in the five years since 1801. Of course, much of this turnover occurred within the traditionally dominant groups of landholders: as Ratna Ray demonstrated, land rights were often bought by the relatives, dependants and former employees of dispossessed zamindars, and at the end of the century the structure of ownership appeared remarkably similar.

However oppressive the pitch of the land revenue, the British soon realized that inflation eventually made nonsense of permanent settlements and turned increasingly to the ryotwari form. In the south, since they had no knowledge of the potential of the land, the British pitched their demands higher than their own estimate of what it might bear, on the principle that it was better to be safe than sorry. In the Deccan, Pringle's settlements in the 1820s and 1830s left the rural economy as denuded and wasted as he claimed the preceding years of Maratha rule had accomplished. The extraction of revenue gave rise to considerable resistance. The Madras Torture Committee of 1855 revealed the extent of physical coercion and violence employed in the collection of revenue, and it was in consequence of its revelations that the police were separated from the revenue administration. After the 1820s and 1830s, the British made attempts to rationalize the revenue administration and to relax its demands. But falling prices between the late 1820s and the 1850s meant that the real incidence of the revenue demand did not appreciably decline. For much of the first century of British rule the dividends from political dominion exceeded the earnings from British exports to India and the proceeds of the Indian trade taken together. 'Even by 1854–55,' wrote Eric Stokes, 'Britain's connection with India still derived from her command of the Indian revenues rather than trade which retained . . . its subservient role as a channel of remittance of the Home Charges and private fortunes.'

The extraction of revenue, the nub of the Company's mercantilism, was intimately related to the high military overheads which it carried. By the early nineteenth century, Britain could already justify to itself these increasingly expensive activities in India by the extent to which it profited from them whether in terms of trade or tribute. But after the 1820s, Lancashire cottons began flooding into the Indian market, creating the promise of fresh opportunities for the industrializing metropolitan economy. If in form the Company state resembled its predecessors, its presence was increasingly driven by wider imperial purposes. At one level the land-revenue settlements were pragmatic accommodations to local fact but they were also at another level more subtly influenced by a variety of British interests which came to be centred on India. The European private traders who destroyed the Company monopoly in 1833 also prevented any attempt to transfer a part of the revenue burden from land to trade. Similarly, the cotton manufacturing interest, with its 'constant complaints that cotton cultivation was unfairly taxed', tried to ensure that the assessment of revenue would be based on the soil rather than its produce.

The logic of the land-revenue settlements was not merely to pay for the Company's bloated, rag-tag army, to entertain fantasies about the Russian menace or to indulge military adventures in Afghanistan, Burma and Sind. Political dominion was the hammer which might beat the Indian economy into the shape of Britain's satellite. At one level, it was supposed, the legal definition of property rights, implemented by a judiciary now separated from the executive, would lay the basis for its exchange; land would offer effective security against debt and capital, and credit would be attracted in larger quantities. In fact, however, the contradictions of the law limited and even retarded the development of the market. The 'elaboration of a legal system which treated and protected landed property as if it was at a remove from the state was', as David Washbrook has pointed out, 'pure farce'. The weight of the land-revenue burden to a large extent determined the value of the land. Privileged tenures enhanced its value and remained essential to the perpetuation of the village elite. Land-revenue demands also forced production for the market.

Without a high pitch of assessment it was likely that cultivators would retreat into subsistence production rather than growing cash crops. This was especially true at the turn of the eighteenth century when circumstances of land surplus and labour shortage prevailed in many regions or in the context of the long agrarian depression of the 1830s and 1840s when the rural produce fetched low returns on the market. To facilitate taxation, the state was drawn into the reproduction of the agrarian economy.

The mercantilism of the Company was also manifested most obviously in the fact that the Company's monopolies influenced the trade in several commodities, most notably opium, over which it established a state monopoly. It was in order to reorganize its lines of supply that the Company had expanded into Gujarat, and political expansion in western India similarly safeguarded its opium trade. The government was deeply involved in lending to the agency houses which financed the cultivation of indigo and in the development of schemes to make India the cotton field of Lancashire. Banking in this period, as Bayly has shown, primarily meant financing the operations of the state.

Similarly, the Company state, while proclaiming its intention of releasing the economy from the dead-hand of the state, intervened deeply in the labour market. Some measures to abolish agrestic servitude in Kerala, to outlaw domestic slavery in North India and to free tied labour were proclaimed. But again in practice the Company's actions failed to match their proclamations. Faced with labour scarcity or rising wage rates, the state acted through caste headmen to extract customary payments in labour for public works. No serious attempt was made to transform agrarian relations based on bonded labour and share cropping in eastern India. By recognizing various forms of serfdom and by helping to catch those who escaped their labour bonds and contracts, as much as through the indirect effects of the revenue system, the state was active in the creation and disciplining of labour supplies.

Finally, in this phase of the colonial state, if surplus appropriation under the weight of the land-revenue burden restricted the accumulation of capital, the role of European private traders as major financiers of the state consolidated the domination of European capital in the Indian economy and conditioned the relationship between Indian and foreign capital in the following decades. By the 1830s and 1840s, European capital had begun to dominate business in Bengal, Bombay and Madras.

While industrial expansion in Britain increased its need to develop India as a source of raw materials and a market for finished goods, it also became increasingly clear that India would not fulfil these hopes. In the early nineteenth century, businessmen who anticipated that there would be no limit to the potential of India's underdeveloped resources and vast population were having to reconcile themselves to the gap between the visionary possibilities and harsh realities of the Indian situation. India's consumption of British manufactures, though expanding, remained a disappointment, rising to no more than one-tenth of Brazil's per capita consumption. Its short-stapled raw cotton offered no substitute for the American crop. The promise of an expanding export economy in cotton, sugar, indigo and opium was shattered by the depression of the 1830s and 1840s, which most severely affected those districts where a high assessment had forced rapid commercialization. In South India, the urbanized, market economy was in retreat and the town of Madras not only declined in size but it did not recover to its 1750 level until at least a whole century later.

By 1847, *The Economist* pondered the 'notorious fact... that there exists some great and serious impediments to the realization of the just and fair hopes entertained with regard to our Indian trade'. The force of British intervention failed to mould Indian society in its own image or fashion it according to its needs. The very pressure of the Company's efforts to open up the Indian economy had undermined its own collaborators, whether the client regimes of the eighteenth century, like the Nawab of Arcot's, or the revenue intermediaries of the nineteenth. Far from releasing private initiative and freeing the markets in land and labour, capital and commodities, the mercantilism of the Company state proved to be a serious impediment to the realization of its aims. Here then was a contradiction between the economic aims and political necessities of British imperialism in India which was to recur repeatedly over the following century. Military conquest and high land-revenue demands were the direct consequence of the problems of ruling India. The purpose of exercising territorial control in India was simply to facilitate the deployment of its resources in the interests of Britain's international system. Yet the mercantilist form of the state constrained the social and economic developments which were a necessary precondition for maximizing the profits of the Indian connection.

II

During the later nineteenth century, the state began to withdraw considerably from direct economic intervention. Much of the apparatus of mercantilism was dismantled. The colonial state passed from the Company to the Crown. More significantly, the weight of the land-revenue burden began to sit less heavily upon the agrarian economy. The trading monopolies of the Company were gradually whittled away or else they became increasingly insignificant. The development of transport and communications created new and wider market opportunities for rural producers, and peasants were pulled increasingly into the orbit of the world economy.

The recovery of the agrarian economy from the long depression of the 1830s and 1840s exposed more clearly a fundamental contradiction in the position of the colonial state. If production was becoming increasingly responsive to the market, India's economic development with a large measure of state encouragement might serve a variety of metropolitan needs and imperial aims. But its attendant social change could also undermine the stability so essential to British rule in India. By injecting some dynamism into the Indian economy, the colonial state could hope to maximize its imperial dividends, but it might also thereby risk or invite its own destruction.

The mid-Victorians were only too aware that the direct returns from India in the early nineteenth century scarcely justified dominion on such a grand scale. As India began step by step to serve a wider range of imperial interests, it also became clear that these gains might have in any case been secured through informal control. The real value of the Indian Empire only became apparent in the context of Britain's global system and it may be worthwhile rehearsing these assets once more. By 1913, India was the most important market for British exports, the foundation of her economic and political dominance in the world. It took 40 per cent of Britain's exports of cotton piece-goods, the most valuable market for its most important industry. India's growing exports of primary products to Europe and the USA, in an elaborate and labyrinthine system of multilateral settlements, paid for two-fifths of Britain's balance of payments deficits between 1870 and 1914. It took nearly a quarter of British overseas investments in 1880, primarily in railway stock, European managing agency houses and government debt, and these were largely underwritten by the Government of India's commitment to guarantee interest payments on these investments. Between 1870 and 1913, British investments in India more than doubled in value, although they declined as a proportion of total British overseas investments. Similarly, the Government of India was committed to keeping the Indian market open to British exports and 'the expansion of the export trade in cotton manufactures was considered an important aim' of imperial policy. For British expatriate businessmen, India was a profitable field of activity. They mainly dominated the export/import sector and industries largely based in Calcutta, including tea, coal and jute, and also a variety of plantations, all of which were developed for the export market. Above all, the Indian Army, supported by the Indian taxpayer and consuming 40 per cent of the Government of India's expenditure, was deployed to police imperial interests between East Africa and China. The fear of another Mutiny was to haunt imperial proconsuls wherever they went in the aftermath of 1857. In India, it led them to enunciate the principle that the Indian Army should always maintain a ratio of at least one Englishman for every three Indians in its ranks. This necessarily increased military expenditure. Between 1853 and 1858, the number of troops trebled and then increased from a total of 61,000 to 130,000 Indian troops and 66,000 British by 1880. India was, in Lord Salisbury's celebrated phrase, 'an English barrack in the Oriental Seas from which we may draw any number of troops as we wish without paying for them'. Furthermore, India's growing foreign trade and military power pushed British influence deeper in east as well as west Asia and served to underwrite informal influence as well as formal empire in south-east Asia and East Africa. The colonial state in India, its social and economic policies or its response to internal opposition, can only be adequately understood in terms of the wider, global imperatives of British imperialism.

If India was beginning to fit more conveniently into Britain's imperial needs, this was in large part the result of changes which were working their way through its domestic agrarian economy. None of these changes were either sudden or dramatic, but their direction was unmistakable. In various ways, market forces, by no means novel, were now playing more freely upon production, and the internal economy was also gradually being more fully exposed to the world market. Several factors lay behind this development. First, the slow but steady growth of population was beginning to register an increasing pressure upon the land, raising its value and intensifying competition for it. At the same time, it yielded a growing supply of labour, reducing its costs as well as its bargaining power. There was no need now for the state to attempt to settle rural groups in order to tax them; social and economic conditions themselves facilitated the tying down of the peasantry and the subordination and cheapening of labour. The effects of these developments varied across the subcontinent. Where population density was low and considerable cultivable acreage available, as in the Punjab for instance, an increased labour supply was valuable to reclaim land on the margins of cultivation. But in already prosperous tracts, like the Doab and the eastern United Provinces, where the population base was already high and the margin of cultivable land rather smaller, the pressure on the land was likely to lead to falling productivity. Smallholding families in such regions were forced to seek supplementary incomes through labour, whether agrarian or urban.

Second, the mercantilist exertions of preceding decades had facilitated the development of transport and communications and created new and wider market opportunities. The price of grains as well as cash crops tended to rise. The markets for land, rent, produce, credit and labour showed promise of expansion. The scarcity of land stimulated the market for its purchase as well as for rentals. Rising prices after the long agrarian depression of the 1830s and 1840s, the growth of the export trade in primary products and the opening out of wider internal markets created a new buoyancy in the market for agrarian produce. The expansion of the export trade was helped not only by the development of transport and communications and the opening of the Suez Canal, but significantly by the falling price of silver. The depreciation of silver made India's exports cheaper and therefore more competitive in foreign markets while the rising trend of prices ensured that the returns to the cultivator and the trader did not decline disastrously. Increasing demographic pressure on the land pulled the peasant out of the subsistence economy and sent him seeking work in the towns, on plantations or in cash-cropping tracts. As land as well as its produce became more valuable, capital was attracted more easily to agrarian production, whether to finance cash-crop cultivation of wealthier peasants or to meet the subsistence or basic agricultural needs of the poorer peasants. Underlying these changes was the decline of the revenue burden. Where assessments could be revised only every twenty-five or thirty years, rising prices and increased commercialization eased the pressure of the revenue demand in real terms, while fierce political resistance to their upward revision prevented the state from keeping their assessments in line with inflation. But the declining weight of the land revenue mitigated its previously depressive effect upon land values.

Yet what is remarkable is how sluggish was the penetration of capital and how superficial the character of agrarian change in this '"golden age" of the rich peasant'. At the outset of colonial rule, Indian agriculture was already characterized by small-scale, labour-intensive farming. The early revenue settlements, particularly in the ryotwari areas, had largely perpetuated this pattern of agriculture. During the late nineteenth century, the 'boom' was characterized in part by the expansion of cultivated acreage and in part by an export trade stimulated by a favourable exchange rate. This exposure to long-distance markets served to accentuate the difference between those who were in a position to exploit the new opportunities and those who lacked the means to do so or the luck to do it effectively. For all the controversy that surrounds them, rich peasants were too scarce on the ground and operated on too limited a scale to provide the driving force of capital accumulation. The consolidation of small-scale agriculture limited the possibilities of growth and heightened the risks of investment. It is not surprising therefore that capital was more readily invested in moneylending or rentals than in agricultural improvement. At the same time, agrarian buoyancy served to consolidate the framework of small-scale farming. The absence of structural change in the agrarian economy left it particularly exposed to the vagaries of the weather and the fluctuations of the market, now increasingly conditioned by international trade. This is why the commercial boom of the late nineteenth century dissolved so rapidly in the agrarian crisis of the 1890s and 1900s.

There were important reasons for the colonial state to shore up this agrarian structure: for the continued generation of revenues so vital to the larger imperial purposes for which India was ruled; for the maintenance of domestic demand for British exports; for the perpetuation of India's export surplus; and in the short-term at least for the preservation of political stability and the social order in India. The colonial state proceeded to protect the smallholder through the operations of its legal system, which did not necessarily serve the interests of capital, as well as through legislation, which increasingly defined tenants' rights, shielded the debtor and resisted land alienation. These factors limited the transformative impact of capital upon the agrarian economy.

In this way, the state acted to blunt the forces of commercialization which it had helped to unleash. The intensification of market competition had not occurred entirely outside the context of official policies. Although the revenue burden had relatively declined, it was still sufficient to force cash-crop cultivation. Moreover, state activity in building railways, roads, canals and wells had invigorated the classic venues for the emergence of the rich peasant in this period. Clearly, the colonial state gained substantially from the agrarian dynamism of the late nineteenth century. And it is possible to argue that it might have gained more if it had more actively assisted the role of Indian capital, both in terms of enabling the more effective exploitation of the colonial economy and in terms of securing wider political collaboration. But the options of the colonial state were limited in the former case by the weakness of capital and in the latter, indeed, in the longer term, by its general commitment to metropolitan capitalist interests.

The development of Indian capital was bound to threaten existing European business interests. Should Indian trading groups increase their domination over agricultural production and marketing, they would come into conflict with expatriate interests in the export trade. Any significant expansion into industry, whether large or small scale, might squeeze the export market of metropolitan capitalists. European business interests in India had long been nurtured beneath the awning of the Company's mercantilism. By the mid-nineteenth century, expatriate businessmen dominated the import–export trade, the plantation crops and raw materials which mercantilism had sought to develop. From the agency houses they had expanded into banking. Once Carr-Tagore had shown the way, they took control of the most productive and profitable sectors of the coal industry. Since the early nineteenth century, they had supplied raw jute to Dundee and cloth and sackings to the British Army, and by the 1870s they launched large-scale jute production. Much of this formidable complex of expatriate business interests was centred in Calcutta and extended through Bengal and North India, their traditional hunting grounds. Here British power had been established the longest and the most securely and here their connections with government were also the most firm.

In western India, the relationship between Indian and foreign capital assumed a different form. European private traders in eighteenth-century Bombay were for the most part poor, diseased and drunk. The Company's power in the region was insignificant until the early nineteenth century. With the expansion of the China trade, European agency houses came to depend heavily upon Indian brokers and dubashes, many of whom traded on their own account. As the phenomenal expansion of foreign trade in the middle decades of the century came to be based upon Bombay, its merchants acquired sizeable fortunes. Ostensibly Indian capital in Bombay commanded a considerably less unequal status with European merchants and a greater access to capital than their counterparts in Calcutta. The first cotton mill in Bombay was built by a Parsi merchant in 1855. It was in the 1870s, however, when the large European agency houses were able to subordinate Indian merchants in the export trade in raw cotton that the first major expansion of the cotton textile industry occurred. These mills largely produced low-count yarn for the Chinese market, where they successfully displaced Lancashire by the 1880s. The effects of this competition between Indian and metropolitan capital were manifested in factory legislation intended to limit India's competitive advantage of cheap labour, and in excise duties on mill production designed as a counterweight to revenue tariffs imposed on yarn and piece-goods imports and thus offsetting any measure of protection to the Indian industry. Behind these developments lay the pressures exerted by Lancashire and the receptivity of the colonial state to them, a response which already opened up differences between the provincial and central governments and was to be more reluctantly forthcoming in the decades between the wars.

If the limited role of rural capital signified the stagnation of the agrarian economy, the inception of industry did not herald a major social and economic transformation emanating from the towns. The fortunes of the Bombay mills were profoundly affected by the agrarian crisis of the 1890s and early 1900s, and by the First World War the industry had not substantially expanded beyond the Presidency. Yet as Indian and British capitalists, whether metropolitan or expatriate, were beginning to conflict, the colonial state was coming into closer relationship with Indian business interests. Its feverish search for revenues was leading it inexorably towards urban-based sources. As it pressed more heavily upon the towns, it prompted the nationalism of business groups as diverse as stultified rural capital, illicit liquor distillers and even millowners, ostensibly 'the best and most loyal of your Majesty's subjects', as Lytton had once described them to Queen Victoria. Seeking to limit capitalism from working its magic in the countryside for fear of the political consequences which it might unleash, the British found that the unintended consequence of thwarting capital was to push various and diverse bourgeois groups into the nationalist fold.

III

Britain swept India into the First World War when its second base of power had been eased into structural stagnation. In both world wars, metropolitan demands of an unprecedented magnitude were placed upon its stagnant economy. Moreover, in the intervening period, its resources were shrinking; at the same time, important changes, taking place in the relationship between Britain and India, suggested that the imperial power would have to pay a high price for the use of its colonial satellite.

In part, this changing relationship was the consequence of metropolitan problems: Britain's economic decline, its subordination as a world power and the domestic constraints of appeasing its own huddled masses now yearning to be free. But to a large extent, it was the price of political constraints being imposed on India. More and more power had to be devolved to Indian politicians. The demand from Indian industries for tariffs meant that it would no longer be easy to keep its markets open for Britain's decreasingly competitive manufactures. The Indian Army, which still consumed two-fifths of government expenditure, could only be deployed for imperial purposes at a price, which the British taxpayer would increasingly have to bear. One consequence of political breakdown was that the division of revenue heads between central and provincial governments ensured that the former would have to depend increasingly on such sources as customs and excise duties or the income tax: some were unpopular in India; others threatened to undermine the oldest imperial aims and the most significant metropolitan interests. Furthermore, in the

1920s, India lost its share of the European markets for primary produce and could no longer meet Britain's balance of payments deficits. In the First World War, the Viceroy commented, India had been 'bled absolutely white' so that it emerged with a national debt of £370 million. The colonial state was faced, in the context of mounting debts, economic stagnation and political resistance, with expanding its revenues and squaring its imperial commitments.

From the late nineteenth century, prices in the internal markets had been brought increasingly into line with levels and tendencies prevailing in foreign markets. Increasingly, the fluctuations of foreign price levels and changes in the international purchasing power of the rupee began to act upon local prices outside the context of local supply conditions. Inflation during the war was followed by the boom of the early 1920s; prices collapsed in the depression of the 1930s and soared once again in the 1940s. Producers, creditors and traders did not readily adapt to these rapid fluctuations. The commitment of the colonial state to balanced budgets, the remittance of the Home Charges and the maintenance of the value of the rupee meant that its deflationary policies in periods of downswing could depress economic activity further. Since it had to print money to pay for the world wars, it stoked the inflation of those periods. There was little that the colonial state could or was willing to do directly to protect the internal economy from these external fluctuations.

Its imperial commitments thus accentuated the pressure upon the state to conserve the structure of small-scale agriculture. The processes which had for some time been at work to relieve the burden of land taxation was carried further. State revenues became increasingly dependent upon customs and excise duties and levies on non-agricultural sources of wealth. Tenancy legislation was extended to Oudh and Malabar in the 1920s. Co-operative credit societies designed as the bulwark against the urban moneylender were revived and extended in the 1930s. When the depression snapped various linkages, the state attempted to arbitrate between debtors and creditors, tenants and landlords, and in the wake of rural riots to create procedures to cancel debts. In the Second World War, it acted to discipline the market to ensure food supply. The expansion of the state apparatus and the devolution of power brought into its structure even more firmly this broad strata of revenue intermediaries, purveyors of what Stokes described as the 'petite culture' of the Indian countryside.

This 'petite culture' was neither very productive nor particularly efficient. In the 1940s, concerned about food supplies, the government made the discovery that they had been declining for nearly three decades. Primary producers lost their export markets and failed to respond adequately to the growing demand in the towns either for food grains, whose prices of course were falling, or for industrial raw materials. Moreover, the general level of demand for industrial goods in the rural markets remained low and many industries had reached the limits of import substitution by the later 1930s. Agriculture, organized around family labour and oriented towards subsistence, scarcely served the needs of industry.

Demographic pressure within the context of stagnation had since the late nineteenth century been working to swell the supply of labour to the towns. At the lower end of the scale of proprietory holdings in the Uttar Pradesh, Stokes pointed out, 'only a very small minority of the rural population was without cultivating rights of some kind', but their 'plots were hopelessly inadequate without another source of livelihood'. In Ratnagiri and Kamara, 'the absurd extent of fragmentation as well as sub-division' was exemplified for one official by the numerous cases in which 'a single cocoanut tree is a hissa and is moreover jointly owned by several persons'. An industrial labour force was taking shape which was rooted in the village but dependent upon the city. If rural poverty forced them to emigrate, urban uncertainties led them to ensure that they retained their rural connections.

The depression served to accentuate these developments. For the ties of credit were increasingly loosened. Those who lent money on the condition that they would receive at the harvest a fixed amount of grain to cover the repayment were left stranded by falling prices in 1929 and 1930. The liquidity crisis in the agrarian economy led to further contraction. As credit dried up, ties of indebtedness were turned into bonds of labour. Yet another trend had been set in motion: as rural landholders were pulled into the state structure, they had become more willing to replace tied labour with casual hands, for they could now deploy the expanding apparatus of the state to discipline labour. The larger landholders responded to falling prices and worsening terms of trade by switching their capital to urban industries. Historians have frequently commented upon the industrial expansion which occurred in the 1930s. But the fact remained that much of this capital was going into what is often and inadequately called the 'informal sector': small workshops with a low ratio of fixed capital producing consumer goods on narrow margins by labour-intensive methods. This accentuated the instability of the urban economy: some workers were buffeted between town and country, others found that their urban earnings could not sustain their village base and, as they became entirely dependent upon urban livelihoods, they swelled the ranks of the town-dwelling unemployed.

Industrial growth brought to the surface the long smouldering contradictions between foreign and domestic capital. The First World War had revealed to the colonial state that modern wars needed modern infrastructures and, if India was to be an effective supply and strategic base, industrial development was essential. The war had in any case provided shelter from foreign competition and enabled some industrial growth. In its wake came the demand for tariffs. It should not be supposed that the colonial state saw itself clearly orchestrating industrial development. Had it in fact shared the vision of development economists, it might have sought to effect far-reaching structural changes in the agrarian economy in the late nineteenth century. Britain was not about to invest in the development of the Indian economy, least of all as it pondered its own decline. But the colonial state was ambivalent towards the demands of businessmen, and only partly for reasons of defence. They were also concerned to attract and retain the alliance of big business, even if they might not care to deal with the men of the bazaar. They were anxious that the rival powers might penetrate the Indian market and carve out their own spheres of informal influence. They were becoming increasingly dependent for their revenues upon customs duties and similar cesses.

This contradiction between foreign and Indian capital came to centre upon the cotton textile industry. Bombay, the most important centre of the textile industry, could not recover its old Chinese market and found it difficult to match its competitors at home. The domestic market was saturated with the coarse goods which Bombay produced. Indian industry had expanded rapidly in these lines of production. It was essential for Bombay to diversify. But the mills in Ahmedabad had already established a grip on higher count production and in this part of the market the competition of Japan and Lancashire was severe. To diversify under these circumstances, Bombay sought protection. For most of the 1920s, the state stayed its hand. Tariff boards argued that the industry should streamline its own organization and especially its pattern of labour deployment before turning to the state for assistance. The Bombay millowners did not need persuading that there were advantages to cheapening labour costs and increasing workloads. But this required investment which was not forthcoming without protection; and it was bound to provoke labour resistance in a situation already characterized by militancy.

In the context of labour unrest in 1925, the state had abolished the excise duties on Indian production. From the early 1930s, measures of protection were extended. It was now becoming clear that it was against Japan in particular that Bombay needed protection; that without tariffs, the depression, which had not promoted expansion in Bombay's textiles, would take much of the industry away with it; that this was a chance which the state could not afford to take in the face of rural unrest, urban upheaval and the revival of nationalist agitation; and that there were revenue gains to be made through tariffs at a time of course when the state was becoming increasingly dependent on these sources. Indeed, Lancashire's interests were by no means abandoned in the 1930s; it was simply that in the pursuit of imperial aims as a whole, political constraints in India had forced Lancashire's interests further down the scale of priorities.

The 1920s and 1930s were also characterized by widespread industrial action. These strikes were neither the consequence of the development of trade unions nor did they give rise to them. But they cannot be construed simply as 'spontaneous' actions either: for at deeper levels, in the neighbourhood and the workplace, they revealed a sophistication of organization which enabled workers to sustain them for remarkable periods of time. Just as rural groups had been able to use their own leverage upon the state to discipline labour, so employers resorted to the same means for the same ends. But the very fact that the state was now becoming less and less colonial and more and more Indian suggests that we need not construe this relationship as any more than an alliance negotiated on terms of limited advantage. Workers' combinations were more effectively disciplined at the point of production. On the other hand, the state did not set its face against trade unions or uniformly repress the workforce. Legislation at times encouraged and even consolidated trade union growth. The state's dilemma in relation to labour was a familiar one: while anxious about the effects of the capture of trade unions by publicists and agitators, it also recognized that it might prove easier to contain organized labour than to negotiate with the inchoate groupings of the street corner. In any event, labour disputes provided another fresh and explosive site of state intervention. Its consequence was often to lend an explicitly political dimension to industrial action and to develop the political consciousness of the working class.

It was within this context of stagnation and turbulence that the colonial state had to discipline Indian society to meet the imperial needs created by the Second World War. It resulted in the expansion of state activity in economic life on an unprecedented scale. For instance, the grain trade was placed under what Baker has described as 'a bureaucratic monopoly'. The price of this intervention was paid in the retreat of the colonial state, but it established a role into which the national state readily slipped.

IV

Historical arguments have for long rested on whether the colonial state on the one hand prised open the Indian economy, loosened it from its traditional moorings and unleashed its dynamism, or, on the other hand, whether it thwarted economic development. This paper has attempted to argue that the colonial state conducted a holding operation which increasingly exposed the contradictions within its own structure. The purpose of the state was not developmental but extractive and exploitative. To this end, it was committed to keep firm the increasingly precarious base of the Indian economy to serve its own increasingly overextended and fragile imperial purposes. The more the state intervened in the economy it had thus guided to stagnation, the less it had to intervene with. The demand for the favours of the state exceeded its capacity to supply them and generated a host of tensions and antagonisms which ultimately undermined it. Had the colonial state embarked on a sustained programme of development, had it carried out structural changes in the economy, it might have achieved the economic aims of its mercantilist phase, of shaping India into a complementary economic satellite. But then should India have served its purposes so neatly, Britain might as well have dispensed with the cares and costs and liabilities of formal rule.

Religion and nationalism in India

From the 1980s onwards, communal tensions and antagonisms in India appeared to increase and violence occurred on a larger scale. Not only did communal riots become more frequent but, in addition, the violence increasingly took on the character of pogroms often conducted on an unprecedented scale. At times, political parties or paramilitary groups acting with the assistance of the police and the state attacked civilians with seemingly an unconstrained ferocity. Waves of violence swept through Gujarat and the North Indian states of Uttar Pradesh and Bihar in the 1980s. There were several days of brutal violence against Sikhs in Delhi and elsewhere in 1984, following the assassination of Mrs Indira Gandhi. Bombay and a few other towns, including Surat in Gujarat, witnessed systematic and, for some days, seemingly unlimited violence against Muslims after the activists of the Hindu nationalist Sangh Parivar destroyed the Babri Masjid, a sixteenth-century mosque which they claimed had been built on the site of the birthplace of the Hindu god, and epic hero, Ram. Perhaps worst of all was the pogrom conducted against Muslims in Gujarat in February and March 2002.

Moreover, this communal antagonism coincided with a shift in the terms of public debate. Until the 1970s, the language of development, nation building and socialism had provided the dominant motifs in Indian political discourse. In the 1980s, there was a perceptible shift towards the definition of the nation in explicitly cultural or communal terms, as a predominantly Hindu nation. This shift was already discernible in the rhetoric of Indira Gandhi and the Congress, but in the longer term, the principal beneficiary was the Hindu nationalist Sangh Parivar and especially its parliamentary front, the Bharatiya Janata Party. In the 1990s, the BJP was elected to power in several states and, in 1998, formed government at the Centre. The consolidation of Hindu nationalism within the institutions of the state and in government at the Centre now meant that for the first time communal antagonism in the street could potentially be backed up by political power and ministerial office.

The intensification of communal antagonism occurred against the background of two seemingly distinct conflicts. First, powerful political movements asserted the state's rights against the Centre. In the 1980s and 1990s, Punjab, Assam and Kashmir were in a state of civil war, in which high rates of violence were matched by sustained and bloody repression. Although these conflicts were not in themselves communal, they were marked by religious difference. In the Punjab, the Congress at the Centre was quick to treat the demand for greater resources for the state as if it was specifically communal. After the Indian forces laid siege to and, with much bloodshed, captured the Golden Temple in Amritsar from 'the militants', Mrs Gandhi declared that the Sikhs had threatened 'the Hindu dharma'. In Assam, conflicts over the distribution of resources between the Centre and the state became inextricably linked to the question of 'illegal migration' into Assam from Bangladesh. Kashmir had become after Partition India's only Muslim-majority state. The intifada in Kashmir was the culmination of several decades of cackhanded intervention from the Centre but it could not be dissociated from the Indian state's anxieties about Pakistan or its doubts about the loyalty of its Muslim citizens. In the 1990s, it is estimated that between 25,000 and 80,000 people died in the Kashmir violence.

This period also witnessed a heightening of caste conflict. It is important to recognize that communal violence between Hindus and Muslims since 1948 has occurred on a surprisingly small scale, entirely disproportionate to the threat it has posed to the Indian political system. For instance, in a population of a billion, about 13 million of whom are Muslim, there have been about 20,000 deaths from communal riots in the past six decades. By comparison, the atrocities committed against dalits, or untouchables, both by upper-caste and intermediate or backward-caste Hindus, has been several times greater. The effect of dalit oppression on the way in which upper-caste Hindus have configured their relationship with Muslims has not yet been adequately examined. In addition, in this period, the competition between forward- and backward-caste Hindus was considerably sharpened over the affirmative action policies of the state. Attempts by various state governments in the 1980s and by the Centre in 1990 to expand the reservation of government jobs and places in higher education for backward castes and dalits have stimulated wider communal conflicts and antagonisms, sometimes leading to Hindu–Muslim violence, for instance in Gujarat in 1985 and in Bombay in 1992–3. Caste and regional conflict helped to mobilize growing numbers behind the banner of Hindu nationalism.

Many of the institutions that made up the Hindu nationalist 'Sangh Parivar' or family of associations had existed since at least the 1920s.

Yet it was only in the 1980s and 1990s that they were able to establish a powerful presence in Indian politics. In the 1980s and 1990s, the rhetoric of Hindu nationalism appeared to capture the ways in which a significant number of Indians understood their immediate situation and to offer a plausible charter of remedies by which it might be transformed. In examining why the rhetoric of Hindu nationalism appeared so persuasive to so many, the firm limits that were placed on its plausibility should also be clarified. This paper will argue that communal antagonism was founded increasingly on the racialization of difference. It registered and addressed a whole range of perceived differences, arising from religion, class, language, region or descent, but its construction was often the outcome of a political process by which adherents of each religious group perceived those against whom they defined themselves to possess essential characteristics unimaginably different from their own.

The investigation of the nature of communalism has given rise to a host of problems around which scholars have continued to circle. For instance, it has proved especially difficult to extricate the analysis of communalism from the teleological legacy of the colonial assumption that religious or communal conflicts reflected the natural, ancient and essential divisions of Indian society. It has also proved difficult to calibrate or specify the weight and significance of religion in communal polarization. What are now enumerated as the major religious communities in India were by no means monolithic. Sikhs and Muslims observed caste, which has no place in the brotherhood of all true believers, and were divided by sects and divergent traditions. Muslims were divided by all the factors that divided all Indians: language, doctrine, caste, class and gender. Some Muslims have had more in common with some Hindus than some of their own co-religionists, a pattern mutually repeated between most religious communities. It was less that religion united each of these 'communities' than that their religion was often all that they had in common. The boundaries between them were highly porous. Ethnographers and census officials alike often noted that 'the various observances and beliefs' of Muslims, Sikhs and Hindus were 'so strangely blended and intermingled, that it is often impossible to say that one prevails rather than the other or to decide in what category the people shall be classed'. In 1891, about one and a half million Sikhs returned themselves as Hindus, while in 1911 in Gujarat, some 200,000 respondents insisted that they were Mohammedan Hindus. For their part, Hindus often described their religion to census enumerators as their particular traditions, which were then reported as individual sects and enumerated as a collective. Indeed, the term Hinduism was first used to connote a single set of religious practices in the 1830s. Until the late eighteenth and early nineteenth centuries, as Romila Thapar has shown, there was only the weakest 'notion of a uniform, religious community readily identified as Hindu'.[1] Of course, religious reform and revival movements combined with the incentives of political representation provided by the colonial state to harden the boundaries between these religious categories. Yet the process had scarcely gone very far by the end of the twentieth century.

Moreover, the relationship of communal conflict to religion was often remote, sometimes coincidental. It was neither always authorized by formal religious organization, nor was it often driven by solidarities fostered by religious belief. Frequently, communal conflicts were the outcome of the quest for local precedence, the assertion of power and rights within a local domain, the defence of status under attack by rival groups or the competition for resources, jobs and political power. Necessarily, such competition for local precedence, status and resources coloured the ways in which participants perceived their rivals who were defined by their difference. Their perception of, indeed their attempt to define, this difference appears to have emerged from political and economic competition rather than from religious practice, ritual or belief. In other words, the communal identity of Hindus, Muslims and Sikhs was not necessarily constituted by their religion. Of course, some Hindus or Muslims drew upon religious ritual and symbolism to communicate more widely or to solidify the sense of their communal identity. But it was also the case that competition over status or resources, like the struggle to maintain local dominance, had led to the definition of similar communities of sentiment around language, caste, region and nation.

Significantly, political movements defined in terms of these shifting identities, for all their differences, have often shared significant characteristics in common: the claim that their members shared a common ancestry; the characterization of those whom they excluded as alien and certainly different in their social and cultural being; a rhetoric which drew upon a discourse of race and sometimes expounded it either to establish the superiority of their claims or indeed to assert their dominance over competing groups. At the same time, their rhetoric and programmes concealed differences within their own ranks, most crucially those arising from class and social inequality as well as from the claims of competing identities upon their constituents. Political associations and solidarities constituted in these terms, whatever their differences, could often appear interchangeable. That communal identity was at times defined along religious lines was the outcome of contingency. It

---

[1] Romila Thapar, *Interpreting Early India* (Delhi, 1992), p. 77, and passim.

was constituted through politics rather than culture or religious practice. For this reason, communal conflicts in India should be conceptualized not simply as the expression of sectarian or religious difference but as its racialization.

This racialization of communal relations was encapsulated in the rhetoric of Hindu nationalism from the outset. Significantly, V. D. Savarkar, the founding figure and principal ideologue of Hindu nationalism, distinguished clearly between Hinduism and Hindutva. In his book, entitled *Hindutva*, and published in 1923, Savarkar argued that Hinduism merely signified all the religions that 'are peculiar and native to this land' and recognized that it might prove impossible 'to reduce the different tenets and beliefs to a single system of religion'. But this did not provide sufficient grounds 'to doubt the existence of the Hindu nation'. For Savarkar, himself a non-believer, 'Hindutva is not a word but a history'. To establish 'what constitutes Hinduism', he argued, 'you must first define a Hindu'. A Hindu was in his view a Hindu without Hinduism. Indeed, to be a Hindu, in Savarkar's view, a person would have to fulfil three conditions. First, he had to be born within Hindusthan, 'the land that extends from Sindhu to Sindhu', that is from the Indus to the two seas. This was the Hindu's Pitrabhu, his fatherland. Second, he would have to be born to Hindu parents, and thus have 'the blood of the ancient Sindhu and the race that sprang from them in his veins', irrespective of his particular sect or religion. Finally, the land of the Hindus would have to encompass his Punyabhu, his sacred or holy land. As a result, 'our Mohammedan or Christian countrymen who had originally been forcibly converted to a non-Hindu religion . . . are not and cannot be recognized as Hindus'. For their Punyabhu lies 'far away in Arabia or Palestine'. As a result, 'their love is divided' and 'they must to a man set their Holy Land above the Fatherland'. In this respect, Muslims and Christians were quite different from Sikhs, Jains, Buddhists, Brabmo Samajists or Arya Samajists, all of whom are bearers of Hindutva in the sense that they fulfilled each of the three conditions that Savarkar set out.

The defining character of Hindutva was the inner essence that Hindus shared and around which they created a community. It was grounded on and legitimized by their history, which in turn was inextricably intertwined with a sacred geography. It provided the spirit which yielded a common culture, enunciated principles of exclusion and necessarily offered the means of creating hierarchy and stratification. While Hindutva enabled Savarkar to establish the fundamental homogeneity of 'Hindus', it also clarified the essential and inherent differences of Others. Savarkar's concept of Hindutva was principally a concept of race, in which doctrinal, sectarian and even religious differences were not only subordinate but also arguably unimportant.

These themes, ranging from the invocation of the sacred geography of the nation to the organic links of the modern Hindu community to its ancient 'Aryan' origins, have continued to recur in the rhetoric, performance and violence of the Sangh Parivar. In a speech delivered in Goa in April 2002, following the state-assisted pogrom against Muslims in Gujarat, India's Prime Minister, Atal Behari Vajpayee, appeared at times to justify the massacres in terms that resonated with Savarkar's Hindutva. He began by referring to a recent visit to Hindu temples in Cambodia. They stood as testimony to 'our culture', which had never destroyed temples or idols, which had no place for forced conversions, religious persecution or religious extremism and which upholds the freedom of worship. It was a 'secular' and tolerant culture even before the Muslims and Christians had 'set foot on this soil'. 'For us,' he explained, invoking the nation's geography, 'the soil from Goa to Guwahati is the same, all the people living on this land are the same.' What happened in Gujarat, in his view, however, had been 'a conspiracy . . . to burn alive the innocent passengers of the Sabarmati Express'. Had this not happened, 'the subsequent tragedy' in Gujarat 'could have been averted'. For all their innocence, the Sabarmati Express carried many RSS and Bajrang Dal activists returning from Ayodhya where they had travelled to urge the completion of a temple on the site of the demolished Babri Masjid. The moral that the Prime Minister drew for his people was clear: 'Wherever Muslims live,' he declared, 'they don't like to live in co-existence with others . . . they want to spread their faith by terror and threats' – in contrast to 'our' secular and tolerant culture. By contrast to the sacred geography of Hindutva, Vajpayee mapped for his fellow citizens, some 13 million of whom are Muslim, the profane, even Satanic, geography of the Other. They would be 'surprised to hear', he told them, as if this had any bearing on the Gujarat pogrom, that Al Qaeda terrorists were now being arrested not simply in Afghanistan or Pakistan, Saudi Arabia or Yemen, but in Singapore, Malaysia and Indonesia. In the many countries he had visited – and now 'everywhere Muslims live in large numbers' – he had met 'rulers' who 'are worried lest those Muslims embrace extremism'.

In the case of communalism in India, it had proved especially difficult to conceptualize conflict in terms of a discourse of race. In part, this is because communal tensions were sometimes localized and limited to particular social groups, without involving their co-religionists even within the locality. The porous boundaries between religious groups and the strength of syncretic religious practices, quotidian social exchange

between different 'communities' and cross-communal political organization have rendered the racial character of communal conflict yet more
implausible. But to some extent it is the resilience of assumptions about
the exceptionalism of Indian society that has led us towards the conceptualization of communal conflict in terms of primordiality, or, failing this,
the malevolent role of political leaders. First, the residual assumption that
one can distinguish between racial groups by their physical characteristics has proved an impediment to recognizing the racial rather than religious character of communal identity. The legitimacy of the modern state
has largely rested on the proclamation of equality between its citizens. As
Todorov and more recently Kenan Malik have argued, the discourse of
race emerged in the West as a means of accounting for social inequality in
a political order grounded on a commitment to equality. The discourse
of race made it possible to characterize, as natural, class differences that
were generated by capitalist development. In this context, the assertion
of the belief in equality in the Enlightenment signified modernity's transcendence of the irrational, parochial, hierarchical divisions of the 'ancien
regime'. But the persistence of these social divisions of wealth, caste and
religion in India signified that its society had been left behind by the
advance of modernity and reason. For this reason, but not this reason
alone, movements of caste solidarity and religious revivalism, the assertion of the rights of 'sons of the soil', regional nationalism and religious
identity in India have often been interpreted as a product of its cultural
particularisms. Communalism, as Gyan Pandey pointed out, entered the
Shorter Oxford Dictionary in the 1940s and 1950s, as a peculiarly Indian
phenomenon.

Moreover, the cultural specificity of caste and religion ensured that ethnic identity in all its forms was dissociated from class. Not so long ago, it
would have been absurd to even consider the question of class in relation
to Indian society. It was taken for granted that, if the concept had any
relevance in India, its application would be limited to special enclaves
of industrialization and modernity. India's unique and defining social
characteristics were believed to lie in the strength of its primordial social
forms, and in particular those of caste and religious community. Finally,
the assumption that caste was an integral aspect, and indeed a function, of
Hinduism also obscured its relationship to communal identity. It became
an aspect of hierarchy specific to Hindus rather than a principle of exclusion and control which played upon their relationship with other social
and religious groups. Scholars, following Louis Dumont, placed the relationship between brahman (priest) and kshatriya (king) at the core of the
caste system and neglected the central issue of untouchability. Arguably,
the central purpose of caste was to provide a mechanism by which rulers

and landowners could obtain and exercise control over the whole being of the labourer, rather than simply the fruits of his labour. The 'caste system', in part, held together a pattern of obligations and dependencies which yielded diverse sorts of labour services to motley groups of dominant peasants, high-caste landowners and rural magnates.

The dalit leader, B. R. Ambedkar, illustrated these interconnections between Brahmanical perceptions of dalits and the hardening of communal identities many decades ago. When the Congress devolved its commitment to improve the conditions of 'the Depressed Classes' to the All-India Hindu Mahasabha, led by Savarkar, precisely on the grounds that 'the question of untouchability concerns the Hindu community', Ambedkar pointed out it was 'a militant Hindu organization'. Its aim was to 'conserve in everyway everything that is Hindu, religious and cultural'. Its main objective is 'to combat the influence of Muslims in Indian politics'. To maximize its influence, it had 'to maintain its social solidarity' and the 'way to maintain social solidarity is not to talk about caste and untouchability'.[2] In other words, the perpetuation of untouchability and the maintenance of caste was a precondition of a Hindu communal identity, the foundation for the construction of a monolithic community and an instrument for the maintenance of its difference from, and hostility towards, Muslims.

Conversely, the politics of communal antagonism could prove difficult to sustain without the suppression of a general awareness of caste oppression. In his classic work, *The Autobiography of an Unknown Indian*, Nirad Chaudhuri observed about his youth in Bengal in the early twentieth century, that 'while we [that is the Hindu bhadralok] had friendliness for the Muslims of our own economic and social status with whom we came into personal contact', they also felt 'mixed concern and contempt for the Muslim peasant, whom we saw in the same light as we saw our low caste Hindu tenants, or, in other words, our livestock'.[3] This relationship between caste and communalism was expressed at a political level not only in the 1930s, when dalits and the lower castes sought political representation, like Muslims, through special electorates but also in the 1980s and 1990s, when controversies over quotas for 'other backward castes' in higher education and government employment showed a tendency to develop into Hindu–Muslim violence. For the assertion of Hindutva, or the quality of being Hindu, the idea of a sacred space which is distinctively Hindu, which other peoples and nations could inhabit

---

[2] B. R. Ambedkar, *What Congress and Gandhi Have Done to the Untouchables* (Bombay, 1945), p. 23.
[3] Nirad C. Chaudhuri, *The Autobiography of an Unknown Indian*, p. 230.

on lesser terms, remained of paramount importance. But this concept of the Hindu rashtra presupposed the subordination of dalits and lower castes while it admitted Muslims so long as they submitted to Hindu supremacy. In a sense, this assertion of the minority status of both Muslims and the lower castes enabled upper-caste Hindus to identify the nation quintessentially with themselves. This process of the subordination of dalits and lower castes should also be seen as a process of proletarianization, which has continued into the late twentieth century. As Satish Deshpande has recently calculated,[4] about 80 per cent of the Scheduled Castes and Tribes in rural India have a monthly expenditure of less than Rs 470 ($10) while a slightly larger proportion in the towns spend less than Rs 775 per month (less than $18). While higher-caste Hindus make up 60 per cent of the urban population in the highest expenditure category, the scheduled castes and tribes, the other backward castes and Muslims, taken together, make up 91 per cent of the urban population and 88 per cent of the rural population below the poverty line (drawn at a monthly expenditure of $7 and $10 respectively). These figures scarcely bear out the Sangh Parivar's repeated claim that the supposedly socialist and secular state under Nehru and his successors in the Congress pampered and unduly privileged India's 'minorities, Muslims, the Scheduled Castes and Tribes and the Other Backward Castes'.

I have tried to ague that the changing nature and growth of 'communalism' in India should be understood in terms of the racialization of social, especially religious, difference. It cannot be grasped as religious conflict in isolation from caste and class, language and 'ethnicity'. The interconnections between these principal categories through which Indian society has been conceptualized was indispensable to the constitution of each of them. For this reason, an explanation of the growth of communalism in the twentieth century demands some reorientation of Indian sociology, which has tended to treat these phenomena in isolation from each other. At the same time, the 'racialization' of communal identity developed as primarily a political process. It occurred alongside and in relation to processes of state formation that can be traced back to the early nineteenth century onwards. Of course, it neither moved inexorably in a single direction nor was it immune to alternative possibilities. Nor do I intend to suggest that, in some teleological sense, it was simply a consequence of modernity and state formation. It was sometimes driven by the tensions between competing elements seeking to secure their own definition of communal identity. Nonetheless, it was in relation to processes

---

[4] Satish Deshpande, *Contemporary India: A Sociological View* (Delhi, 2003), pp. 102–24.

of state formation that communal identities acquired a clearer political definition.

By the mid-twentieth century, communal identities had begun to harden. Between 1946 and 1948, communal violence, especially in North India, took on the character of a civil war. About 200,000 people died in riots that extended from Bengal to the Punjab and swept further south to central India and to Bombay. But communal violence was not so much a cause as a consequence of the Partition, an expression of the panic and uncertainty with which it was anticipated. Nor can it be said that the fact of Partition simply resolved the communal problem and defused the mounting tensions and antagonisms of the mid-1940s. Significantly, more Muslims remained in India than moved across the border to Pakistan. After Partition, India became the world's second largest Muslim country. Once the communal violence of 1946–8 subsided, its incidence was negligible until the late 1960s and then it declined once more until the 1980s. Communal violence when it occurred manifested itself as localized cycles of violence and showed few signs of the 'racialization' of difference witnessed during Partition.

The Indian nation, contrary to its mythologies, had been rather arbitrarily assembled. If its external borders were artificial, it was far from clear how its provincial units might appropriately be composed. The task of marking out the territory of the independent nation raised diverse questions about communal identity, whether of religion or language, caste or region. These unresolved issues remain at the heart of Indian politics today. Not only was the question of how power would be distributed between the Union and its provinces open to question but also the principles by which the provinces would be demarcated. In determining these boundaries, both national and provincial, and, thus, necessarily the social and political character of each province, numerous groups stepped forward with competing claims, often grounded on an ethnic principle. The Congress was at first reluctant to redraw the boundaries of the existing provincial units in case it led to the dismemberment or even the weakening of the Union. Eventually, it was forced to concede the principle that, while it would not countenance claims on the basis of religion, language was an acceptable basis for the creation of provinces. Yet no one could be sure where this principle would lead. In the early twentieth century, the Linguistic Survey of India had with magisterial simplicity declared that 179 languages and 544 dialects were spoken in the Tower of Babel.

At the same time, the Indian constitution was strongly unitary and concentrated impressive powers at the Centre. The Congress, always a party of the strong centre, acted after 1947 to strengthen and reinforce central powers. In response, regional elites organized around linguistic, caste and sometimes religious identity in order to extract greater power and resources from the Centre or to seek the revision of state boundaries in the expectation that they would gain some advantage over their rivals. As Indian elites strove to create a domain for the exercise of their power, powerful regional interests organized to resist the Centre. The widespread appeal of regional nationalism suggested that the identity of the Indian nation remained unsettled and open to revision and redefinition. It was within this shifting framework that various social groups attempted to imagine their past and envision their future, and ethnic identities were created, revised and advanced.

This process gave rise to various outcomes. The anti-Brahmin, Tamil nationalist Dravidian movement offered, between the 1920s and 1960s, an alternative vision of a secular, egalitarian and decentralized polity. It was committed to the abolition of caste and untouchability, and accommodated Tamil Muslims as yet another Tamil non-Brahmin caste. After forty years in power, the results have been unexpected. It has acted to entrench caste as a basis for social conflict, maintained social exclusion for the Adi-Dravidas, sometimes by repressive force, marginalized Muslims and incorporated Brahmins into the Tamil nation. Similarly, the fascist Shiva Sena Party emerged in the mid-1960s out of the Samyukta Maharashtra Samiti movement whose aim was to retain Bombay city within Maharashtra when it was divided from Gujarat. It claimed to protect the interests of the Marathi-speaking 'sons of the soil'. But states' rights and 'nativism' were quickly transmuted into animosity and violence directed against Muslims. In 1984, the Sena played a systematic role in a pogrom against Muslims in the weaving town of Bhiwandi and then repeated this in Bombay in 1992–3, following the destruction of the Babri Masjid at Ayodhya. In both cases, the Sena acted with the connivance, indeed the assistance, of some of the police and local government and with the complicity of a wide range of the population. In effect, cultural nationalism, deployed against the Centre, yielded a rhetoric that was exclusionary and, if it was directed against Brahmins or untouchables, Tamil or Gujarati speakers, could be turned against Muslims, or dalits, or indeed any other category that it characterized as marginal. Political organization around any form of ethnic identity often absorbed and seemed liable to bend before the exclusionary rhetoric of Hindutva.

If the Dravidian movement and the Shiv Sena widened the focus of their antagonism from Brahmins and Hindi speakers, or South Indians to Muslims, Hindu nationalism seemed to confine its major protagonists to the North Indian plains until the 1980s. The Jana Sangh, an earlier incarnation of the BJP, secured four-fifths of its votes from upper-caste, urban Hindus, mainly from a salaried lower class and small traders and shopkeepers, in the Hindi-speaking belt of North India. Its attempt to identify the nation primarily and quintessentially with Hindus was accompanied by its determination to ensure the acceptance of Hindi as the national language, but its advocacy of Hindi left it marooned within the region. As a party of regional nationalisms, it could scarcely claim prior rights over the sacred geography of Hindustan.

In 1980, the Jana Sangh reinvented itself as the BJP and sought to expand its influence beyond the North Indian plains. It abandoned its commitment to the national language and attempted to parade its moderation and its modernity. But its cadres grew increasingly impatient with the BJP's attempt to emulate the Congress. At this point, it began to reconcile itself to its roots as an explicitly anti-Muslim party. It could unleash its cadres against Muslims, while seeking to safeguard the privileges of its upper-caste constituencies by adopting a right-wing liberalism. This twin strategy had already laid the basis for associating policies that threatened upper-caste privilege through positive discrimination for backward castes and dalits with the Congress government's alleged 'appeasement' of Muslims. By the end of 1989, a wave of anti-Muslim pogroms occurred across North India. At the same time, in parliamentary and provincial elections, the BJP's performance improved substantially. It was elected to power in a number of northern and western states. In 1998, it formed a minority government at the Centre.

Two characteristics of the BJP's ascendancy in the 1990s need to be considered. Both suggest that there were limits to the plasticity of the language of communalism. While the widespread currency of regional nationalism or some configurations of caste identity helped to make the exclusionary rhetoric of Hindutva more plausible, it also served at times to mark the limits of its acceptability. First, the rhetoric of Hindutva played differently in different regions. Its state-level parties were often doctrinally rather different from each other. In UP, which had the highest concentration of Brahmins and other forward castes and a substantial Muslim population, its support came from rural, upper-caste elites and the urban lower middle classes threatened by the political influence and prosperity of backward-caste peasants and town dwellers seeking their quotas of places in higher education and government employment. In Rajasthan, the BJP was the party of a specifically Rajput identity, which focused more fully on distinguishing itself from the rising 'backward castes' than on the claim to embody the true essence of the nation or even to express an antagonism against Muslims. In Gujarat, a forward-caste rich peasantry seeking to retain its grip on lower-caste rural labour and their caste fellows in the town, deploring the limits placed on their mobility and their life-chances by reservations for the backward castes, combined to act against the Congress in Delhi which had not only forsaken them but championed the backward castes, Muslims and dalits in their own backyard. Second, the BJP's share of the vote increased from about 10 per cent in 1967 and 11 per cent in 1989 to 21 per cent in 1991. It seemed as if the BJP was admirably placed to establish itself as the majority party in India. But its vote share increased no further over the next decade and a half. When the BJP formed the government in Delhi in 1998 and 1999, it coalesced with a host of regional parties on terms of limited advantage to each. The regional parties, often proponents of cultural nationalism, hoped that by allying with the BJP they would keep the Sangh Parivar out of their states, and that if they won a majority, they could leverage their share of seats in the coalition to extract power and resources from the Centre to wield against their own rivals and to consolidate their own local position. The BJP calculated that their alliances would open up for them a political space in the regions in which it had thus far made no headway.

If the interplay of Centre–state relations had entrenched a vocabulary of ethnic identity and competition in Indian politics, the developmental projects of the state sharpened the perception of difference. At one level, India's ruling elites attempted to legitimize the new state through its efficiency in promoting economic development. Planned development, socialism and the campaign to abolish poverty were the themes around which the nation was defined. By the 1980s, it was clear that development planning had ground to a halt. Socialism and poverty alleviation appeared to amount to pretty words and modest achievement. It was no accident, therefore, that by the 1980s and 1990s, the definition of 'the nation' took an explicitly cultural form. Moreover, the development policies of the state had already begun to consolidate caste and communal identities in unexpected ways. For one thing, development expenditure and plan allocations were directed through the central government. They gave the government in power at the Centre – throughout this period, the Congress, with one or two interruptions – very substantial powers of patronage in relation both to the states and to particular politicians of any party, whether in parliament or in the state legislatures, in whose constituencies these projects might be located. At the same time, since development projects were never sufficient to provide lasting pleasure for all, this process of negotiation was always likely to build up regional or particularist resentments against the ruling party at the Centre. Since the Indian government, whether at the Centre or through its provincial and local agents, played such a decisive role in the allocation of patronage, particular interests mobilized to compete for the regards and favours of the state. Sometimes these allocations were made to individuals who belonged to particular social categories, whether defined by caste, language or region. Its effect was to encourage pressure groups, lobbies and political networks to organize themselves around these categories. In the case, for instance, of expenditure through block-development grant schemes, the allocations were geographically specified and so, in effect, distributed through the dominant caste 'bloc' of the village. The Indian state was not averse to 'divide and rule'. By ensuring that local and regional interests engaged with the state in this process of bargaining, it deflected threats to the fragile territorial unity of the nation. By ensuring that local elites or ethnically constituted pressure groups competed with each other, it weakened the thrust of any concerted attack against the centralized state or the class interests that dominated it. As the state withdrew from its highly interventionist role in development, or to the extent that it did, it left behind an infrastructure of political organization and consciousness and action that was both habituated to and cohered around ethnic or cultural particularism.

Moreover, planned development recorded a number of achievements, which in turn stimulated social mobility. For instance, the green revolution enabled intermediate or backward-caste peasants to prosper. Similarly, some elements of the backward castes and dalits were able to take advantage of the opportunities for higher education and government employment created for them by reservation policies. Employment in government or public-sector enterprises had conventionally offered important avenues for social mobility to forward as well as backward castes. Finally, the presence of the state in the Indian economy expanded massively in the 1970s. In part, this was one way of accommodating the clamour for patronage among social groups that organized to realize their claims on the state. Of course, upper-caste Hindus were the major beneficiaries of these opportunities for social mobility. They already commanded the education and social networks and took advantage of them. Their relatives and caste fellows were already firmly entrenched in the major professions. On the other hand, the take-up rate among the backward castes and dalits for their reserved places was modest and, indeed, fell rapidly as the prestige, status and income from employment increased. Around these processes of state formation a wide range of social conflicts were engaged. Peasant lobbies for higher procurement prices for grain or subsidies for water, electricity or fertilizers compromised urban profits. Prosperous peasants from the backward castes proved highly repressive towards dalit landless labourers. Muslims gained nothing from positive discrimination, since there were no reservations for religious communities. In fact, they gained little from state patronage and, among the poorer strata, were further marginalized.

Social mobility was also facilitated by the rapid growth of the parallel economy. Its size has been estimated in the 1980s and 1990s to exceed the 'real' economy by several multiples. But the expansion of the black economy created considerable uncertainty for its beneficiaries. It raised the subventions that had to be paid to secure services. To the extent that these capital costs or service charges were propelled by the black economy, they often appeared more unpredictable than they were. The growth of reservations for the OBCs and dalits, for instance, left the forward castes competing for fewer prizes. As the advances and supplements that the forward castes had to pay to secure admission to medical and engineering colleges increased, so did their resentment at being crowded out of institutions and rewards that they believed, sometimes justifiably, were theirs by merit. It did not require much extrapolation to conclude that the Sangh Parivar's explanation was that they had been victimized in their own Punya bhoo by those who, like the OBCs, had lesser claims upon it or those like the Muslims who had none.

How far religious identity was capable of being racialized was most fully reflected in periods of communal violence. Historians and social scientists have often analysed the nature of communal relations through the study of communal riots. Necessarily, this rather episodic approach has distorted our understanding of communalism. In particular, it has sometimes lent credence to the view, drawn from dramatic and exceptional moments of crisis, that Hindus and Muslims constitute monolithic and naturally antagonistic communities. By contrast, there have until recently been few ethnographies of communal violence. In part, writing about periods of communal violence poses fundamental ethical problems. How does one write 'an ethnography . . . of violence', as Valentine Daniel recently asked in a rather brutal fashion, 'without its becoming a pornography of violence?'[5] The scale and brutality which has driven scholars to investigate them has also rendered them morally, even accurately, impossible to represent. On the other hand, the interpretative cost of this neglect lies in our often inadequate grasp of the

---

[5] E. Valentine Daniel, *Charred Lullabies: Chapters in an Anthropography of Violence*, p. 4.

peculiarities of communal violence. Unless social groups were able to draw in their political imaginary upon a distinctive sense of their own essential characteristics and the distinctive essence of the other 'community', the peculiarities of communal violence would not have manifested themselves.

Communal riots rarely constitute a single event. They usually conceal a host of disparate struggles waged under the cover of social breakdown: from the rivalries of neighbourhood toughs to land-grabbing by slum lords against their tenants and the attempt by merchants and traders to put their rivals out of business. They have also varied considerably in character. Some are localized and their protagonists have roughly clear objectives. It is possible to discern in them both an economy of violence and a means of reconciliation. However, the pogroms that occurred in the 1980s, 1990s and 2002 were characterized by the participation of organized political groups, often assisted by the police. For most people, especially but not exclusively their victims, they took the form of a generalized period of anarchy in which fear bred violence and diffused panic, which, in turn, initiated further spirals of violence and panic, fear and anarchy. The riots often entailed murderous violence on an extensive scale, and the cycles of violence they manifested were apparently without limit or economy. Everybody appeared to be at risk and nobody could anticipate who might turn upon whom. At another level, these periods of violence implicated everybody either as potential victim or as potential aggressor. Merchants and shopkeepers seeking to protect their property could only do so by the same means as those who threatened them. The respectable who were concerned to secure their neighbourhoods had no option but to adopt the methods of the rough. Above all, few could make sense of the riots. Whatever the degree to which communal identities had been racialized, none could make sense of the starkness and brutality of this antagonism that consumed whole cities. Nonetheless, these riots constructed, and in turn were constructed by, the generalized essentialization by religious groups of themselves and their antagonists.

Under these circumstances, anxieties about 'the Other', fortified by social prejudices harboured in ordinary times, now acquired an awesome and menacing shape. The difficulty was that the Other now became everybody else. The rich feared the poor; Hindus and Muslims feared each other; women feared men; everybody feared the hooligan. In particular, the responsibility for the violence was displaced onto 'the hooligan'. His presence allowed those who aspired to respectability to excuse their own complicity in the riots, to absolve themselves from responsibility for the violence and to dissociate themselves from its brutality. Explanations of communal violence that lay their emphasis, as many social scientists have done, on the primordial compulsions of ordinary people, the machinations of political leaders or the criminality of the poor have often proved attractive precisely because they absolve wide swathes of society from their complicity, whether passive or active, in the events that lead to these periods of apparently unlimited violence.

In the nineteenth and twentieth centuries, the nature of religious identity in India was transformed, largely in relation to processes of state formation. In the twentieth century, religious groups took on more clearly than before the shape of enumerated communities. But they remained internally divided. Some of their members continued to share more in common with the adherents of other religions than they did with their own co-religionists. As it developed in relation to the state, communal identity in the twentieth century became less dependent on religion, even if it was closely identified with it in public discourse. Communal antagonism became more secular and substantively less religious in character. As religious identity was shaped in relation to politics, communities were defined or defined themselves in relation to each other. Communal conflict, like aspects of the relations between Hindus and Muslims, became increasingly capable of racialization. This racialization was partly the resolution of the complex problem of identity in a society in which the boundaries between religious groups were porous and contained syncretic traditions in which the pious of every faith shared rituals and observances with every other.

At the same time, religious identity was inextricably intertwined with discourses of caste, region, language, descent and nation. Communities, or more explicitly 'minorities', constructed around each of these categories of identity played upon the others. Everybody in India could, according to one or other of these categories, claim to belong to a minority. The processes of state formation in the late twentieth century continued to encourage and proliferate these categories of identity. The political definition of a 'Hindu' community, for instance, either polarized caste differences or struggled to subsume them. Religious communities were constructed in different ways in different regions and sometimes fractured along lines of language or regionalism. Conversely, constituencies mobilized around discourses of caste, language or regional nationalism have sometimes found the claims of religious nationalism readily plausible. 'Hindutva' developed explicitly as a racial rather than a religious doctrine. This multiplicity of ethnic identities might explain in part why so many people seemed so quickly susceptible to the racist discourse of Hindu nationalism in the 1990s. But the diversity and contradictions which these various conflicting ethnic identities embodied might also explain the social limits of Hindutva's appeal and the social constraints that have appeared to tighten upon the expansion of Hindu nationalism's constituency.

From neighbourhood to nation: the rise and fall of the Left in Bombay's Girangaon in the twentieth century

If you stand at night on the roof of one of the recent, still under-occupied high-rise buildings erected on the property of a defunct mill in central Bombay, and often named with a surreal flourish like Kalpataru Heights, or the Phoenix Towers that sprang from the ashes of a spinning mill, you will be treated to an instructive, indeed, allegorical, view of the city. Immediately at the base of the Heights upon which you stand will be a discernible circle of gloom. Further afield, a mile or two away, whether towards the bustling suburbs to the north or the old town and the business districts to the south, the city will be awash with electric light. As the city's textile mills have closed down, so the residents of Girangaon are enveloped in darkness in the geographical centre of one of the world's largest cities.

Two events in recent times have marked the ways in which Bombay's residents view their city, its culture and character, its position in the wider world and the social and political relations by which it is constituted – the decline and in large measure the closure of the textile industry since the late 1980s and the brutal pogrom against Muslims in December 1992 and January 1993 that followed the destruction of the Babri Masjid at Ayodhya. Bombay's prodigious growth in the late nineteenth century and its claim to be a major metropolitan centre has until recently been inextricably tied to the rise and growth of the cotton textile industry. The apparently precipitous decline of the industry has not only proved calamitous for some of its residents but has unsettled the city's sense of it own identity.

No sooner had the orgy of violence in 1993 ceased than Bombay's residents began to wonder how communal violence – perhaps an endemic feature of the wild and backward plains of the north – could have

This essay was first published as the Introduction to *One Hundred Years, One Hundred Voices: The Millworkers of Girangaon: An Oral History*, by Neera Adarkar and Meena Menon (Calcutta, 2004). It is re-published here with the kind permission of the authors and the publisher, Seagull Books.

consumed their modern, cosmopolitan city. The city's inhabitants, including those who had declaimed at the time that the Muslims needed to be taught a lesson or two, now picked over the causes and assessed who was to blame. Some perceived the manipulations of politicians and underworld bosses at work. Others saw in it the malevolent hand of 'anti-social' or 'lumpen' elements, thus absolving themselves from any complicity in the violence. Many took it for granted that both these events were closely linked. De-industrialization and large-scale unemployment, it is said, gives rise to anger and frustration, lawlessness and anomie, and communal hatreds and elemental violence. Mounting evidence about the involvement of the 'respectable' middle classes, skilled workers, sometimes police and other officials – in itself wholly compatible with, and rendered plausible by, what we know about the appeal of Hindutva among high caste, urban middle class groups – suggests that such brisk conclusions might profitably be postponed.

On the other hand, these two determining events of the past twenty years – industrial decline and communalism – may be linked in a different perspective. They reflect fundamental changes that had been working their way through the city's social fabric. Perhaps the most significant of these changes has been the increasing marginalization of the urban poor and the working classes. Their claim to a stake within the city's social framework, never very secure, has been increasingly undermined, sometimes seemingly brushed aside. At first sight, the notion that the working classes could lay a stronger claim to inclusion within the social contract of the city in the early twentieth century may seem as implausible as the notion that it had weakened in the context of a vibrant, raucous democracy. But it merits some consideration. The rights and claims of the working classes in the early twentieth century, weak as they may have been, were neither created by the colonial autocracy nor granted by the city's ruling elites. They were seized by the momentum of popular political and industrial action. Conversely, the marginalization of the city's poor reflected the gradual breaking down of workers' resistance. At various times in the history of the cotton mills, workers' resistance has been contained and beaten back. Its revival in the form of the general strike of 1982 hastened the flight of capital, as the millowners sought to diversify their investment, outsource production to power looms and garment factories and realize the value of their vastly inflated real estate.

The closure of the industry was thus intimately related to the defeat of labour, the clawing back of their employment rights and the dissipation of their stake in the city. At the same time, the Shiv Sena, characterized by its explicitly communal agenda, actively contributed to, and was, at times, even instrumental in undermining workers' resistance and in breaking the communist trade unions. The marginalization of the claims of the working classes and the urban poor to citizenship could not have been achieved without a wider degradation of governance. The closure of the industry was the culmination of political choices to which in effect some communal organizations contributed. Moreover, the stripping down and dismantling of the industry, and the handling of its consequences, reflected the ungenerous parameters within which the ruling elites and employers weighed up and calculated the rights which the poor and the working classes deserved. Conversely, the dismissal of the rights of the poor has sometimes, as one of a range of responses, elicited a communal turn. For it is through some communal organizations, in their assertions of community, that the urban poor have been able to declare, and sometimes no more than momentarily display, their claims to equality. In this sense, if de-industrialization and communalism are closely linked, it is not directly as economic cause and social effect but because of the immediate and intimate connections between the processes by which the stake of the poor in the city has been swept aside and the quickening degradation of governance.

In this book, Neera Adarkar and Meena Menon offer a perspective on these transformations in the social relations of the city by examining the recent history of Girangaon, the mill village, as the cotton mill districts of Bombay city came to be known to its residents. Their history is based on the oral testimonies of mill workers, Girangaon residents, trade union leaders, political commentators and political activists. Since these interviews were conducted at the end of the twentieth century, the oral testimonies reach back into the 1930s but necessarily tell their most concentrated story for the period between the 1940s and the general strike of 1982. Neera Adarkar and Meena Menon have made a vital contribution to the recent history of the labour movement and of Bombay city. As a work of oral history, its significance is pioneering. The oral testimonies collected here illuminate not only the past but also the crises that the city and its working classes face today.

The book makes its most powerful contribution by enabling 'a hundred voices', frequently silenced in the archives and the historical records, to be heard. Indeed, for the most part, the working classes have remained silent in Indian history. The voices of their political representatives have sometimes been treated inter-changeably with their own expression of their concerns, aspirations and social experiences. Workers' concerns are thus often made available through the petitions mounted on their behalf by lawyers and activists. Their acts of resistance and protest are transmitted through newspaper or police intelligence reports. The significance of their strikes and political activism is sometimes gleaned through the assessments of civil servants, political commentators and trade union leaders. Their motives and ideologies are briefly glimpsed through the prism of collective action or in the claims and the rhetoric of their spokesmen.

As a result, historians who have sought to unravel what they saw as the specificities, even peculiarities, of working class culture have often found themselves replicating the stereotypes and social prejudices of its many interlocutors: civil servants and employers, police reporters and political commentators, social observers and political leaders. The sometimes unexamined assumptions of contemporary elites, whether these have related to the characterization of the 'rural mentalities' of the workers, their caste, 'communal' or 'pre-industrial' consciousness, their inherent religiosity, their filial dependence on their patrons and leaders or their volatility and inherent propensity to violence and roughness, have thus often passed seamlessly into the conclusions of historians and social scientists. For this reason, by systematically recording the testimonies of workers, as well as those who led, fought, observed or attempted to control them, Adarkar and Menon have moved our inquiries forward in promising directions. Moreover, oral history remains an unduly neglected field, and an under-used technique, in the study of Indian society. It is to be hoped that this book will stimulate a greater interest in and engagement with the methods and possibilities of oral history.

It has become increasingly apparent that urban space has exerted a major influence in shaping the history of the working classes in India, as indeed elsewhere. For this reason, it is important for historians to pay particular attention to the social relations of the neighbourhood. Terms like 'neighbourhood' or 'community' have often nudged historians and social scientists towards an assumption of their homogeneity or even of an inherent social harmony. However, collectivities, shared values and a sense of mutuality is not necessarily predicated upon proximate living. Indeed, to a large extent, close connections are forged in the neighbourhood most extensively in conditions in which the survival strategies of its residents force them to draw heavily upon their friends and relatives. Yet it is precisely in these conditions that social relations are most explicitly characterized by competition and conflict. It is by recognizing how far the social relations of neighbourhood are constituted by antagonisms and conflicts, rather than by assuming a natural harmony, that it might be possible to discern and delineate more accurately the bonds of commonality that are forged within them. The social relations of Girangaon were constituted primarily by its daily tensions and conflicts and increasingly by its experience of political and industrial struggle. The making of Girangaon was in a fundamental sense an explicitly political process.

The character of social relations in Girangaon, as well as its place within the city as a whole, changed substantially since its formation in the late nineteenth century. In the early twentieth century, the neighbourhood represented the most crucial social arena in which the solidarities of the working classes in Bombay were forged. In fact, in important ways, the social relations of the neighbourhood, particularly in the case of Girangaon, were constituted neither by social homogeneity nor by a harmony created by the act of living together but by political conflict, at various levels from the family and the chawl to the mill and the state. At the end of the twentieth century, as the cotton textile industry was dismantled, the politics of urban space impinged upon the residents of Girangaon and indeed of the city as a whole in a radically different way. For the residents of Girangaon, and for the mill workers among them, the portentous question was, as it remains today, how they might extricate an equitable settlement from the debris of industrial collapse. At the same time, the deployment and usage of the mill lands, as well as, indeed, the vast expanses of dock lands, pose important questions both for the fate of those who live within them as well as for the character of the city and its future. The strategic utilization of these lands in the centre of one of the world's largest and fastest growing cities could determine how far its urban future can be secured, how sustainable its growth might be and how habitable it will be for its residents and its workers over the next few generations.[1]

The making of Girangaon[2]

From the earliest days of the industry, Girangaon had witnessed extensive industrial action. Commentators observed the frequency of strikes since at least the 1880s. In the early 1890s, workers coordinated strikes across several mills, for instance, in the Heeramaneck and, subsequently, the Sassoon group. When mills began to extend the working day competitively, with the introduction of electricity, they also manipulated wages and thus provoked further strikes, which culminated in a general strike when Tilak was sentenced to transportation in 1908. During the First World War, and in its immediate aftermath, strikes occurred with increasing frequency, both within the industry and outside, until the mill workers

---

[1] For a recent investigation of these themes, see Darryl D'Monte, *Ripping the Fabric: The Decline of Mumbai and its Mills* (New Delhi, 2002).

[2] This section draws substantially on the arguments and evidence presented in my earlier work, *The Origins of Industrial Capitalism in India: Business Strategies and the Working Classes in Bombay, 1900–1940* (Cambridge, 1994) and *Imperial Power and Popular Politics: Class, Resistance and the State in India, 1850–1950* (Cambridge, 1998), ch. 4.

mounted and sustained industrial action on an unprecedented scale and for extensive periods in the general strikes of 1919 and 1920. Between 1918 and 1940, eight general strikes occurred in Girangaon. None of them lasted for less than a month. The general strikes of 1928–29 lasted in effect for eighteen months.

From the late 1920s onwards, especially during the general strike of 1928, the labour movement came to be dominated by a communist leadership. Around these general strikes in the 1920s and 1930s, there occurred over one thousand strikes in individual mills and departments. Not surprisingly, Girangaon sometimes came to be seen by the city's elites, especially in the late 1920s, as an insurrectionary centre. By the late 1940s, the support that the communists commanded among the workers had begun to dwindle, by comparison with the heady days of the late 1920s. Nonetheless, they continued to elicit substantial support in Girangaon until the 1970s. The communists played a prominent role in the general strikes of 1950 and 1974, and they remained a major electoral force in the area. They were capable of mobilizing votes and winning seats, and at the very least of determining the outcome of elections to the municipal corporation, the state assembly and indeed the Lok Sabha. This scale of industrial action, especially that witnessed between 1918 and 1940, could only be sustained because workers were able to draw heavily upon the social organization of the neighbourhood. Similarly, the decline of the Left, and indeed the weakening of workers' resistance, was closely connected with fundamental changes in the social character of Girangaon and its relationship to the city after the Second World War.

There was clearly an important spatial dimension to the development of workers' politics in Bombay. The neighbourhood was a crucial arena in which the solidarities of the working class politics were forged. Indeed, the workplace and the neighbourhood cannot be treated as neatly distinguished social spheres in examining the development of workers' politics in Bombay, and indeed, perhaps anywhere. Rather, the social contours of Girangaon were shaped by the nature of the labour market, the division of labour and the organization of work. They were also influenced by the close connections that workers' families maintained between the urban neighbourhood and their rural base.

Girangaon began to take shape in the late nineteenth century. Between 1840 and 1880, Bombay city grew rapidly and first acquired the character of a major metropolitan centre. By the early twentieth century, its claim to be an industrial centre turned wholly on the cotton mills. Although the first mills were built in the 1850s, the industry expanded substantially only in the 1870s and 1880s. Mills now proliferated to the north of the 'native' town. The average number of workers employed daily in the mills increased from 13,500 in 1875 to nearly 76,000 in 1895 and then doubled again by the early 1920s.[3] But this figure conceals the fact that at least a third as many additional workers were needed to sustain this daily average through the year. In the late nineteenth century, workers moved out of the northern areas of 'native town' and into Girangaon. The mill districts expanded rapidly in the early twentieth century. The population of Parel and Byculla, for instance, doubled between 1891 and 1921, while Sewri and Worli expanded nearly five-fold.[4] Increasingly, those who hoped to work in the mills began to settle in their vicinity. A survey conducted by the Labour Office in 1925 revealed that 90 per cent of the mill workers lived within a fifteen-minute walk from their place of employment.[5] As Bombay's population grew exponentially after independence, workers slowly began to disperse and larger numbers travelled into Girangaon from further afield in the city.

This growing concentration in Girangaon of mills and ancillary work-shops, millworkers and job-seekers in the late nineteenth and early twentieth centuries reflected in some measure the inadequacy of the city's infrastructure, especially the cost and scarcity of transport and housing. But it was also influenced by the labour policies and business strategies of the millowners. Inhospitable and sometimes arbitrarily changing conditions and hours of work, uncertain and irregular employment and low wages made it essential for workers to live near their place of employment. The mills hired labour according to need, which varied not only from day to day, but at times also fluctuated on a single day within the same mill. Notionally, at least, workers were hired at the mill gates each day. By virtue of their connections with a jobber, their particular skills and experience or their role within a team, some workers acquired a semblance of a grip on their jobs. But only the most optimistic and the foolhardy could rely upon the permanence of their employment. Their social connections, built up in the neighbourhood, often originating in affinities of caste, kinship and village, became vital to workers both in their attempts to find jobs, housing and credit, and in seeking support in times of unemployment, sickness or family crisis.

Most workers were migrants to the city. In 1921, about 84 per cent of the city's population had been born outside Bombay.[6] Fifty years later, the city's labour force still consisted largely of rural migrants.[7] The

---

[3] Figures from the *Annual Reports of the Bombay Millowners' Association*, passim.
[4] *Census of India, 1931*, Vol. IX, part ii (Bombay, 1933), pp. 158–59.
[5] *Labour Gazette*, Vol. IV, no. 7 (1925), pp. 745–47.
[6] *Census of India, 1921*, Vol. IX, part I (Bombay, 1922), p. 16.
[7] K. C. Zachariah, *Migrants in Greater Bombay* (Bombay, 1968); H. and V. Joshi, *Surplus Labour and the City: A Study of Bombay* (Delhi, 1976).

predominant pattern was for young males to come to the city in search of wages, generally leaving their families behind in the village to look after their holdings. They came to the city to work and often returned to their village in old age, and in periods of sickness or unemployment, and of course each year to help with the harvest.[8] For many working class families, the purpose of migration was to enhance the family's resources in order to enable them to hold on to their stake in the village, not generally for the individual to escape from its clutches.[9] The access to cash and credit which urban employment, especially industrial wages, sometimes afforded them, also enabled them to settle their debts in the village, buy seed and hold on to their plots. It sometimes enabled their families to subsist even after the village plot had become a fading memory. It was a matter of the utmost significance for the social relations of Girangaon that migration was driven not by social mobility but by poverty.

Not surprisingly, therefore, workers rarely migrated alone, but usually within the framework of their caste, kinship and village connections. They came to the city along already established routes. It was with the help of relatives and friends, co-villagers and caste fellows that they tried to find work, shelter and sometimes credit in the city. Workers who were already established in the city maintained and renewed their rural connections by helping kin and caste fellows when they first arrived. This pattern of migration thus forged for most workers a nexus of social connections which integrated not only the rural and urban economy, but also workplace and neighbourhood. They served to constitute the working class neighbourhoods and, indeed, to shape the organization of work, even if they were by no means the only or the determining influence upon these social arenas. These social connections provided the basis of their welfare protection in times of crisis. To be known in the neighbourhood eased workers' paths in raising credit in a period of unemployment or sickness, and in finding shelter when they could no longer pay their rents. It enabled them to organize to defend their wages or conditions of work or to protect their jobs when they went on strike. It is not intended to suggest that their place in the working class neighbourhoods was sufficient to provide such protection, but it was often a necessary minimum to help tide them over a crisis.

This nexus between workplace, neighbourhood and village was further soldered by the methods of recruitment that prevailed in the industry.

[8] A more detailed analysis of patterns of migration is offered in my *Origins of Industrial Capitalism*, ch. 4.

[9] Some women who came to the city to escape the shackles of the family remained an exception to this rule. See also Samita Sen, *Women and Labour in Late Colonial India: the Bengal Jute Industry* (Cambridge, 1999).

In the early twentieth century, certainly until the 1930s, the millowners depended very largely upon jobbers to recruit and discipline workers. They looked to the jobbers to maintain an adequate supply of relatively docile labour, with an optimum level of skill and experience, in the face of fluctuating demand. This was never easy to achieve. To ensure a regular supply of labour and to exert their control over the workers, the jobbers in turn recruited within networks of kinship, caste, village and neighbourhood. Through these networks, jobbers often acquired considerable influence in Girangaon. They sometimes acted as creditors, as landlords or as the intermediaries for grain dealers, moneylenders and landlords. In this way, they performed a significant role and acquired considerable influence in the housing, credit and labour markets. No jobber could expect to impose his authority in the workplace unless he also cut a figure in the neighbourhood. In any event, the jobber's connections were valuable to the workers whom he hired when they sought credit or housing. The jobber's patronage was particularly crucial for workers who had recently arrived in the city. In this way, as Girangaon formed, the jobber's role served to integrate the workplace and the neighbourhood. It should not be supposed that the jobber was the only kind of patron in the working class neighbourhoods. However, by straddling workplace and neighbourhood, his role became symptomatic of the social relations that developed around the textile industry and that served to constitute Girangaon and to shape its social character.

By enumerating his functions, it would be easy to conclude that the jobber was a monolithic and homogenous institution. In fact, there were many kinds of jobbers and their influence in the neighbourhood often varied according to their place within the labour process in the mills. Conversely, not all jobbers sought and developed extensive social and political connections in the neighbourhood. Some jobbers obtained their position because they were dadas, who led and organized gymnasiums, and built up links with other greater patrons, politicians and power brokers in Girangaon. Others were more modest figures, whose reputation did not extend far beyond the mill or their chawl and immediate neighbourhood. While the jobber's role was not monolithic, nor was it unchanging. The power and influence of the jobber, and his place within the workforce, changed substantially in the late nineteenth and early twentieth centuries. As general strikes occurred with greater frequency across the industry, it soon became apparent to the millowners that the jobbers could no longer be relied upon to deliver a docile and pliant labour force. More crucially, perhaps, the jobbers could no longer serve as an effective bulwark against industrial action. By the 1930s, the millowners had begun to look for alternative methods of labour control in the industry. By the

1950s, the jobber's influence was considerably diminished and his role within the mills was radically transformed. The jobber now ceased to be the agent of recruitment and discipline and was integrated into the structure of supervision and pacemaking in the mills. Workers with aspirations to influence in the neighbourhood now no longer saw their appointment as jobbers as a necessary, let alone a significant, step towards their goal.

Clearly, labour migration was a highly gendered process. Women's experience of migration cannot be readily assimilated to these generalizations.[10] The sex ratio of the population of the city reflected the fact that it was primarily young males who came to the city. Until the mid-twentieth century, there were at least two men for every woman living in the city. Girangaon was, in particular, a predominantly male space. The predominance of adult male migration was not simply the consequence of traditional, culturally specific inhibitions on women's work and migration. Certainly, it reflected a continuing attempt by families, castes and villages to retain control over female mobility and labour. However, it was determined largely by the gendered character of employment opportunities. After factory legislation began to restrict the hours of women's work in the cotton mills in 1891, their employment dwindled. Until then, the proportion of women employed in the cotton mills had been increasing. In the 1890s, the proportion of women employed in the mills declined. Subsequently, the introduction of maternity benefits in 1929 further dissuaded millowners from hiring women, except in defined and restricted occupations. As Rukmini Ainpure and others testify in the pages that follow, the millowners 'did not like to employ women mainly because they did not like to give maternity benefits'. In other words, millowners prized their freedom to deploy labour as flexibly as they chose, and on their own terms. When categories of workers, such as women and children, were protected by legislation, they preferred to exclude them as far as possible from the labour force. Women's employment in the Bombay cotton mills was thus restricted from the late nineteenth century onwards to the two occupations of reeling and winding.

Once the cotton mills began to hire fewer women, it left no large, staple employers of female labour in the city. From the late nineteenth century onwards, women who migrated to the city often found themselves consigned to the casual labour market, or what later came to be called the 'informal sector'. Low wages, irregular employment and poor conditions, and thus low skill and low status, characterized women's work. Thus, when men migrated to the city, women frequently remained in

---

[10] Chandavarkar, *Origins of Industrial Capitalism*, pp. 94–99 and passim.

the village to cultivate their plot or supplemented their earnings through agricultural labour. For the most part, women migrated to the city only in distress. Whole families migrated either only when they were sufficiently prosperous to live together or when they had no other options, for instance during famines or when they had completely lost their stake in the village. Thus jobbers and skilled weavers sometimes brought their families to the city. Similarly, women migrated to the city when they had no other options – for instance, when they were widowed or deserted by their husbands or when they were cast out of the family. It would be folly to underestimate the number of women who came to the city to escape the control of their families.

Since women's work was associated with low status, low skill and low wages, it was often a mark of status and respectability for male workers in the city to withdraw the labour of their wives and daughters when they could, especially in periods of economic buoyancy. Conversely, it was when their husbands, sons and fathers were thrown out of work, when the market slumped, or when their village base was undermined by a crop failure, that women were forced to seek employment. Thus, it was frequently the case that women sought to enter the labour market when jobs were scarce and to withdraw in times of buoyancy when their bargaining position was strong. As a result, their efforts to entrench themselves within the labour market were undermined. In the long run, it became impossible to remedy and transform the structural weaknesses in their bargaining position.

Women's work and mobility thus became subject to, and dependent upon, the circumstances of the family and especially its adult males. Necessarily, this also limited their control of the family's resources. In this way, patriarchal control over women's mobility and employment created the conditions for the exploitation of their labour as well as their bodies. Just as social aspiration was expressed through the withdrawal of women's labour, their commitment to the labour market was, because of the association of women's work with low status, meagre wages and poor conditions, accompanied by the withdrawal of respectability from working women. Women, who worked in the cotton mills, often single, widowed or deserted, were often assumed in public discourse to lack respectability and to be promiscuous and morally tainted. The weakness of their position in the labour market often served to undermine their status within the household. Moreover, this discourse about women's work was often elaborated in times of labour resistance and political conflict. In effect, it fortified attempts to limit their claims to, and control their use of, public space. Sexual taunts, for instance, were commonly used both by women against those who attempted to cross the picket lines and against women when they attempted to go to work during a strike. Similarly, in periods of communal violence, women were taken to sym- bolize their 'community' and both venerated and violated accordingly. Political assertiveness, indeed labour activism, often proliferated simi- lar representations of women. As Prema Purao recalls, 'When women become [politically] active, the first thing that people would say was, she has questionable morals.' Indeed, this is how, according to Prema Purao, they spoke about the redoubtable Parvatibai Bhor, one of the legendary figures of the city's labour and communist movements since the 1930s (Ch. 2, pp. 20–21; also p. 53).

It was not simply the means by which workers found and defended their jobs but especially the widespread and shared experience of unemploy- ment that brought workplace and neighbourhood closely into relation with each other. To deal with the inherent insecurity of their existence and arbitrary and unpredictable changes in their circumstances, most workers had to organize outside the mill by maintaining close connec- tions with their villages, their caste fellows and kin. Frequently room – and rent – sharing arrangements in the city were organized along lines of caste, kinship and village, whereby those who were earning would help those who were unemployed to tide them over periods of difficulty. Several testimonies in the pages that follow describe the workings of the galas, the khanavalis and the gaonkari mandals around which these arrangements for mutual help were based. Similarly, when grain dealers, moneylenders and landlords extended credit or rolled over debts, they were acting in part in their own commercial interests. But they were also thereby paying heed to their debtors' social connections in the neighbour- hood or responding to and respecting the familiarity of neighbourhood acquaintance. Sometimes, they recognized that they could by tighten- ing credit incur the wrath of the whole neighbourhood. In an important sense, therefore, the social organization of Girangaon was shaped by the survival strategies of its residents. This social organization had, after all, formed around the struggle to secure and retain jobs, gather and defend wages, find housing and obtain credit.

Caste, kinship and village connections were therefore vital to work- ers as they organized for life in Girangaon and not surprisingly their significance has endured. Since recent migrants as well as longer estab- lished inhabitants of Girangaon found a measure of security and pro- tection through these affinities, it followed that caste clusters formed both in occupations and in residential patterns. But this did not mean Girangaon was neatly segregated by caste and religion. The patterns of association and sociability of Girangaon's residents formed around over- lapping and intersecting affinities of caste and kinship, village and urban neighbourhood, religion and occupation. Caste and religion were not by any means the sole organizing principle of social life. In any case, caste differences were neither defined nor deployed in a systematic and consistent manner. In the early twentieth century, the caste groupings that contemporary observers identified within the working classes were often large caste blocks rather than endogamous jatis and sometimes nothing more than loosely defined regional, religious or even linguistic groupings. Caste associations in Bombay sometimes brought together those related by jati and kin who belonged to a collection of villages in the district from which the workers had migrated. Sometimes they limited themselves to the residents of a particular neighbourhood in the city. Some caste mandalis operated across the boundaries of jati. In the 1960s, the majority of caste mandalis among migrants from Ratnagiri were organized by village rather than by jati, while no more than two-fifths of their number bothered to join mandalis defined by caste.[11] Migrants from Maruti Satkar's village, already established in Bombay, had set up and organized the room in which he lived on coming to the city. 'Only people from our village', he recalled, 'are allowed to stay in these galas. There are people from all castes' (Ch. 1). Maratha, and to a lesser extent Muslim, weavers fought to defend their skilled position within the workforce partly by keeping dalits out of the weaving shed. Despite the very considerable restructuring and reorganization of work, which occurred from the 1930s onwards, and which quickened after the 1940s, weavers continued successfully to sustain these exclusionary practices. Since these reforms, passing under the label of 'rationalization', sought to undermine the status and bargaining power of weavers, it is especially remarkable that they were able to continue to insist upon the exclusion of dalits over such a long period. Indeed, in view of the millowners' attempts to break the bargaining power of weavers since the 1910s, it is even more surprising that they tolerated the latter's stance of caste exclusion.

Forms of caste exclusion were indeed practised, not only by weavers, seeking to avert the dilution of their skilled status, but by various workers across the industry. It is still sometimes too readily assumed that urbanization dissolved caste differences or that workers' perception of their common interests allowed them to transcend its divisions. In practising caste exclusion, workers sometimes expressed no more than a narrow bigotry and sometimes a general social aspiration. As Datta Iswalkar points out, 'upper caste workers' would not drink water from a pot filled by a Mahar, or indeed, eat with dalits.

[11] K. Patel, *Rural Labour in Industrial Bombay* (Bombay, 1963).

They would sit and chew paan with him [Vishnu, a Mahar worker in the Modern Mills] but they would not drink water from his hands! They never treated him badly, they were friends with him, but they would never go to his house. Or eat out of a lunch box brought by any of the Mahars. The funny thing is, the Maratha workers were unable to judge the caste of North Indian workers. So they could not practise untouchability with them (Ch. 1, p. 23).

Similarly, Sheikh Janu Chand, a communist and one of Girangaon's leading shahirs, recalled that the khanaval at which he boarded when he first came to Bombay in the 1940s was run by a Hindu woman from the Ghat and attended by 'Hindus, Muslims, Buddhists etc. . . . The textile workers would eat very well. No, there was no untouchability or casteism in the khanaval' (Ch. 1, p. 48). Although Sheikh Janu Chand's khanaval may not necessarily have been exceptional, it would be unduly optimistic to suppose that workers practised no caste exclusion. In any case, as he pointed out himself, it was only after the communal riots of 1946–47 that 'Muslims lived together for security.' Social segregation was necessarily accentuated by communal violence, but it rarely endured.

The physical structure of the working class neighbourhoods ensured that the distinction between private and public space was sometimes worn to the point of obliteration. Social life often acquired an essentially public quality. This was the consequence in part of proximity and over-crowding. It also followed from the patterns of building and settlement. Girangaon was by no means among the most densely inhabited areas of the city in the 1920s and 1930s. Nonetheless, its ramshackle, jerry-built chawls were often packed closely into spaces between streets and municipal thoroughfares. Since land was expensive, tenurial conditions complex and, most crucially, returns on rentals for the poor invariably low, builders sweated sites with chawls and squeezed them into as many tenements as they could. They also sought to economize on the quality of materials and construction and on the provision of sanitation. Since the late nineteenth century, observers noted 'the sacrifice in durability' in these buildings. Chawls which boasted more than the most minimal plumbing were, as if for their hubris, subjected to 'the speedy dilapidation of timber-frame buildings' as 'the constant soaking from the washing places produces rapid rot of pillars and posts'.[12] Nonetheless, several of these older chawls have endured better than more recent attempts to build low-rent accommodation for the poor.

Chawls were usually one- or two-storeyed buildings in which rooms ran off an ambulatory corridor or verandah. Common washing facilities

---

[12] *Gazetteer of Bombay City and Island* (3 vols.) (Bombay, 1909), Vol. I, p. 199.

and lavatories were located at one end of the corridor. Taps were scarce, quickly ran dry in the summer (and even more consistently as the city's water problems grew in the 1950s), and often became a flashpoint of conflict between neighbours. Over-crowding of chawls and rooms within them made it even harder to gain access to the tap. Anxiety about the water running out or the fear that they would not get to the mill on time added an edge to the often frenzied competition among neighbours for their moment at the tap. Water probably generated more feuding, enmity and violence than any other aspect of chawl life. The tap should douse cold water upon any romantic assumptions about the natural warmth and camaraderie of neighbourhood life. In fact, fighting around the water pipes in the chawls contributed to a steady flow of assault cases to the city's police courts.[13]

The extent of over-crowding ensured that the distinction between the home and the street, between private and public space, could not easily be sustained. The residents of Girangaon's chawls spilled out into the verandahs, the wadis and the streets. In view of this over-crowding, the Census Commissioner in 1931 found 'nothing remarkable in the fact' that 'the streets are used at night as sleeping places'. For three-quarters of the city's population lived in single-room tenements in 1931 in which 'the average floor space available for each occupant cannot be more than what can be covered by a small mat'.[14] Already at the time, between 30 and 40 per cent of the residents of Girangaon lived in one-room tenements inhabited by more than six people. In Byculla, barely 1 per cent of the population, and in Parel and Mazagaon no more than 12 per cent, lived with fewer than three others in a single room.[15] This density of occupation only became greater as the twentieth century wore on. The implementation of multiple-shift working from the late 1930s, a practice that increased considerably in the 1940s and 1950s, enabled landlords and rent collectors to pack their chawls yet more intensively. Shivaji Date describes below how in the 1960s and 1970s as each shift set off for work from the gala of the Pimpalgaon Gaonkari Mandal, another returned from the mills to sleep. 'There are 20 to 30 people in each room. How do we manage? Well, because there are three shifts.' Once night shifts ceased, the number of tenants became yet harder to manage. If a mill closed, if there was a public holiday or if a strike occurred, 'we had a real problem' (Ch. 1, pp. 6–7). The social organization of the neighbourhood was so closely integrated with the rhythms and imperatives of work that the decline and the closure of the textile industry in the 1980s posed major,

[13] *Indian Textile Journal*, Vol. XXIX (August 1919), p. 209.
[14] *Census, 1931*, Vol. IX, part i, pp. 88–89.   [15] *Ibid.*, Vol. IX, part I, pp. 88–91.

often insuperable problems for the institutional arrangements and social relations of Girangaon.

The popular culture of Girangaon

The public spaces of the street and the neighbourhood thus had a private dimension, just as the private spaces of the family and home were constituted by public processes. Moreover, the processes that acted upon the social organization of the neighbourhood in the early twentieth century transcended locality and linked Girangaon to the villages of the desh and the Konkan coast, or, increasingly, further afield to the Gangetic plains and the Tamilnadu countryside. The arena of the street and neighbourhood did not simply derive from the material needs of the working classes. It was substantiated by leisure and sociability as well. It was in particular constituted in important respects by the politics of Girangaon and especially the traditions, memories and experience built up by decades of industrial conflict and political struggle.

In the context of over-crowding, the street corner offered a meeting place. Street entertainers, from monkey players to kadaklakshmis, were a recurrent feature of Girangaon's daily, public theatre.[16] The tea vendor, it was said, provided an information exchange, acquiring and dispensing news and gossip. At the teashops and the pleaders' offices, those who could read the newspapers out to those who could not.[17] Liquor shops and akhadas drew their members from the neighbourhood. Landlords sometimes owned grain shops on the ground floor of their chawls and required their tenants to patronize them. In this way, the landlord hoped that his tenants would deepen their debts and their dependence upon him. Chawls, streets and neighbourhoods organized communal activities, including occasions of religious observance whether satyanarayan pujas, Mohurram tolis, Gokulashtmi melas or what became the increasingly popular observance of Tilak's invention, the Ganeshotsav. Often, chawl committees and gaon mandalis even acted as tribunals, settling disputes between neighbours and, on occasion, imposing their moral expectations upon tenants and members. Chawl committees sometimes organized to represent the interests of the residents against landlords and his rent collector, or in their dealings with municipal officials or the police. Local and neighbourhood organization thus reached into the more rarified spheres

---

[16] Parvatibai Bhor, *Eka Rannaraginichi Hakikat*, as told to Padmakar Chitale (Bombay, 1977).

[17] *Bombay Confidential Proceedings*, 1917, General Department, Vol. 25, p. 15. Oriental and India Office Collection, The British Library; Patel, *Rural Labour*, p. 151.

of institutional politics in the early twentieth century.[18] The growth of democratic politics and electoral competition after independence further developed and elaborated these connections.

Several voices in the pages that follow attest to the long historical memory of Girangaon's culture. Speakers identify the changing character of Ganeshotsav across the twentieth century. Tilak had sought to establish the festival to wean Hindus away from participation in Mohurram. Its observance imitated many of the collective and popular aspects of Mohurram which British officials, ashraf elites and high-minded reformers had darkly perceived as 'saturnalian'. The final procession, which led to the immersion of Ganpati in the sea, was its high point. Like the waaz delivered in the mosques, lectures on political themes were often associated with the festival. Until the 1970s, the public observance of Ganpati had an important secular dimension. The characteristics for which Ganpati elicited both admiration and affection was his irreverence, his benign sense of mischief and his good-hearted fallibility. As Vijay Khatu recalled,

The Ganeshotsav was not just a religious festival, but a means to gather people for a comparatively harmless purpose . . . There was a pride of one's own locality, which is the case even today.

Khatu, a leading sculptor of Ganpati idols, linked himself, with considerable historical precision, to 'the second oldest' Ganeshotsav mandal in Bombay. He was able to date the growing 'practice of making huge Ganpati idols' precisely to 1953 and the institution of chakri vyakhanmalas and lectures on political and moral subjects, akin to the waaz heard during Mohurram, to the days of the Samyukta Maharashtra movement in the late 1950s. However, political discourses were, to a greater or lesser extent, associated with the festival from the outset. The observance of the festival acquired increasingly a religious significance as well as a narrowing communal definition. By the 1980s, in the wake of the Shiv Sena's increasingly prominent public presence, what had been an open, all-comers ritual of inversion and celebration of mischief and irreverence became an expression of 'Hindu' triumphalism.

As various artists and performers describe their lives in the 1940s and 1950s, Adarkar and Menon disclose, for the first time, the depth and liveliness of a popular artistic culture in Girangaon. The 'theatre of the street' now acquired an increasingly organized shape. The popular entertainers of the 1910s that Parvatibai Bhor recalled in her memoir had given way by the 1940s to increasingly differentiated and sophisticated

[18] See Chandavarkar, *Origins of Industrial Capitalism*, ch. 5.

forms of cultural production.[19] Significantly, the artists themselves, in their testimonies, differentiate specialisms within their art forms, distinguish carefully between them, locate themselves rather precisely within its history and identify the provenance and complex development of their art forms. Performers had a lively sense of their own artistic history. Annabhau Sathe's Mumbaichi Lavni was a conscious tribute to Patthe Bapurao. The Loknatya tradition explicitly drew upon and closely associated itself with the tradition of the Satyashodhak jalsas. Nivrutti Pawar recalled how his first visit to see Patthe Bapurao's tamasha shaped his future as a 'shahir': 'with the very first beat of the dholak, I felt a tingling throughout my body'. Subsequently, he took his first steps towards becoming a singer when he began to accompany Shahir Haribhau Bhandari as he peddled khaja through the streets of Girangaon. As a result, he began to acquire a reputation as a singer. 'I started getting invited to sing at functions' and thus, gradually became a professional singer and poet. '"Shahir"', as he pointed out, 'is a title people give you. It is not a title conferred by any institution.' In this sense, it was not very different from those who came to be known as dadas. In much the same way, Vijay Khatu was closely aware of the legends of his own craft as a sculptor of Ganpati statues and indeed his own artistic lineage: Shyam Sarang from the Chinchpokli Ganeshotsav Mandal and 'then there was Welling – he was a great artist. He was the guru for our generation, a perfectionist.'

Several people testified to the range of artistic performance that inundated the streets and wadis of Girangaon by the mid-twentieth century. As Shahir Pawar described it,

When you walked down in the streets [of Girangaon], you would hear bhajans and kirtans. We would go and watch the sculptors at work on the Ganesh idols in Lalbag for Ganeshotsav in September. There were Rangoli artistes who made beautiful paintings. They were so life-like, when you looked at them, you felt they would open their mouths and speak. They were drawn on the roads, and people would come to see them. Where is the space to do that now, when the cars even climb the footpaths.

Similarly Vijay Khatu recounts the range of cultural activity around Ganeshotsav itself: 'bhajans, songs and dance competitions, Loknatya, one-act plays, fancy dress competitions and folk art on every street. There were painting competitions in Peru Chawl.' Moreover, both producers and consumers of this output were fully aware of the differences between,

---

[19] Bhor, *Eka Rannaraginichi Hakikat.*

and the manifestation of, the distinct cultural forms of the Konkan and the Ghats.

By 1946, when the Hanuman theatre was started, there were already nineteen tamasha theatres in Bombay. Some operated on a significant scale and were commercially successful. The city's tamasha players also possessed a highly developed, complex and socially differentiated sense of their craft. According to Madhukar Nerale, the owner of the Hanuman, the theatre distinguished between a proletarian 'lok sangeeth' and a middle class 'natya sangeeth', between the 'baithakichi lavni' in which the players sat down and sang for a polite audience and the 'bahurangi tamasha' which was often improvised, rambunctious and bawdy, and more closely approximated to the style that was popular in the rural Deccan. In this form, 'there was a lot of ad-libbing and there was hardly any written script. There would be topical comments, the language and lyrics were colloquial, the music folk' (Nerale). The performative genre of the tamasha was associated largely with the Deccan districts. The traditional genre of the Konkan, known as 'the dashavatar', entailed improvisation upon stories and characters from the epics and had its own variations along the coast. In Girangaon, these genres adapted to and borrowed from each other. Although some attempted to retain their distinctiveness – the Hanuman theatre, for instance, maintained its affinity with tamasha, they often fused, or at least like their performers entered into a lively and engaged dialogue.

The influence of this cultural renaissance could scarcely be contained within Girangaon. The Loknatya tradition which emerged in the mid-twentieth century brought together the form of the tamasha with the formal disciplines of the theatre. It was associated with many of the leading figures of the Marathi literary canon. Among the great poets of the canon were some of the shahirs of Girangaon, like Annabhau Sathe, Amar Sheikh and Gavankar, who also wrote and performed tamashas and who emerged and remained within the city's Leftist tradition. Through Dada Kondke, Vasant Sabnis and Shahir Sable, tamasha was brought, with its own transformations, to the heart of the Marathi cinema.[20] Leading figures of the nascent Bollywood were closely associated with the city's communists and many with the Progressive Writers' Association. As Vasant Bhor, Parvatibai's son, recalls, Balraj Sahni, Kazi Azmi and Dina Gandhi lived for a time in the party commune in Sandhurst Road. The smell of urine that pervaded the building made the communist gentry feel especially high minded and self-conscious about the righteousness

---

[20] Communication from Neera Adarkar.

of their cause, the seriousness of their struggle, the purity of their beliefs and the gravity of their sacrifice.[21] Progressive writers, dramatists and actors became in the following decades the interpreters and purveyors of India's indigenous and authentic aesthetic. In this elusive quest for authenticity, they enshrined loknatya within the increasingly standardized canon of an Indian folk tradition that they had in effect begun to invent, freeze and invite the middle classes to revere. Similarly, mainstream Hindi cinema in the 1950s, on the verge of developing into a behemoth, could scarcely escape the influence of Girangaon's high culture. Following its own agenda of nation-building, Bollywood sought to borrow, incorporate and pay homage to what it imagined as India's folk tradition and popular culture.

In the 1940s and 1950s, Bombay city was the locus of a wide range of creative and artistic activity. This burst of creative activity often emerged from an explicit political engagement. The Progressive Writers' Association had originally formed in a Chinese restaurant in Denmark Street in London, but in India it found its home in Bombay.[22] It was here on the eve of independence and partition that many of its leading figures, Sajjad Zaheer, Ali Sardar Jafri, Sadat Hasan Manto and Mulk Raj Anand, worked, wrote and organized. The IPTA flourished in the mid-twentieth century as the city's communist intelligentsia favoured the theatre as a powerful means of spreading their political message. Between the 1930s and 1950s, Bombay city witnessed the emergence of a modernist movement in architecture and revelled increasingly in the exuberance of art deco. At this time, too, the Bombay modernist painters came together around Ara, Hussain, Gaitonde and, above all, Raza, who must belong among the great painters of the twentieth century.[23] The range and vitality of this cultural production could not have taken shape in isolation from the similar vibrancy that was witnessed in Girangaon at the same time. They emerged from similar influences and from connections and contexts that were closely related and unavoidably in dialogue with each other. Their inter-connections remain yet to be fully explored. Some of the voices heard in the pages that follow indicate the urgency of this task.

The prodigious cultural production of Girangaon had significant political roots. They were in important ways formed by the political and

[21] For memories of the smells of the commune in Sandhurst Road and its effect on herself and her comrades, see Raj Thapar, *All These Years: A Memoir* (New Delhi, 1991).
[22] *Golden Jubilee of the Progressive Writers Association UK, 1935–1985: Brief Report, Statement, Declaration and Resolutions of International Conference held on 3rd and 4th August, 1985 at GLC County Hall, London* (London, n.d. [1985?]).
[23] Yashodhara Dalmia, 'From Jamsetjee Jeejeebhoy to the Progressive Painters' in S. Patl and A Thorner (ed.) *Bombay: A Mosaic of Modern Culture* (Bombay, 1995), pp. 182–93.

industrial conflicts waged in Girangaon in the early twentieth century. Many of the leading performers in Girangaon clearly conceived of their art in explicitly political terms. Some played a prominent role in political mobilization. Amar Sheikh, Annabhau Sathe and Gavankar wrote and performed as members of the Communist Party. Annabhau Sathe's troupe, which was formed in 1943 and with which Narayan Surve came to be associated, was in fact known as the Lal Bawta Kalapathak. Amar Sheikh was said to have trained several kalapathaks in Girangaon. Shahir Sable and Raja Mayekar ran their own troupe in DeLisle Road. Narayan Surve and Krishna Desai became leading members of the Lalbag Kalapathak. The communist shahirs 'did much to propagate the party's politics amongst the ordinary people', as Madhukar Nerale recalled. They wrote songs about 'the problems of workers who lived here and on political issues'. Indeed, 'the communists', he suggested 'were able to reach the workers this way'. Socialist shahirs, however, characteristically concentrated their efforts on 'sermonising on moral and ethical issues'. Similarly, there were others like the rangoli artist Gunvant Manjrekar who saw themselves as artists rather than political agents. Nonetheless, as he pointed out, 'my art is not separate from my political opinions. I am not an activist, but my association with political leaders and organizations have been important to me.' Indeed, he proclaimed that rangoli 'is a socialist art form' not only because 'it can be appreciated by rich and poor alike' but especially because it is 'a social art, one that is practised by every woman, rich or poor outside the house' (Ch. 1, pp. 28–29). It was commonplace for kalapathaks to perform at public meetings, to sing political songs or lay on a tamasha. Crowds pulled in by these performers, so the theory ran, then usually stayed behind to hear the speeches and watch the main act of the tamasha that followed. As Vasant Bhor put it, in the 1950s, 'we would sing in order to gather the public, then after the speeches, there would be a tamasha announced so that no one would run away during the speeches' (Ch. 1, p. 45). It is at least open to speculation that the crowds that collected at public meetings, which Bombay's communist leaders addressed, had gathered to hear the legendary shahirs and to watch the staging of the real, rather than the figurative and political, tamasha. Perhaps, the communists who immersed themselves in the arcane revolutionary discourse and embarked upon the political adventurism of the late 1940s and early 1950s had in fact mistaken the passion for tamasha for a popular revolutionary zeal. Nonetheless, it was clear that the highly active and vibrant cultural life of Girangaon had been shaped by its own entrenched political traditions that looked back to the struggles of the 1920s and 1930s.

Workers' politics and Girangaon

If the social organization of Girangaon was constituted by its political traditions, politics in turn formed a part of the theatre of the street.[24] Regular processions, demonstrations and public meetings contributed to the pageantry of political activity. Increasingly, in the 1920s and 1930s, the Congress agitations consisted of specifically chosen symbolic and ritualized acts: prabhat feries, the picketing of liquor shops, the manufacture of salt or the bonfires of foreign cloth. These public actions were characterized by their dramatic, even theatrical quality.[25]

Frequently, there was also a theatrical side to the beginning and the end of strikes, especially when they were conducted on a significant scale. Some of the theatre of industrial action arose from the fact that it could only occur in the face of formidable opposition. Mill managers, supervisors and jobbers in the early twentieth century often treated complaints, let alone the expression of grievances, by workers as a breach of discipline. Workers who went on strike were liable to be dismissed. Industrial action placed jobs in jeopardy. Faced with a strike, the employers' first option was simply to replace those who had refused to work. If the mood of the strikers was too determined and the strike too complete to be broken with a few dismissals, the employers could declare a lock-out and wait for the workers to be hounded to return by starvation, by their landlords or by their moneylenders.

The threat to jobs was greatest when a strike was partial. In the face of workers' solidarity, it was difficult for employers or their jobbers to recruit strike breakers. But it was difficult to estimate how complete a strike would be, soon after it was called. Because industrial action jeopardized their jobs, the strength of the strike was an important element in the decision of workers and jobbers to join it. For this reason, the beginning of strikes was marked by hesitancy and vacillation. Workers would appear at the mill gates on the morning of the strike to check whether the general tendency favoured a stoppage. In many ways, this constituted a vital stage in the conduct of a strike. Workers thus collected might join the stampede to cross thinly manned pickets, or alternatively turn upon those who were trying to go to work. At every stage of a strike, the commitment to industrial action imposed complex calculations upon the workforce. They had to consider not only their immediate chances of success, but

---

[24] This section draws upon my earlier work, *Origins of Industrial Capitalism* and *Imperial Power and Popular Politics*.

[25] Jim Masselos, 'Audiences, Actors and Congresss Dramas: Crowd Events in Bombay City in 1930' in Jim Masselos (ed.) *Struggling and Ruling: The Indian National Congress, 1885–1985* (New Delhi, 1987), pp. 71–86.

also the extent to which their urban as well as rural resources would enable them to bear the costs of industrial action. At the same time, to obtain concessions from the employers, to create the possibility of negotiations, or even to preserve their jobs, it was imperative for the workers that the strike be complete.

Employers attempting to end a strike swiftly often sought to keep production going, essentially by recruiting blacklegs, shepherding them into the workplace and working as many machines as possible. Necessarily, the employers hoped that, faced with this threat to their jobs, the strikers would drift back to work. As soon as some workers returned, the danger of losing their jobs might bring several others back. Once set in motion, this reaction could overcome a sizeable section of the workforce. The employers could then dictate the terms on which the rest of the workers might return. Frequently, of course, under such circumstances, they simply replaced their most militant workers. When workers sensed that their solidarity was ebbing away, or suspected that some groups of workers might be offered favourable terms to return to work and that the strike might be broken, they would assemble at the mill gates. Once more, as they gathered, their aim was to judge the general mood, watch developments closely and decide whether to continue or abandon their struggle. Once more, the excitement and anger that marked the beginning of strikes – the arguments, the debates and, at times, the violence – would necessarily characterize its final stages.

Thus, strikes frequently spilled out of the mills and into the streets and neighbourhoods. It was in the neighbourhood that mills and their jobbers recruited blacklegs and strikers mobilized pickets, moneylenders extended or withdrew their credit and landlords demanded their rents with menace or waived them with apparent magnanimity. Large-scale strikes often encompassed the social organization of the whole neighbourhood. For grain dealers, moneylenders and landlords could not simply call in their dues when a large proportion of their customers were on strike and therefore, in effect, unable to obtain their wages. The neighbourhood connections of the workers, which helped them to survive when they were jobless or sick, could also provide a basis for organizing industrial action. The repression of workers' combinations in the mills often forced them to organize in the chawls, tea shops and akhadas. Workplace and neighbourhood were closely integrated not only by the business strategies of the millowners and by the workings of the labour market but also by the patterns of industrial action. These intimate connections between workplace and neighbourhood ensured that even the daily conflicts and minor disputes in the mills were repeatedly placed before Girangaon and, in the process, acquired an explicitly political meaning. In turn, the political concerns of limited groups of its residents often swiftly became public knowledge in Girangaon as a whole.

The politics of Girangaon was integral to the public performance of the neighbourhoods. It was not unusual for political meetings to be choreographed as entertainment. Indeed, sometimes, public performance and political action came to be even more directly connected. Shahir Sheikh Janu Chand described in detail how he developed his passion for singing after attending a dramatic public meeting at Kamgar Maidan probably in the late 1940s. The meeting occurred at the end of 'a big morcha'. Before the meeting, rumours circulated that Dange, who had 'gone underground' to avoid arrest, would make an appearance. At the meeting Amar Sheikh, Annabhau Sathe and Gavankar sang

without mikes to this huge crowd. The communists were powerful then; they could do whatever they wanted. All this was new to me. It was an illegal meeting, no stage, no mikes. If the police came they would have to flee . . . There were some songs where the whole crowd would sing along.

When Dange was announced, 'fire crackers went off, for almost half-an-hour'. Presumably, Dange had felt no need to make a discreet entrance or, perhaps, the option was taken away from him. Janu Chand recounts how Dange's speech was integral to the magic of the moment. 'Everyone was talking about the speech the next day in Girangaon. I had the songs in my head. I bought the song book for 2 annas.' After that he would plead illness with his employer and go to communist rallies, to hear the shahirs and to sing along with them. Thus entranced, Janu Chand began to attend the meetings every day. Eventually, he persuaded 'my friend Hassan who sold eggs' to introduce him to Amar Sheikh and they in turn became friends. Janu Chand was with Amar Sheikh when they met with the car accident that killed the latter.

The intense militancy that Girangaon witnessed in the 1920s and 1930s, and the forms that it took, were in part the unintended consequence of the millowners' repressive response to workers' discontents. It was also shaped by the extreme reluctance, even outright hostility, of the employers to the formation of trade unions. The Bombay millowners, like most employers in India, assumed that it was inherently difficult to pin workers down to their machines. Max Weber had expressed this conventional wisdom when he claimed that increased earnings led Indian workers to stop working, take holidays or decorate their wives with ornaments.[26] Thus, employers remained liable to calculate rather

[26] Max Weber, *The Religion of India*, translated by H. H. Gerth and D. Martindale (Glencoe, Ill., 1958), p. 114.

harshly what they deemed to be the margin of fairness in the returns to, or conditions of, labour. Similarly, the millowners took it for granted that workers' discipline was difficult to secure and impossible to maintain. They often feared that if they showed signs of weakness, say by submitting too readily to workers' demands, they would encourage a spiral of unreasonable claims from which they would not escape. As a result, they often showed a propensity to 'face down' their workers' demands and to lock out strikers. Sometimes, these lockouts caused the millowners considerable losses but they also calculated that the corresponding gains from better discipline would compensate in the long run. The consequences for the industry and for individual millowners, however, were often highly counter-productive. By treating workers' grievances as simply a problem of discipline, worked up and fomented by troublemakers, the millowners rendered the politics of the industry highly confrontational. Indeed, throughout its history, the industry paid a high price for its inability to institute adequate systems of bargaining and negotiation and its refusal to countenance trade union organization. The Currimbhoy group never fully recovered from the general strike of 1925, which lasted three months, when the state of their finances would have made it imperative that they keep production going. Similarly, the strikes of 1928–29 ensured that the industry lost a considerable share of their market to their Japanese rivals.[27] By adopting a similar approach to the strike of 1982, the millowners hastened the demise of the industry.[28]

While the millowners were determined to face down seemingly truculent workers, they also took it for granted that there was no real need for trade unions to exist. Since the earliest days of the industry, the millowners had relied upon jobbers to reconcile workers to their imperatives. In a sense, by delegating responsibility for the recruitment and disciplining of labour to the jobbers, the millowners also expected them to manage workers' discontents and thus to prevent or, if necessary, break strikes. When these grievances could not be satisfactorily resolved on the shopfloor, the millowners often claimed to be available to lend a sympathetic ear to their workers or to adjudicate upon disputes. In this line of reasoning, trade unions appeared redundant. Indeed, there seemed little need to tolerate the meddling of trade unions in the affairs of their mills. However, workers who lost their jobs by appearing troublesome or truculent recognized

---

[27] *Report of the Indian Tariff Board Regarding the Grant of Protection to the Cotton Textile Industry* (Calcutta, 1932), p. 118.

[28] D. Bhattacharjee, 'Unions, State and Capital in Western India: Structural Determinants of the 1982 Bombay Textile Strike' in R. Southall (ed.) *Labour and Unions in Asia and Africa: Contemporary Issues* (London, 1988), pp. 211–37; H. Van Wersch, *The Bombay Textile Strike, 1982–83* (Delhi, 1992).

another harsher reality. The risks that workers incurred in expressing their grievances too vehemently led them inevitably to seek the help of 'outsiders' – lawyers and social workers, publicists and politicians – to act as their champions and their spokesmen. In the 1910s, an increasing number of politicians and publicists grew increasingly interested in organizing labour. For some, this was part of a widespread strategy among Indian politicians to expand their constituencies in preparation for the political reforms and the wider electorates that they anticipated.

Politicians and publicists who thus developed an interest in labour problems brought with them a range of objectives, styles and ideologies. Some hoped to widen the social base of particular competing nationalist factions, for instance, the Home Rule Leagues or the extremist rump of the Tilakites or the emergent non-Brahmin group. For others, like N. M. Joshi, their interest in the labour question emerged from their dedication to 'social service'. Such publicists often hoped to represent the labour interest in the councils of state, or, indeed, before employers, while also interpreting the policies of officials and the millowners to the workers. They met with varying degrees of success. Most, however, found themselves squeezed between the militancy of the workers and the intractability of the millowners. Indeed, their position often seemed untenable. They were called upon to secure both, and at the same time, the trust of the workers and the confidence of the employers. To retain their credibility with the working classes, it was necessary at times for these publicists to confront the employers in the interests of their followers, but it was also essential for them that the employers accept and accredit them as the bargaining agents on behalf of labour. Yet, from publicists with whom they were willing to treat, most employers required compliance. Moreover, the millowners for the most part remained averse to surrendering to 'outsiders' the freedom to represent the grievances of their own workers. As a result, in their intermediary role, these publicists rarely succeeded in persuading the employers to accede to the workers' demands. But the more limited their influence with the employers appeared, the less compelling were the reasons for workers to accept their leadership. Conversely, the repeated failure of these publicists to secure the workers' acceptance for deals they had negotiated on their behalf rendered them unreliable intermediaries for the millowners. Thus, during strikes, their leadership was often thrown over by the workers. Yet in ordinary times, their inability to secure concessions from the employers limited their value for workers and sometimes propelled, even necessitated, industrial action.

Into this setting, the young communists of the Bombay labour group brought a novel political style. Perhaps, the point is more accurately made in the opposite way. They entered the labour movement on a rising tide of militancy. In 1925, the textile workers had succeeded, after a general strike that lasted three months, in securing the restoration of a substantial wage cut. Three years later, the attempts in individual mills to cut wages, increase workloads and retrench workers provoked a wave of strikes across the industry, which culminated in a general strike by April 1928. It was during the course of this general strike that the communists entrenched themselves as the leading force on the joint mill strike committee and developed a substantial following among the workers and more generally in Girangaon. When the strike had ended, the millowners sought as far as possible to exclude the communists from the workplace and to victimize their followers. They had often adopted this strategy against all but the most pliable trade unions. What made it so difficult to sustain in 1928–29 was the massive support that the communists had evoked. To beat back the tide of communist support in Girangaon, the millowners needed the sustained intervention of the colonial state. From 1929, whether through police actions justified by the imperative of public order, legislation to control picketing or to define the conditions in which a trade dispute could be conducted, or, most dramatically, through the Meerut Conspiracy Case, the colonial state acted increasingly, together with the employers, to narrow the space within which the communist Girni Kamgar Union and the millworkers were able to manoeuvre.

In the late 1920s and 1930s, the millowners tried to exclude the communists from the workplace, dismissed their followers within the labour force and, whenever they could, refused to countenance representations made by them as well as their claims to negotiate on their behalf. Despite the extensive support they gained in Girangaon, the communists were only intermittently able to establish and never really to sustain a permanent organizational presence at the workplace. For the communists, it became clear that the most effective method of developing a base within the industry, in the face of employer hostility and state repression, was to intervene relentlessly in every dispute and to seek to generalize it beyond the individual mill and department. This energetic intervention was wholly compatible with the larger political strategy to which the communists were committed. To various degrees, the communists expected that industrial action, trade union struggle and repeated confrontation with the employers would serve to develop the political consciousness of the working classes. Their theory about their current political position and the best means by which it might be developed in the future led them to the same conclusion as their assessment of the pragmatic and optimal means of overcoming the very severe constraints that employers and the state imposed on workers' organization and action. This conclusion was that they should give workers' militancy its head, to encourage it where it existed, to foster among workers a clearer consciousness of their class interests and to heighten their levels of political action. They expected thereby to establish themselves so powerfully across the industry as well as in the neighbourhood that the millowners and the state would no longer be able to exclude them from conducting disputes in individual mills and departments. At the same time, it would enable them, by repeatedly leading strikes, to generate an enthusiasm for revolutionary action. It was only by repeatedly and tirelessly intervening in individual disputes that they could hope to build up a following across the industry. By establishing themselves across the industry, they could effectively exert pressure on the owners and managers of a particular mill. At the same time, the vulnerability of workers to disciplinary action when they went on strike in small groups, jobber gangs, specific departments or even whole mills had developed the propensity among workers to generalized action. In other words, in the 1920s and 1930s, there was a symbiosis between the militancy of workers and their growing propensity to act on a wider scale, on the one hand, and the political strategy adopted by the Bombay communists.

That the public spaces of Girangaon became a site of acute class conflict in the early twentieth century was in part the outcome of the nature and practice of industrial relations in Bombay. As workers organized and took action on a wider scale, and especially when they did so, after 1928, under the red flag, colonial officials and the police began to perceive their threat to the public order. Sometimes they simply anticipated it. In the 1920s and 1930s, the state intervened increasingly in the conduct as well as the negotiation of industrial disputes. The police now escorted blacklegs across the picket lines, while fresh legislation defined the conditions of picketing so stringently that it became almost indistinguishable from 'intimidation'. Violence on the picket lines, at the mill gates or the chawls, between strikers and blacklegs resulted in increasing police intervention.

As strikes proliferated in the mills, they were lodged in the collective memory of Girangaon. Strikes, their causes and conduct, the ruthlessness or generosity of the millowners' responses to workers' demands and the nature and style of state intervention informed the political consciousness of the working classes. They became an integral part of the social experience of Girangaon. In this sense, too, Girangaon was constituted as a social arena by industrial action and political struggle. As these struggles furnished the collective memory of Girangaon, the cumulative experience of these conflicts in the past provided a yardstick by which the responses of employers and officials, patrons and political leaders, jobbers and dadas, policemen and the state in the present could be judged. From these elements, the political consciousness of the working classes was forged.

Of course, the increasing intervention of the state was neither singularly nor consistently hostile to all forms of trade union organization. Indeed, by the 1930s, as colonial officials found that the Congress and mass nationalism appeared rather less threatening than they had once feared, they began to contemplate the possibility of associating labour more fully with their rule. Nonetheless, the fact remains that the working classes encountered the state most immediately in the form of police actions, often during strikes. Perceptions of the repressive, unjust or arbitrary character of the state fostered for workers at particular moments a sense of their shared interests and informed a political understanding of their situation and how it might be changed.

These possibilities of change were captured and reflected most clearly in the rhetoric and political style of the communists in the late 1920s and 1930s. By contrast with other politicians and publicists who had begun to take an interest in labour questions, the communists appeared to be motivated by nothing more than an interest in the issues that confronted the working classes. They paid close attention to the daily issues of the workplace, rarely set out to act as a brake upon workers' militancy and often showed a willingness to lead them in confrontation, and, above all, appeared consistently to refuse to collaborate with employers and the state. The stance of continued opposition to employers and the state, which the Girni Kamgar Union adopted in this period, was matched by the unremitting hostility that they encountered in return. Frequently, their leaders were themselves subjected to state repression. Indeed, the repression to which they were subjected was a familiar part of the experience of most workers on strike. In this period, the communists emerged as the only political group associated with labour that remained untainted by their association with the state. They were unique in Girangaon for being able to present themselves plausibly as the only element within the labour movement that acted in the interest of the working classes alone. This is not to suggest that the communists found uncritical acclaim and unswervingly loyal devotion in Girangaon. Their insistent claim that they were above all the party of the working class was challenged and interrogated by some of their constituents even in the late 1920s and 1930s. What was perceived as their adventurism after the 1928 general strike and their refusal to associate with the Congress during civil disobedience in 1930–31 cost them considerable support. Their failure to consistently address the dalit question and their inability to encompass the rural as well as the urban context of workers' lives were exposed by the success of

Ambedkar's Mahar movement and the Independent Labour Party in the late 1930s. In the 1940s, their conciliatory posture towards the employers and the state in the shadow of the People's War began to unsettle their pre-eminence within working class politics and contributed to their slow decline after independence.

Nonetheless, even as they were repeatedly subject to scrutiny and challenge, the communist leaders of the Girni Kamgar Union established a massive following in Girangaon after the general strike of 1928 and dominated the politics of the labour movement for the following decade. From the late 1920s onwards, Girangaon appeared to be a communist stronghold, at times even an insurrectionary centre. What the communists had created in Girangaon was an extensive community of political sentiment. Their rhetoric, their actions and their political strategies appeared to the working classes in Girangaon not only to grasp the nature of the problems that they encountered and reflected a plausible understanding of their social and political conditions but also seemed to offer a realizable method by which they might be transformed.

The decline of the communists

The communists of the Girni Kamgar Union had acquired a position of dominance in the labour movement in the 1920s and 1930s largely because they had emerged as the only political group that appeared to the working classes to be untainted by their association with the employers and the state and to be motivated solely, even exclusively, by their concern for the workers' interests. The communists had understood the workers' interests largely in terms of the workplace and in terms of their relations with the millowners. Yet the political solidarities of the working classes had also been forged by their changing experience of the state. Their support for the communists, invariably a matter of constant scrutiny and debate, arose in part from their understanding of where they stood in relation to the state. The solidarities of the working classes in Girangaon had been formed through politics, and shaped by their experience of the state.

It was in this wider context that the limitations of the communist leadership were most fully exposed. The communists entered the labour movement with the belief that the working classes had an inherent propensity for revolutionary action. The considerable political momentum that the labour movement had already acquired in Bombay, and especially in Girangaon, by 1928, even before the communists rose to prominence, seemed to uphold and justify their axiom. In a sense, the Bombay communists, suddenly catapulted into prominence during the general strike of 1928, were undone by their own success. In the late 1920s and 1930s, their leadership had been characterized by a certain pragmatism and flexibility in the conduct of strikes and in the organization of labour. Increasingly, this pragmatism came to be overlaid with a more rigid theory that derived its wisdom from the Comintern. This theoretical rigidity dogged their footsteps as they addressed wider political issues. This was especially apparent as they attempted to define their relationship to the nationalist movement. The Communist Party now set itself the task of both promoting 'bourgeois nationalism' in its struggle against imperialism and asserting its hegemony over it, so as to direct it in the revolutionary interests of the working class. In practice, this posed a major problem. The Communist Party of India was small and its influence localized. If it sought to encourage bourgeois nationalism, it might quickly be submerged by the Congress within the 'anti-imperialist' movement. If they tried to retain their distinctive political identity, what was there to prevent the bourgeois nationalists from simply ejecting them from the Congress? Their problems were complicated and deepened by the fact that the civil disobedience campaign evoked a massive popular response in Bombay city in the early 1930s. Having adopted the language of the Comintern, the communists found themselves taking their own political bearings in relation to the Congress. Over the next four decades, they found that the more they took their political bearings in relation to the Congress, the more fully they passed, kicking and screaming, under its hegemony. It is possible to see in retrospect how far this process had advanced by the 1970s.

In the 1930s and 1940s, their relationship with the Congress and bourgeois nationalism still posed major theoretical and, therefore, tactical problems for the Communist Party. Its decision, following the Sixth Comintern line, to liberate the masses from the thraldom of bourgeois nationalism at the height of the civil disobedience campaign in 1930–31, had considerably weakened their position. Far more damaging, however, as several workers and activists recall in the following pages, was the decision to follow the Comintern into the People's War. In the 1940s, too, Bombay city was one of the most significant centres of nationalist resistance directed against the colonial state. After all, the political experience of the working classes had been constituted in relation to the state. The communists had developed an extensive following in Girangaon over the preceding decade and a half largely through their willingness to pick up the daily disputes of the workplace and the neighbourhood and to pursue redress through industrial and political action. Once the People's War was underway, the communists, and the leadership of the Girni Kamgar Union, adopted a conciliatory attitude towards both the employers and

the state. While they had barely a few years earlier assiduously intervened in workplace disputes and energetically championed the workers'
interests, now they advocated restraint and sought to mediate conflicts.
Similarly, when workers expected them to fight for their interests, severely
threatened by the tensions, scarcities and disruptions of war, the communists seemed to ask their followers to endure immediate hardship
in the name of 'historical necessity' and long-term salvation. 'Wherever
there were strikes, party members would stand at the gates and tell the
workers, don't strike because the war is on. That alienated workers from
the Communists,' just as, in the previous decade, their willingness to
stand at the gates and support the workers in their disputes had helped
to build their following. Gangadhar Chitnis, subsequently the General
Secretary of the GKU, recalls this simple reasoning: 'Russia was a bastion
of the workers' movement . . . So it was necessary to protect this bastion'
(Ch. 2, p. 27). Yet, as Narayan Samant, then a clerk in the Tata Mills,
put it:

The communists said, 'we must defeat fascism and defer the struggle against the
British government' . . . Ordinary people could not understand the concern with
fascism. All they knew was that the communists were supporting the British. Mill
workers felt deeply about independence, so they were not happy with the party's
stand (Ch. 2, pp. 3–4).

By the end of the war, the communists had lost their position of unchallenged dominance in Girangaon. Mill workers had begun to drift towards
the Congress union, the Rashtriya Mill Mazdoor Sabha.

Looking back from the vantage point of independence in 1947, the
communists' achievement had been considerable. They had consolidated
and developed a nascent labour movement in Bombay and established
their presence in Girangaon. Their offices in Dalvi building remained a
landmark in Girangaon until at least the 1970s. Their connections in the
neighbourhoods and the mills had survived waves of severe repression
by the state. By leading a powerful workers' movement in the city, they
had ensured that the working classes had secured a substantial public
presence in the politics of the city. As a consequence, Girangaon had
acquired a certain social and political identity. This identity had been
shaped by politics and in particular by numerous conflicts over wages and
working conditions. It had yielded by the 1940s and 1950s, a flourishing
artistic and literary culture in Girangaon. This vigorous cultural life in
Girangaon, from the Loknatya tradition to rangoli art and Ganeshotsav
sculpture, had effects beyond the neighbourhood. It contributed to, and
stimulated, the very significant artistic and literary movements which
emerged in the city in the same period.

The communists, however, entertained explicit revolutionary objectives. It would be pertinent to ask, therefore, how successfully they were able to transform the political culture of Girangaon, once they had established themselves within it in the 1920s and 1930s. Whether their influence would yield fundamental, even revolutionary, social and political change would depend largely on how far they were able to create and develop a new and transformative political vision. By this measure, the communist achievement was in their heyday in Girangaon rather more limited.

In the aftermath of the 1928 strike, they had appeared to develop a political language which allowed their followers to interpret their discontents within its terms and to identify a realizable means of remedying or even resolving them. By the 1940s and 1950s, it would seem that their political language was no longer sufficiently capacious or flexible to provide an equally wide and diverse constituency in Girangaon either a means of political interpretation or a method of transformation. Whereas in the late 1920s, the communist leadership had remained alert and sensitive to the particularities of local circumstance, now they were more constrained by their wider theoretical alignments. By the 1940s and 1950s, it was to become increasingly difficult to reconcile the complex needs of the locality with the Comintern's interpretation of Marxism. As this task grew more demanding, and their efforts to fulfil it more heroic, the communists surrendered a considerable measure of interpretative flexibility and they came to rely increasingly upon authority for grasping the changing social and political predicament of the working classes.

At the same time, their political methods and practices became increasingly hierarchical. In part, this submission to hierarchical practice arose from their concern to maintain discipline in their ranks. In part, it was an effect of ideological compulsions and the fancy of theory. The more difficult it became to interpret the particular social and political circumstances of the working classes in Girangaon in the increasingly remote and arcane discourse of the Comintern, the deeper grew their dependence upon the authority of theoretical orthodoxy. The authority of theory and the imperative to maintain discipline acted upon each other to deepen hierarchical practices, which in turn were sometimes absorbed unwittingly and enforced by their members, and sometimes resented by them. Vasant Bhor, the son of the redoubtable communist leader Parvatibai Bhor, illuminated the nature of this hierarchy that was almost taken for granted. There were, he observed, 'three different levels' of communists. There were those 'at the top whom you cannot expect to live in a chawl. They do what is possible for them to do.' There was a second level of member 'who earned money and worked free of cost of the party'. He put his mother in a third category, who were 'not very educated, who lived in a chawl in Lalbag and who worked full time for the party'. As Bhor observed,

the middle class women cadres and leaders were different from her. They were not so involved. The ways of the middle class women are completely different and even if they become communists this cannot change (Ch. 1, pp. 43–44).

Yet, it may at least in theory have been their ambition to generate a political culture in which these differences would have been broken down and dissolved.

For similar reasons, Soloman Kudgaonkar left the communists 'because I did not like their attitude' (Ch. 2, pp. 37–38), particularly when they attempted to dictate terms to the mill committee in the China Mill strike in 1954. The leaders increasingly perceived signs of independence from the mill committee as 'arrogance' that had to be contained and disciplined. In the 1920s and 1930s, the communists had entered the social networks of the neighbourhoods and mobilized them in their struggles. They had been able to strengthen the hand of workers as they acted to constrain their patrons, landlords, jobbers, grain merchants and dadas, and to force them to operate within the moral economy of the neighbourhood. The mill committees, that had been thrown up for the first time in the general strike of 1928, now embarrassed the leadership in 1954. Similarly, B. D. Parab described how 'we looked down upon' the neighbourhood toughs in the 1950s and 1960s. 'We only used them' and 'never gave them any place in the organization'. This was, as he pointed out, in marked contrast to the Shiv Sena. For, 'if there is a dashing activist in the organization, and he is known to be goonda, the [Shiv] Sena gave him status and prestige'. The Sena, according to Parab, provided 'those who were in the bottom rung of the organization' a substantial stake within it, while the Communist Party only 'talked in theory of doing this, but never did'. Thus, 'earlier, all the gymnasiums were with us, but we did nothing for them. We were only concentrating on millworkers.' By the 1970s, 'the new generation', not only the younger members of the party but even 'the children of the communists', abandoned the party, so that it was no longer possible to raise enough union dues for the subsistence of their cadres (Ch. 4, pp. 39–40).

The strategy of immersing themselves in the social organization of the neighbourhood had in the late 1920s represented a highly innovative move by the communists in their approach to popular politics. In the 1950s and 1960s, this engagement with the neighbourhoods was gradually crushed by the weight of supra-local party organization, its attention to orthodoxy and its hierarchy, the compulsions of ideological rectitude and a propensity for reciting the slokas of high theory that only a few could possibly know. Behind their growing distance from the neighbourhood lay a wider problem. As L. Y. Shinde, who joined the party in 1940, put it,

The party had a one-line struggle. They paid attention only to the trade union, not to culture. The party should have paid attention to social norms and rituals which are part of people's lives. Now everyone from Moscow onwards is trying to analyse what went wrong.

Where there had once been a hundred party supporters in Tejukaya Mansion, he observed, 'now I am the only one' (Ch. 4, pp. 38–39). Communist orthodoxy stifled the systematic and serious consideration of the various social identities to which the working classes subscribed, whether these formed around kinship or village, language or gender, caste or religion. They refused to address questions of caste and religion, not always the case for instance among their comrades in Malabar,[29] because they feared 'it would divide the class struggle' (Ch. 2, p. 60). As a result, to many dalits, it seemed that 'the traditional left parties never really understood or paid proper attention to the dalit question' (Ch. 4, p. 52). Similarly, Muslim workers seemed intermittently reluctant, especially, for instance, during the general strike of 1929, to follow the lead of the Girni Kamgar Union. In effect, the communists in Bombay focused so closely upon strikes and trade unions that they lost sight of their own wider political objectives and more crucially ceased to subject them to critical scrutiny.

In an extended reflection upon the communists' failure to transform and create a new more progressive political culture, Narayan Surve, among the leading literary figures that the city has produced in the late twentieth century, offered illuminating insights into this process of decline (Ch. 2, pp. 57–61). The Left 'read Marxism', as he put it, but they had 'no idea as to how to link it with the specific cultural and social and historical questions of this country's history'. Indeed, their engagement with this history continued to grow weaker. 'Marx did not write much about India', as Surve points out. 'It was *our* duty to have done that, not anyone else's.' The failure to engage effectively with India's history weakened the communists' grasp of its society and its culture and culminated in theoretical banality and political bankruptcy. 'We kept on talking about the working class', Surve recalls, 'but they only related to us on economic issues, and sometimes on political issues, but we were

[29] D. Menon, *Caste, Nationalism and Communism in South India: Malabar, 1900–1948* (Cambridge, 1994).

not with them at the social and cultural level' (Ch. 2, p. 60). The Left propelled itself towards 'economism' and obscured its political imagination by an adherence to an increasingly arcane theoretical orthodoxy. Indeed, it had been largely as innovative and effective trade unionists that the communists had developed an extensive political following in Girangaon. But it was precisely as trade unionists that they were most readily undermined by their rivals, by employers and by the state.

As the Girni Kamgar Union established its hegemony in Girangaon, the millowners and the state, successively 'colonial' and then 'national', between 1930 and 1960, devised novel strategies for containing the threat of labour. The repressive actions of the state against both strikers and communists, combined with the propensity of employers to dismiss workers who associated with trade unions, severely constrained the development of the labour movement. But repression alone was insufficient to break what had become in Girangaon a bastion of the Left. Between the 1930s and 1960s, the employers and the state adopted two strategies in order to contain the threat of labour. They served to fundamentally alter the structure of labour relations and determined the terms on which trade unions could organize and act.[30] In the process, they eroded the foundations on which the communists had built. First, they developed an increasingly elaborate legal framework for the conciliation and arbitration of trade disputes. The effect of this legislation was largely to blunt the instrument of the strike and to narrow the space with which trade unions could manoeuvre. Of course, this was not a necessary consequence of trade disputes legislation. It could have served to strengthen collective bargaining. But these measures were introduced against a background of hostility against workers' organizations. Lightning strikes, for instance, especially if they were sufficiently widespread, protected workers who took action. Conversely, strikes, localized to a particular department or even a whole mill, undertaken decorously, after due notice, usually enabled the employers to sack the protagonists. Similarly, if trade unions found themselves excluded from individual mills, it was only establishing their presence across the industry as a whole, usually by proving their value to workers during strikes, that they could force individual employers to deal with them. In this political context, it is hardly surprising that workers' organizations rarely acquired a formal and permanent institutional shape, however extensive the following that they commanded at particular times. Trade disputes legislation since 1929 attempted to create an official mechanism for addressing workers' grievances that would

---

[30] I have treated these issues in greater detail in *Origins of Industrial Capitalism*, chs. 8 & 9 and in *Imperial Power and Popular Politics*, ch. 3.

tend to distance trade unions yet further from the daily problems of the workplace and, thus, to gradually render them superfluous. It also defined more stringently the conditions under which strikes would be deemed legal and trade unions would qualify to represent workers and negotiate on their behalf. Not surprisingly, these definitions tended to undermine those unions which were not favoured by the employers and especially those which adopted a more militant and confrontational style. Arbitration procedures did not always provide a mechanism for justice. For they often tended to favour the stronger side in an industrial dispute, in this case, mostly the millowners. After all, no arbitration award could be implemented if it was obstructed by the stronger party to the dispute.

This series of trade disputes legislation culminated in the Bombay Industrial Relations Act of 1946. It was passed before independence by the Congress government elected to power in the Presidency immediately after the war. The provincial Congress government explained that its aim was 'to supply a very real impetus for the growth of sound organizations of industrial and other workers' and 'to ensure that . . . efficient production is not hampered by thoughtless and needless stoppages of work'.[31] By the provisions of the Trade Disputes Act of 1938, passed under the aegis of the previous Congress ministry, only those unions whose membership included a quarter of the industry's workforce qualified as a representative union. Given the nature of industrial relations in Bombay, it is hardly surprising that no union, not even the Girni Kamgar Union at the height of its popularity, could claim this proportion of the workforce as its members. The new legislation in 1946 sought to establish a single union within the industry. It introduced a new category of 'approved' unions. To qualify, trade unions had to renounce the option to strike until all other means of resolution had been exhausted and they could initiate action only when it was sanctioned by a majority vote by secret ballot. In practice, this meant that the union would have to renounce strikes in return for 'approved' status. An 'approved' union was allowed access to the workplace. It could collect dues from workers on wage payment day. It could deploy conciliation procedures on behalf of the workers. Most crucially, it could gain 'representative' status by enrolling a smaller proportion of the workforce – 15 per cent – than the trade unions that were not 'approved'. An approved trade union that gained representative status also acquired the exclusive right to negotiate for the workforce and to represent it in conciliation and arbitration proceedings.[32]

---

[31] *Labour Gazette*, Vol. XXV, no. 9 (1946), pp. 670–71.
[32] See M. D. Morris, *The Emergence of an Industrial Labour Force in India: A Study of the Bombay Cotton Mills, 1854–1947* (Berkeley and Los Angeles, 1965), pp. 185–94.

As the Girni Kamgar Union began to lose its appeal in the shadows of the People's War, the Congress hoped to acquire for the first time a significant base among the millworkers through the Rashtriya Mill Mazdoor Sabha, founded in 1945. In 1949, the RMMS was officially granted representative status on the basis of the membership list it claimed. No ballot was held to establish the preferences of the workers. The fact that the RMMS could collect its dues at the pay desk was a convenience for the union. That it was allowed access to the workplace and to seek redress for the daily problems of the workers proved a major advantage. As Bhai Bhonsle, later the General Secretary of the RMMS, recalled, workers

felt that all they have to do is give twelve rupees a year to these people and we have our problems solved; so what is the loss in doing this? Textile workers always know where their interests lie' (Ch. 2, p. 45).

The representative status of the RMMS was challenged almost immediately. Certainly, the general strike of 1950, called by the Girni Kamgar Union and the socialist Mill Mazdoor Sabha and sustained for over two months, cast grave doubt on the 'representative' character of the RMMS. As unions scrambled to claim 'representative' status, in the wake of the Bombay Industrial Relations Act, fierce competition to enrol members led to considerable turmoil and violence in the mills in the late 1940s. The advent of independence, and, with it, the prospect of universal adult franchise, provided an incentive for political parties to create their own unions as means of gathering workers' votes and mobilizing support during elections. As unions proliferated, the competition for members and for a foothold in the industry and in Girangaon only intensified. In the long run, the BIR Act created a highly sclerotic and increasingly corrupt system of industrial relations, which favoured and entrenched the official union, the RMMS, while obstructing channels for the expression and representation of workers' grievances. For the communists, their strategy of relying increasingly on the workplace, precisely at the moment when they were most effectively excluded from it, served to accelerate their decline.

The second strategy for managing labour was adopted increasingly in this period between permanent and casual labour. Until the 1930s, the millowners had relied upon jobbers to discipline labour and break strikes. The growing propensity of millworkers to coordinate strikes across the industry from 1919 onwards had increasingly shown the weaknesses of the jobber system as a bulwark against industrial action. Legal measures for strangling unions at the workplace were a necessary pre-condition for replacing jobbers. The jobbers' power had derived from their ability to increase or reduce the supply of casual labour. To replace the jobbers, it would also be necessary for the millowners to find a method of ensuring that a large pool of casual labour came into the industry and then were held within it. This was precisely what the badli control scheme of the late 1930s sought to achieve. In return, the millowners recognized they might have to accept labour legislation that expanded the employment rights and benefits of 'permanent' workers, while marking them off more clearly from the badli workers who were excluded from these gains. In the boom of the 1950s and 1960s, the wages and conditions of permanent workers improved considerably.[33] Even more substantial wage increases were granted in the new industries, especially pharmaceuticals where, in addition, skill thresholds were higher.[34] At the same time, employers regulated entry to the permanent workforce with great care. In other words, employers, politicians and officials had begun rather actively to create within the industry what has, as a term of art, been described in a wider context as the 'informal sector'. Here conditions of work remained insecure and wages low. Badli workers depended even more fully on contractors and intermediaries, patrons and caste fellows, and assorted pedlars of influence, power and credit. Before 1930, the line that divided 'permanent' and 'badli' workers was extremely thin. Workers who seemed securely employed one day could lose their job the next, for a wide range of reasons, from participation in a strike, to a downswing in trade or the changed composition of output or the dismissal or, most arbitrarily, even the death of a jobber. Conversely, the barriers to entry onto the permanent muster were relatively low from badli workers. The creation of an abyss between 'permanent' and 'badli' workers had portentous consequences. Obviously, it divided the working class. More fundamentally, for permanent and badli workers, the relationship between their village and urban networks and between workplace and urban neighbourhood diverged significantly. No longer was the experience of irregular employment common to the working classes as a whole. Yet this experience had largely shaped the institutions of Girangaon. It had provided the foundations on which the labour movement of the 1920s and 1930s had developed and which had created the Girni Kamgar Union and its communist leadership. As the political conditions of Girangaon changed, the communists remained tethered to an old style that now appeared increasingly inadequate and vulnerable to the initiatives of their rivals, the millowners and the state.

[33] M. Holmstrom, *Industry and Inequality: Towards a Social Anthropology of Indian Labour* (Cambridge, 1984).
[34] J. Banaji and R. Hensman, *Beyond Multinationalism: Management Policy and Bargaining Relations in International Companies* (New Delhi, 1990).

The rise of the Shiv Sena

The Indian communists in the 1920s and 1930s consisted largely of leaders without followers. They operated as small circles of intellectuals who feverishly debated the labour theory of value, the nature of the revolutionary vanguard or the coming proletarian consciousness. By contrast, the communists in Bombay had developed a significant working class base by the late 1920s. By the late 1940s and 1950s, when the Left elsewhere in India began to attract substantial support, largely by leading peasant struggles in east UP and Bihar, in Kerala, West Bengal and parts of Andhra,[35] the Bombay communists began to lose their position of dominance in Girangaon. Of course, it is only with hindsight that the slow decline of the Left in Girangaon becomes most apparent. Its decline was neither inexorable nor inevitable. Indeed, in the late 1940s, as in the following decades, the Left witnessed significant moments of revival.

The communists hoped that their intervention in the naval ratings' mutiny in 1946, for instance, would help them recover some of the ground that they had lost during the People's War. The RIN Mutiny has often been represented as a potentially revolutionary moment, when the millworkers came out onto the streets in support of the naval ratings. For the communist leadership, it seemed, in retrospect, that the naval mutiny had 'saved us' (Kusum Ranadive Ch. 2, p. 30). At least, by calling for a general strike in support of the naval ratings, they had been able to find some correspondence once more with the old core of their support. On the other hand, the Congress, aspiring to inherit the state from the British, held aloof. It could scarcely be seen to be fomenting mutiny in the armed forces on the eve of independence. In their demonstrations in support of the naval ratings, the millworkers expressed their long-standing antagonism to the state rather than any lasting wish to make common cause with the armed forces. The revival of the Left continued during the general strike of 1950, led largely by the socialist Mill Mazdoor Sabha and, following their initial opposition, the Girni Kamgar Union.[36] The collapse of the strike led to a further drift of support from the Mill Mazdoor Sabha, and especially the RMMS, to the communists.

The performance of the communists in the general elections of 1952 provided further evidence, albeit of a negative kind, that they still

---

[35] D. N. Dhanagare, *Peasant Movements in India, 1920–1950* (Delhi, 1983); A. Satyanarayana, 'Rise and Growth of the Left Movements in Andhra' *Social Scientist*, no. 152 (1986); A. Cooper, *Sharecropping and Sharecroppers' Struggles in Bengal, 1930–1950*; Stree Shakti Sanghatna, *'We Were Making History': Women and the Telengana Uprising* (New Delhi, 1989).

[36] V. B. Karnik, *Strikes in India* (Bombay, 1967), pp. 341–44.

commanded considerable influence in Girangaon. The decision by the socialists and the communists not to forge an electoral pact, let alone join together to combine with Ambedkar's Scheduled Caste Federation, against the Congress lost them the Central Bombay seat. Dange, for the CPI, Asoka Mehta for the socialists and Ambedkar each stood separately and fell together. Significantly, Dange instructed his supporters to spoil their ballots in the reserved constituency for Central Bombay rather than vote for Ambedkar. Indeed, Ambedkar duly lost and attributed his defeat to the communist campaign. Although the communists could not win the Central Bombay seat, their influence in Girangaon, including its dalit voters, was sufficient to decisively influence the outcome. The election campaign created a lasting bitterness. As Dinoo Ranadive recalls, 'the differences between the dalits and the communists became so sharp that even today it has become difficult for the communists to appeal to the Republicans' or at any rate to some sections of dalit voters.

In a sense, the election campaign of 1952, and its outcome, illuminates the predicament of the communists in that decade. Although they had begun to regain some of the ground that they had lost in the People's War, their base had begun to fragment. The advent of universal adult suffrage provided an incentive for every political party to organize more extensively in Girangaon. At the same time, trade union rivalries had sharpened considerably in the late 1940s and early 1950s. It was precisely as their position of dominance in Girangaon, and thus in the city as a whole, grew weaker that the issue of states' reorganization acquired an increasing prominence. The Bombay State after independence comprised diverse regions, joined, like most Indian states, by little more than historical accident, the residue of colonial habits of administration and the arbitrary nature of Partition. It did not reflect either administrative convenience, geographical unity or cultural coherence. As the pressure for the linguistic reorganization of the states gathered force, the political future of Bombay city was thrown open to debate. This debate necessarily provided a stimulus for the city and its residents to define their identity. Yet the city's ethos was eclectic. Neither did it derive from nor did it dominate its immediate hinterland. It streets teemed with people of every faith. Its wadis and gullies echoed with the sound of every language spoken in the subcontinent. Its residents had migrated from all over the subcontinent. To some, this suggested that the city could plausibly be deemed a Union territory and administered from the centre. To others, it seemed that, if Gujarat was to be separated out, it might also have a large claim to the city by virtue of long and close association. About two-fifths of the city spoke Marathi as their mother tongue and perceived its spirit to be quintessentially Maharashtrian. In the controversy that followed, the communists now discerned the shape of a populist cause that might enable them to regain their position of dominance. In retrospect, this judgement seems to have expressed the triumph of hope over diffidence, if not as yet despair.

The issue of states' reorganization highlighted the arbitrary nature of the Indian Union as well as its particular mix of strength and fragility. In the 1940s and 1950s, as Indian elites strove to create a domain for the exercise of their power, powerful regional interests organized to resist the Centre and, in asserting states' rights, to extract a larger share of its resources. Some regional elites threatened secession from the Union, rather as Jinnah had done in the 1940s,[37] as a means of acquiring a stronger grip on its power and resources. Others sought to redraw state boundaries on a linguistic principle in the hope that the new arrangements would suit them better than their political rivals. The widespread appeal of regional nationalism suggested, of course, that the identity of the Indian nation remained unsettled, labile and open to revision and redefinition. Conversely, by competing for the political and economic resources of the centre, regional elites served to strengthen and legitimize it and, indeed, paradoxically revealed their own commitment to it.

In the 1950s and 1960s, linguistic nationalism sometimes evoked considerable popular support.[38] By identifying a state, and, especially, its administration and its educational institutions, with a particular language, its agenda promised to create new and wider opportunities for some in education and government employment. Those whose mother tongue was the language of the proposed state but who lacked the education or the literacy to seize the new opportunities themselves recognized nevertheless that their relatives and friends might, by securing jobs in the bureaucracy, get things done for them or offer them patronage and protection. In the long run, their own children might profit from the opportunities for social mobility. Thus, cultural nationalism sometimes secured the passionate support of some among those who stood to gain little directly from its programme.

It was soon apparent that there was a considerable and widespread antipathy in Bombay to the alienation of the city to a central

---

[37] A. Jalal, *The Sole Spokesman: Jinnah, the Muslim League and the Demand for Pakistan* (Cambridge, 1985); J. Chatterji, *Divided Bengal: Hindu Communalism and Partition, 1932–1947* (Cambridge, 1994).

[38] There is of course a large literature on linguistic nationalism and the nature of centre–state relations in India. See F. Frankel and M. S. A. Rao (eds.), *Dominance and State Power in Modern India*, 2 vols. (Delhi, 1990); and in relation to Maharashtra, J. Lele, *Elite Pluralism and Class Rule: Political Development in Maharashtra* (Toronto, 1981).

administration. There was also by the mid-1950s a significant groundswell among Marathi speakers, including the working classes, in favour of the city's incorporation into a Maharashtrian state. In Bombay, the question of states' reorganization deepened the suspicion for some that the provincial Congress, dominated by Gujaratis, might swing the city into their state or that Gujarati capital would acquire a closer grip on the city. As G. L. Reddy, a communist activist, recalled, workers identified the industrialists and the millowners with Gujaratis. Bombay's workers 'of all castes and religions – even the Muslims in Madanpura' supported the Samyukta Maharashtra movement because they 'wanted that administration and government should be in Marathi and workers should have power in the new state. They were for a socialist state.' This was why 'the people of Girangaon came out of every house, every chawl to fight for Bombay' (Ch. 3, p. 13). Similarly, Sahdev Jagre, a former jobber from the Swan Mills, described their fears that if the city was centrally administered, 'it would not remain a working class Bombay. This was more important to us than Marathi and non-Marathi.' Thus, workers from UP 'also supported the movement' (Ch. 3, p. 14). According to Ahilyabai Rangnekar, 'the women of the poorest classes . . . knew that if they went to an office, they should be able to speak in their mother tongue' (Ch. 3, p. 16).

For the communists, and for other intellectuals on the left, it was possible to perceive the aspirations of the Samyukta Maharashtra movement as largely progressive. It seemed to attract considerable support from the predominantly Marathi-speaking working classes and it appeared to transcend caste, religious and regional identities. The benefits of making government more accessible, perhaps, even, more accountable to all its citizens could scarcely be decried. Yet perhaps the most compelling and recurring theme of the movement was the definition of a Maharashtrian identity. No less than caste, religion and nation, language offered an ethnic identity that could be counterposed to class. It is paradoxical, therefore, that the communists, who had been quite so averse to engaging with the question of caste and religion, because of its potential for dividing the working classes, should have so fully advanced the cause of the Samyukta Maharashtra. Shanti Patel, the socialist politician and trade unionist, offered at least a partial explanation when he pointed out the communists 'wanted to utilize the mass upsurge on this issue' and by doing so 'they got political mileage', at least for a while (Ch. 3, p. 26).

However the nature of the mass upsurge may have been grasped in Girangaon, the fact remained that the Samyukta Maharashtra movement had its widest appeal around the symbols of regional nationalism. In some measure, the communists were pulled into the movement by the tides of popular opinion. By contrast to their stand against popular opinion in the early 1930s and in the 1940s, their submission to it in the mid-1950s suggests a growing diffidence about their own standing within their old stronghold of Girangaon. In addition, the Communist Party of India was now committed to a strategy of working democratic institutions and of allying with the progressive elements of the 'national bourgeoisie' to push it leftwards. Under the circumstances, they prized highly the electoral dividends that participation in the movement might yield. Undoubtedly, their espousal of the Samyukta Maharashtra movement brought them some immediate gains. It may even have enabled the communists to halt their apparent decline and to protect their position in Girangaon and among the working classes. But this venture into regional nationalism, associated inevitably and closely with the prior claims of 'a people' defined by language, posed complex problems for the development of a political agenda built around class and seeking to transcend ethnic, regional and religious differences. As Shanti Patel put it, in explaining his own opposition to the movement,

Actually, I don't agree that language is the basic history of the masses. This thinking is against progressive concepts and philosophy. The agitation served no purpose. The exploitation and difficulties of the masses have remained the same (Ch. 3, p. 26).

In fact, in important ways, their 'exploitation and difficulties' may have got worse. The discourse of linguistic nationalism necessarily also carried chauvinistic and racist themes. The principal beneficiaries of this discourse in the long run were not the communists, but the Shiv Sena. In the late 1960s, the Communist Party of India (Marxist) was to achieve massive success in West Bengal as the champions of regional nationalism. For in the specific political circumstances of West Bengal in the 1960s, they emerged as the only plausible bearers of this mantle. In Bombay, the communists had entered the Samyukta Maharashtra movement largely on the terms that were set out for them and they had failed to swing it to their own advantage in the longer term. In the 1957 election campaign, the Samyukta Maharashtra Samiti fought on the basis of 'a common minimum programme' for a 'socialist Maharashtra'. By signing up for it, the Right, especially the Jana Sangh and the Hindu Mahasabha, may have shown they they had interpreted the trajectory of the politics of cultural nationalism with greater accuracy than the communist leadership. The Marathi manus, with all his rage, was nurtured in the womb of the Samyukta Maharashtra movement. He emerged fully formed with a belief in his own victimhood and in the injustice meted out to his folk.

The Shiv Sena, founded in 1966, was the legacy of the Samyukta Maharashtra movement, whose aims had seemed to some of its protagonists at the time to be progressive.[39] The Sena drew upon the programme of Samyukta and developed it to its furthest extreme. First, it built upon the Samyukta Maharashtra movement's emphasis on the exploitation of the 'sons of the soil' and its quest to secure their rights. Its agenda to ensure justice for the Marathi manus sometimes proclaimed the imperative for direct action. Of course, there were substantial, sometimes fundamental, differences between many of the political parties that coalesced around the Samyukta movement and the Shiv Sena. Indeed, from the outset, the Sena treated the communists, together with Muslims and South Indians, as their principal antagonists. However, the fact that the major political parties, including some factions of the Congress and the communists, had embraced, and sometimes subscribed to, the nativist rhetoric of Samyukta Maharashtra made it impossible for them to adequately confront, let alone plausibly counter, their fundamental differences with the Shiv Sena. In the mid-1960s, the communists still constituted a formidable force in Girangaon. At first, as long as the Sena appeared to be marginal – and, outside Bombay and Thana, so it remained for a while – the Congress hoped to deploy it against the communists and divide their followers. Increasingly, employers too began to see its value as a strike-breaking force. The encouragement provided by some employers and the ruling party provided an impetus for the Sena's early growth.

In addition, the Samyukta Maharashtra movement had orchestrated the revival of the symbols and iconography of regional nationalism, which had not been deployed on this scale since Tilak first brought them into play in the early twentieth century. The Shiv Sena played upon and developed this imagery. It recalled, and made central to its own iconography, the glories of Shivaji's heyday and his resistance against the Mughal Empire. It also offered itself as the repository and arbiter of a pristine Maharashtrian culture and the purity of its values. Thirdly, Samyukta Maharashtra, by securing the creation of the state and the inclusion of Bombay city within it, had enabled Maharashtrian politicians to acquire a tighter grip on power and an easier access to the massive resources of India's leading industrial and commercial centre. Necessarily, the politicians and political networks that dominated the new state used its patronage to favour their friends and constituents. Yet since the resources of

---

[39] In a large and swiftly growing literature on Shiv Sena, see the fascinating study by Thomas Blom Hansen, *The Wages of Violence: Naming and Identity in Postcolonial Bombay* (Princeton, 2001).

even the Maharashtra Government were insufficient to provide lasting pleasure for all, the serried ranks of its disappointed clients grew rapidly. On the one hand, the city's Marathi-speaking middle classes discovered a certain confidence from the triumphs of Samyukta Maharashtra as well as from tasting the fruits of state patronage. On the other hand, they could not overcome the feeling that they had as yet gained little from their struggle to create a 'Maharashtra for Maharashtrians'. The Sena's nativism tapped into precisely these rapidly accumulating resentments. In the early 1960s, Bal Thackeray's journal, *Marmik*, both fed and expressed the general anxieties of middle class Maharashtrians in the city, whose fears for being so unspecific became all the more haunting.

The Shiv Sena's rhetoric, with its assertion of power, its spectacular display of violence and racism on the one hand, and its sense of victimhood and injustice and its invocation of the fear of domination by 'outsiders' and by bureaucrats, corporate interests and politicians beyond their control, found its resonance not primarily in Girangaon, but especially among the upwardly mobile Maharashtrian middle classes in general. Their ranks included the growing army of clerks in the 1950s and 1960s, the children of skilled industrial workers and those who were the first generation in their families to finish secondary school or acquire university degrees. Some had gained substantially from the expansion of employment and rising wages in the 1950s and early 1960s and found themselves forced to confront the limits of their opportunities for social mobility. Others found themselves buoyed up by this period of expansion and then left stranded by the slump of 1965–66, which hit many millworkers especially hard. Yet others found themselves competing for clerical jobs in a shrinking market. In the Bombay municipal elections of 1968 and 1973, the Shiv Sena candidates performed best in constituencies like Girgaum and Dadar that were dominated by the Maharashtrian middle classes.[40] In Girangaon, and in working class constituencies, they won fewer seats by smaller margins. In 1968, the Sena received nearly a third of the votes cast in the municipal elections. Clearly, it had also attracted substantial working class support. The communist stalwarts among the millworkers often lamented the fact that their children had joined the ranks of the Shiv Sena. Nonetheless, the working classes did not support the Sena necessarily for the same reasons as the voters of Girgaum and Dadar. As the surveys conducted by Dipankar Gupta and Mary Katzenstein in the early 1970s showed, working class Sainiks

---

[40] Mary F. Katzenstein, *Ethnicity and Equality: The Shiv Sena Party and Preferential Policies in Bombay* (Ithaca and London, 1979), especially chapters 4 & 5.

showed little antipathy towards the communists.[41] The Sena's ferocious anti-communist rhetoric played far better with their more prosperous, middle class members. Similarly, Katzenstein's survey suggested that the working classes in 1971 on the whole showed 'positive attitudes' towards Muslims and non-Maharashtrians and adopted 'a more tempered and moderate outlook' than the Sena.[42] Significantly, while working class voters who held extremist views were more likely to join or vote for the Sena, Congress voters among the working classes on many issues, notably on the use of violence, or the need for authoritarian rule, subscribed to beliefs rather similar to the Sainiks, and sometimes in larger numbers.

Bal Thackeray, and indeed the Shiv Sena, as a whole, had from the outset claimed to eschew politics. Rajkaran, as Thackeray proclaimed, was gajkaran. The Sena was not to be thus sullied by political participation. Yet from the outset, the Sena intervened in the political process, made and switched political alliances with some facility and competed in municipal and state elections and attempted to influence the outcome of elections to the Lok Sabha. Its early experience of elections indicated that to secure a closer grip on power, the Sena would have to expand its working class following and to extend its appeal beyond the enraged Marathi manus. To reach out beyond the disaffected Maharashtrian lower middle classes, the Sena concluded that it would have to develop its Hindu nationalist agenda and began to focus its antagonism more sharply against Muslims. More immediately, in order to develop its working class constituency, the Sena had to establish itself in Girangaon. In turn, the attempt to do this brought them directly into conflict with the communists.

In the late 1920s, the communists had discovered just how closely inter-related were the social organization of the workplace and the neighbourhood. They had quickly grasped the significance of organizing in the neighbourhood to sustain strikes and, indeed, to strengthen their position in the politics of the industry. As a result, they had begun to immerse themselves in the social and cultural institutions of the neighbourhood. Ironically, the Shiv Sena extended their influence by the same means, but often proceeded in ways that had scarcely been traditional in Girangaon and, as they did so, the political economy of the neighbourhood itself was being transformed.

Since discrimination against Marathi-speakers in the job market, whether for clerical or blue-collar employment, was a recurrent motif in the Sena's nativist rhetoric, it is scarcely surprising that it offered itself

---

[41] Katzenstein, *Ethnicity and Equality*, pp. 90–93; Dipankar Gupta, *Nativism in a Metropolis: the Shiv Sena in Bombay* (New Delhi, 1982), pp. 144–45.

[42] Katzenstein, *Ethnicity and Equality*, p. 90.

in Girangaon, as elsewhere in the city, as the champion of 'the unemployed youth'. The Sena blamed the condition of the young unemployed Maharashtrians on the presence of 'outsiders' and migrants, especially from Uttar Pradesh and South India. 'We could see it all before our eyes,' as Bal Nar, then a Sainik himself, recalled,

> the street vendors, the traders were all outsiders, Madrasi, Gujarati, Telegu. They would not treat us with respect, they would do *dadagiri* and they were organized . . . As the Shiv Sena grew, some of them who got beaten started behaving with respect.

Violence, and the threat of violence, was, from the outset, crucial to the Sena's strategy. It was also deployed to coerce employers to hire Marathi speakers. *Marmik*, Bal Thackeray's newspaper, published lists of appointments made, usually to government, public sector and corporate posts, to show how Maharashtrians were being denied jobs. When Sena demonstrators assaulted the General Manager of Air India, it shocked the city, but 'convinced the youth that the Sena stood for Maharashtrians' (Bal Nar, Ch. 4, p. 6). An important object of antagonism were the restaurants run by 'the Shetty community' from Udipi in Karnataka. They garnered a large share of the business in cheap eating-houses but brought along their own employees, so that Maharashtrian boys could not even get 'the job of waiters in these hotels' (Dinoo Ranadive, Ch. 4, p. 5). Thus, Vijay Gaonkar, a local dada who later represented the Sena in the Municipal Corporation, explained that 'we burnt the Visawa Hotel' in 1969, 'because it had been taken over by the Shettys by force from a Maharashtrian. The Shettys always got workers from their villages, and they would not employ local people' (Vijay Gaonkar, Ch. 4, p. 13). Alongside these spectacular demonstrations of violence, the Sena cultivated a reputation for helping 'to find jobs for unemployed Marathi youth' (Bal Khaonekar, Ch. 4, p. 7). Similarly, when the signboards on shops 'were not written in Marathi, we smeared them with tar' (Bal Nar, Ch. 4, p. 7).

At the same time, Sena activists attempted to draw Maharashtrian youth into their ranks by entrenching themselves within the neighbourhood. They opened a number of 'shakhas' or local branches in Girangaon as indeed they had elsewhere in the city. Characteristically, the Sena opened one of its first shakhas in the old communist stronghold of Lalbag. It would be easy to exaggerate the degree of organization in these shakhas, and in the structure of their relationship to each other or to the Sena as a whole. They often depended upon a few dominant figures and dadas and a loose network of followers and friends who collected around them. The shakhas most commonly operated as a meeting place on the street corner. They served as a centre for collecting dues for

Shivaji Jayanti or for Ganeshotsav mandals. Sometimes, such collections resembled extortion and the youth who gathered around the shakhas ran what were more or less protection rackets. The money for the local shakha was collected 'naturally', as Bal Nar explained, 'from the liquor and matka operators' (Ch. 4, p. 33). Sometimes, subscriptions were taken from 'local baniyas' and shopkeepers. This money was used to fund the Sena's local activities, including various festivals and public events, and sometimes to pay off the police and other officials or to stand bail for sainiks who had fallen foul of the law. Thus, money collected from the liquor distillers and matka operators by the Parel shakha paid for

everything – all expenditure of those accused in the Krishna Desai [murder] case, including their clothes and even their slippers and underwear. . . including money for their families (Ch. 4, p. 24, Prakash Bhogle).

Some shakhas acted as 'trouble shooting' and 'problem solving' centres. 'Local people', Bal Khaonekar, General Secretary of the Girni Kamgar Sena declared, 'would also bring their grievances to the shakhas' (Ch. 4, p. 8). Bal Nar recalled the activities of his shakha near the Modern Mills:

We would solve domestic problems, say arising out from alcohol. We would advise the families to try and resolve the situation amicably. If not, then we would slap the chap around a bit and the problem would get solved. There would be cases of harassment on the road or at work; we would investigate under the guidance of the shakha pramukh and then we would act.

Often, they acted with the same brisk violence. In 1972, when the Sena agitated against rising prices, shortages and hoarding, 'we hijacked the lorries taking grain for the hotels and sold it at the shakha at two rupees a kilo to the people'. But since they could not distribute all the grain in this way, they 'handed the lorry over to the police' (Ch. 4, p. 33). Thackeray liked to claim that the Sena was not a political organization. It did not dabble in politics. Rather, the Sena and its shakhas often revealed a preference for direct action.

At the same time, the shakhas also undertook what their activists called 'social work'. According to Bal Khaonekar, they opened 'health camps, vocation guidance and eye camps' (Ch. 4, p. 8). The Sena 'did a lot of community work. . . We have ambulances. When there is an accident, Sainiks are the first to donate blood' (Vijay Gaonkar, Ch. 4, p. 14). By intervening in festivals like Ganeshotsav and Shiv Jayanti, the Sena tried to appropriate them and 'gave them a social content and made them grand and colourful' (Bal Khaonekar, Ch. 4, p. 8). The Sena tried to place 'their cadres in Ganeshotsav Mandals', which also helped the organization (Ch. 4, p. 7). Local youth, attracted by the prospect that the Sena would rescue the Marathi manus, invited them to their akhadas and their kho-kho clubs (R. S. Bhalekar, Ch. 4, p. 7). From the outset, as Bal Khaonekar described it,

Balasaheb [Thackeray] was confident that the movement would grow through activities in the cultural field. That is why we concentrated on capturing the vyamashalas and with their help, he held meetings in the *chawls*, in small halls and the maidans of Girangaon where he propagated his views (Ch. 4, p. 8).

By the late 1960s, the communists could not claim to lead 'a single Ganeshotsav mandal' (Datta Iswalkar, Ch. 4, p. 15). As the Sena gained prominence and popularity within Girangaon, they appeared to have captured precisely those social and cultural organizations of the neighbourhood that had allied themselves so closely with the communists in the 1930s and 1940s. The relative ease with which the communists were substituted in the social organization of the neighbourhood suggests how shallow their cultural penetration had been during their period of political dominance.

The Shiv Sena's capacity to fulfil the expectations that it generated, to find jobs for its boys, to resolve disputes in the neighbourhood and to do favours for its clients depended upon acquiring political power. Although Thackeray often claimed to eschew politics, the Shiv Sena participated in municipal and state elections. Within a year of its founding, it had emerged as the single largest party in the Thana municipal council. In the following year, the Sena won 42 seats in the Bombay Municipal Corporation and constituted the largest opposition party. Over the next few years, it intervened often decisively in state and parliamentary elections. In the process, the Shiv Sena showed an enthusiasm for making political alliances across the ideological spectrum and breaking them as expediency and opportunism dictated. The Sena in this respect matched every other political party whose opportunism it derided. Between 1967 and 1974, the Sena made various alliances and associated for electoral purposes with both 'the Requisitionist' and 'the Opposition' Congress, the Praja Socialist Party, the Republican Party of India, and the Swatantra Party and rarely held back from joining forces with parties that it had in the recent past attacked mercilessly.[43] Of course, the Sena's objectives had always extended well beyond Girangaon. However, its growing proximity to political power, especially in the Bombay Municipal Corporation, which commanded resources equivalent to a middle-ranking state,

---

[43] Gupta, *Nativism*, pp. 159–66.

gave the Sena greater access to patronage and served to consolidate its position within Girangaon.

In the late 1960s, and early 1970s, Girangaon became the scene of an intensive struggle for supremacy between the Shiv Sena and the communists. This conflict was not merely a battle for political ideas or a social vision. It was also fought for supremacy in the public spaces of Girangaon and it brought to the surface the rivalries between dadas and the toughs of the neighbourhoods and their followers. It was as much the case in the late 1960s, as it was in the 1930s, that 'all the parties use dadas to some extent'. As the Sainik, Prakash Bhogle, explained,

what is called terrorism on the part of the Sena is not that at all. These things have to be done, or how to deal with the aggression of the other side? (Ch. 4, p. 19)

Indeed, 'the lal bawta did as much tod-phod when they were the main opposition union in the mills' (Ch. 4, p. 32). The dominant figure among the communists in Girangaon was the charismatic Krishna Desai. According to Sahdev Tawde of the Rashtriya Seva Dal, Desai, 'had a tough reputation . . . At first, he was a dada . . . Not like Arun Gawli or Ashwin Naik and those mafia people. He was not an extortionist nor was he a contract killer. But he was tough and violent' (Ch. 4, p. 11). He was also 'known to be militant and fearless' (Sitaram Jagtap, Ch. 4, p. 29; R. S. Bhalekar, Ch. 4, p. 28). It was said that, if he took a patient to hospital, Krishna Desai would warn the staff from the Dean to the ward boy that 'if my patient dies, you are responsible so you'd better get cracking'. His objective was to ensure that they took 'proper care'. As a result, 'the moment people knew Desai had come, everyone would be galvanized' (R. S. Bhalekar, Ch. 4, p. 28). Krishna Desai could place his followers in jobs and get his friends released by the police.

In the political economy of the street, personal allegiances were important but political boundaries were often opaque. Certainly, the dadas of Girangaon were sometimes closely connected, irrespective of their political differences. Thus, R. S. Bhalekar, a Shiv Sena dada, revealed that Krishna Desai was supposed to take him to the Coca Cola Company to get him a job. But he was murdered the day before their appointment. Bhalekar remained forever devoted. 'I always voted for him', he said,

even after he died. I say that I am a Shiv Sainik, but I have always voted in his name for the Lal Bawta. I don't care if my vote is wasted. When the Sena is elected, I dance on the street but I don't give it my vote (Ch. 4, p. 29; R. S. Bhalekar).

Similarly, the testimony of Govind Phansekar, a Congress dada from Prabhadevi, suggests the intimacy that marked the connections and the rivalries between these neighbourhood bosses. Phansekar regarded Krishna Desai 'like a family member'. He had in the past helped Desai secure his election to the Municipal Corporation. But Phansekar's political commitments to the Congress prevented him from supporting Desai in the elections to the state legislature in 1967. During the campaign, 'they [the communists] had sent a hundred people after me – but I too had a hundred people after Krishna'. Phansekar's mother 'got angry with Krishna' and reminded him that 'I have looked after you with as much love and affection' as her own son. Despite her exhortations, they fought after the election. 'I was known to be militant,' he recalled,

Krishna was too. I had an influence in my territory. No one messed with us. But we were both on the side of justice.

But when Phansekar thrashed the communists after the elections, he said, they had no one to blame but themselves: 'they had given me such a bad time [during the campaign] – and they were supposed to be friends of mine' (Ch. 4, pp. 26–27).

At least in part, these political rivalries turned on the reputation, skill and prowess of particular bosses. The outcome of these rivalries was likely to be explained in terms of their personal role. When Krishna Desai was murdered in 1970, several prominent Sainik toughs were charged. The murder of Krishna Desai has been regarded on the Left but also by other political groups as a major turning point for the communists. In retrospect, at least, Sainiks as well as communists agreed that 'the Sena would have found it difficult to grow had Krishna Desai been alive' (Ch. 4, p. 24, Prakash Bhogle). His comrades in the party, according to Phansekar, were 'good people but no guts' (Ch. 4, p. 26). Already in the late 1960s, as B. D. Parab recalls, 'the terror was so great that we [communists] could not move about freely' (Ch. 4, p. 39). Even the communist leaders were reduced to 'hiding their faces behind a newspaper' when they walked the streets (Ch. 4, p. 39). Successively, the general election of 1967 in which the Sena ensured the defeat of Krishna Menon in north Bombay by their support for the Congress candidate, S. G. Barve, the attack on the communist offices in Dalvi building and the murder of Krishna Desai (followed by the defeat of his wife by a Sainik in the subsequent by-election) suggested that the battle for territorial dominance in Girangaon had turned decisively in favour of the Shiv Sena. Left-wing activists as well as Sainiks attributed the Sena's successes in Girangaon to the role of individual dadas. Prakash Bhogle, a Sainik, who believed that Krishna Desai was the Left's last bulwark, similarly declared that 'the Sena is as it is now in Lalbag-Parel because of the work that Wairkar master did' (Ch. 4, p. 58). Wairkar, a prominent Shiv Sena dada, was one of the accused in the Krishna Desai murder case. Similarly, Neena Sarmalkar, a CPI activist, attributed the success of Shiv Sena in Girangaon to Bandu Shingre 'their goonda in Parel' and Wairkar Master, who were both 'part of the first batch of gangsters' (Ch. 4, p. 36).

Of course, the Sena's expansion in Girangaon did not pass unchallenged. Roza Deshpande's victory as the CPI candidate for Parel in the state assembly election in 1974 suggests that the Left still commanded substantial support in Girangaon. Similarly, in the same year, mill workers across the whole industry and indeed the whole political spectrum came together to effect a general strike under the leadership of the Girni Kamgar Union. The strike lasted for nearly six weeks. There was considerable dissatisfaction in Girangaon when Dange called off the strike with very modest wage increases. Some suspected his decision was driven by the communists' increasing proximity to Congress. Others believed that it was a tactical masterstroke, worthy of his leadership of the strikes of the 1930s and 1940s. His aim, according to Iswalkar, was to maintain 'the morale [of the working class] to be able to fight another day' (Ch. 5, p. 9). Bhai Bhonsle, at the time General Secretary of the RMMS, likened Dange to the tiger who 'looks and calculates before attacking' (Ch. 5, p. 21). However, by the end of the decade, it was becoming increasingly the case that 'the Lal Bawta exists only in name' (Bhalekar, Ch. 4, p. 29).

Similarly, from the mid-1970s onwards, the Shiv Sena's fortunes appeared to have waned. When Thackeray supported the Emergency, suspicion of and hostility towards the Sena began to grow in Girangaon. More widely, in Maharashtra, the Sena's vote began to shrink. Thackeray's justification of Indira Gandhi's benevolent authoritarianism as the system of government best suited to Indian conditions did not convince his followers or fill the electorate with enthusiasm. Some even discerned that 'the Sena was almost finished at that time'. Thackeray calculated that its revival lay in 'playing his Hindutva card' (Iswalkar, Ch. 5, p. 17). The Shiv Sena began to shift its emphasis from fighting for the rights of local people to advocating the claims of Hindutva. The Sena propounded its new programme with the same stridency and violence that marked the old. The Bhiwandi riots of 1984, which extended to Thane and parts of central Bombay, appeared to entail the systematic participation of the Shiv Sena. In the organization and forms of violence, and the role of the police and the state government, the Bhiwandi riots seemed to prefigure the pogrom against the Muslims in Bombay in 1992–93.[44] This shift towards Hindutva was in part forced upon the Sena and it suggested the fragility of its own place within the political economy of the neighbourhoods. The volatility of its methods and organization enabled it to stage dramatic displays of power and influence but it did not always enable the Sena to embed itself within the institutions and social practices of the neighbourhood. Nonetheless, its adoption of an increasingly aggressive and violent anti-Muslim politics coincided with its growing association with the new style of dadas, increasingly observed in political life, who operated within wide networks of power and enterprise, usually on the margins of legality. In the 1980s, the Shiv Sena was reputed to be the party represented by the most candidates with a criminal record.[45] Once the Sena secured a majority for the first time in the Bombay Municipal Corporation in 1985, it gained access to vast resources and extensive webs of patronage. In the late 1980s, the Shiv Sena established a presence in the wider political arena.[46] It began to win a larger number of seats in the state assembly and founded branches outside Maharashtra. Barely two years after the pogrom of 1992–93, the Shiv Sena was elected to power in Maharashtra in a coalition with the BJP.

The party that had dismissed rajkaran as gajkaran now embraced politics and state power with enthusiasm. Having built its base on the rage of the Marathi manus, it now proclaimed the virtues of Hindutva yet more vociferously from the 1980s. The primary focus of their antagonism, 'Madrasis' and 'bhaiyas', were to be accommodated within their fold so long as they were Hindus. Muslims, whether they spoke Marathi or not, became the primary focus of their antagonism. The Marathi manus was in danger of being swamped by the Hindu nation. As a local and neighbourhood movement devoted confessedly to 'social work', the Shiv Sena attempted to develop a more elaborate political machine that could effectively contest elections, run governments and at the same time nurture their patronage connections in neighbourhoods and the localities. These tensions and contradictions which arose from the expansion of the political arenas in which the Sena operated clearly generated discontent and turmoil among the oldest and most loyal cadres. As Prakash Bhogle comments:

Now the Sainiks beat up and kill for money. Every Sena leader, even an ordinary corporator needs a bodyguard now, otherwise he cannot move around . . . That is what social service has come to (Ch. 4, p. 59).

---

[44] Hansen, *The Wages of Violence*; see also *Report of the Srikrishna Commission*, 2 vols. (Bombay, 1998).
[45] Hansen, *Wages of Violence*, pp. 98–99.
[46] U. Thakkar and M. Kulkarni (eds.), *Politics in Maharashtra* (Bombay, 1995).

Necessarily, as the Sena projected its presence into wider political arenas, its methods of patronage as well as of coercion became more complex and more attenuated from the moral economy of the neighbourhood. This discontent among its old cadres may suggest that, as its own strategic emphasis reached beyond the locality, its own links with the neighbourhoods of Girangaon, its informal institutions and its power structures, had begun to atrophy. In this respect, in relation to the neighbourhoods, it may have run into the difficulties that the communists began to encounter in the 1950s and 1960s. As the nature of their neighbourhood connections was transformed, the Shiv Sena established a greater public prominence, exercised greater leverage on the state and gained greater access to the power and resources with which they could shore up their position in the city.

The changing political economy of Girangaon since the late 1960s

By the 1960s, however, the social organization of Girangaon had begun to change. These changes certainly unsettled the foundation on which the communists had built since the 1930s and they may have served to undermine the solidarities they had helped to forge. First, the social character of Girangaon had begun to change as the city expanded. Certainly, a city that had grown slowly as Girangaon formed in the preceding fifty years now expanded rapidly as it absorbed a substantial inflow of migrants, as a consequence of the social dislocations of partition and later of rural immiserisation. Between 1941 and 1971, the city's population grew fivefold and then doubled again in the next two decades. The scarcity of housing, rising rents and improved transport meant that a growing proportion of millworkers lived beyond Girangaon. Of course, Girangaon was still very much a mill district. Nonetheless, it was no longer the case as it had been in the 1920s that nearly all who worked lived within walking distance of the mill. Moreover, the new migrants who streamed into Bombay often came in distress. Yet the social economy of Girangaon had been formed by a particular set of relationships between town and country. Workers who came to Bombay to earn cash and hold on to their village base developed institutions in Girangaon, like the khanavalis and the goankari mandals, that were geared to the maintenance of their rural connections. Those who arrived in the city because they could no longer maintain their village base perceived their position in the city and in the countryside in rather different terms. Workers without a village base had always been more easily recruited as strike-breakers. They depended more heavily upon their patrons and their kin, caste and village connections to secure jobs, credit and housing as well as help in times of crisis. In this way, the changing economy of Girangaon had begun to threaten social connections and networks that transcended caste, kinship and village. As a result, it was probably becoming easier to mobilize along lines of caste and language, religion and nation. At the same time, the effect of increased state regulation of working conditions, together with the response of the employers to the new laws and practices, had exacerbated differences between permanent and badli labour. Casual workers relied more extensively upon caste, kinship and patronage networks for organizing their lives in the city. They also found it more difficult to maintain their rural connections without sacrificing their position within the urban labour market. There was, as a consequence, a greater diversity of social experience within Girangaon, not only in terms of their conditions of work, but also in the way in which workers related to the institutions of the neighbourhood, from the employers, landlords and creditors to the dadas, 'social workers' and politicians.

Second, it would seem as if many of the cultural institutions and social practices that workers created as Girangaon formed were now in decline. These institutions, and the social relationships that they forged, had underpinned the particular style of industrial and political action that had emerged in the 1920s and had created the communist leadership of the Girni Kamgar Union. Jobbers had primarily acted as agents of labour recruitment and discipline. But their role had been crucial in linking the social organization of the workplace and the neighbourhood. In the 1920s and 1930s, the millowners valued and deployed them as strike-breakers. Nonetheless, jobbers could not perform their essential functions of recruiting and disciplining workers if they stood aloof from the workforce and several were drawn into the labour movement by the momentum of industrial action. This bridge between workplace and neighbourhood, between permanent and casual labour, gradually cracked under the weight of workers' militancy. By the 1950s, their role had largely been reorganized and their powers severely curtailed.

Similarly, the khanavalis, where single male migrants took their meals, had once flourished in Girangaon and had provided a vital focus of sociability. At their height, there were, according to one count, about 650 khanavalis in Girangaon. From the mid-1970s, they began to fold up (Indubai Patel, Ch. 1, p. 8). Ganeshotsav, which had once simply been 'a joyful and collective celebration', began to acquire religious and Hindu nationalist overtones in the 1970s and 1980s. This religious dimension was, according to Vijay Khatu, reputed to be the best sculptor of Ganesh idols in Bombay, 'created by political vested interests' (Ch. 1, p. 27). Gunwant Manjrekar, the great rangoli artist, who had characterized it as 'a socialist art form', decided that 'it has no future that I can see' and stopped teaching it in 1975 (Ch. 1, p. 29). The Hanuman Theatre where tamashas were performed in Lalbag since the mid-1940s finally closed down by the mid-1980s. Madhukar Nerale, its last owner, lamented the fact that 'our audiences have become almost extinct. The tamasha artistes are unable to survive. This artistic tradition is likely to die out' (Ch. 1, p. 34). No longer could they muster patronage from political parties, political 'movements or from the state'. Even the Shiv Sena which 'talks of Marathi culture' never did anything 'to encourage Marathi folk forms' (Ch. 1, p. 34). Similarly, along with the decline of tamasha, the shahirs began to disappear. 'Everything has been swept away now,' declared Shahir Sable,

The cultural movement is almost dead. The shahirs of today are starving... Today Marathi culture is almost gone from the city... On the streets you don't hear Marathi anymore. Only Hindi (Ch. 1, p. 39).

This, then, was where the nativist agenda had led. From the 1970s and 1980s onwards, the Loknatya tradition withered away. At one level, this evidence suggests that the cultural effervescence that was witnessed in Girangaon in the 1940s and 1950s, built upon its older political traditions, had begun to peter out. But at another, it also suggests that social ways of being that had underpinned this cultural activity, and that had been the product of the political momentum of the 1920s and 1930s as much as it had fostered it, were now being fundamentally transformed.

Finally, by the late 1960s and 1970s, the political economy of local dominance, and indeed the place of violence within it, had also begun to undergo significant change. Local dominance had often depended upon the use of muscle. The 'dada' had been an important, even ubiquitous institution of the neighbourhood. Respected for their physical strength, their fearlessness and their ability to get things done, dadas were often called in by landlords to collect rents, by creditors to recover debts, by politicians to acquire votes, by trade unionists to organize strikes and by employers to break them. Govind Phansekar, a Congress dada, active in the 1960s and 1970s, explained that he attracted support and loyalty

because people respected me; then of course I also had the reputation of being a dada and a goonda. So what is wrong with that?... See the way to do it was, however big a leader he may be, if he comes in your way, you must hit him (Ch. 4, p. 27).

Dadas also sought to perform services within the neighbourhood that were not dissimilar – even if they were conducted in a smaller scale – to those which the Sena provided: getting young men jobs, securing medical help for their neighbours, rescuing their friends from the clutches of the police or the grip of other institutions of the state. Necessarily, dadas sometimes entertained connections with the police, neighbour-hood patrons, more powerful and prominent bosses and politicians. By the 1960s, some neighbourhood toughs discovered fresh opportunities and challenges by involving themselves in wider networks of enterprise and power.

The workings of democracy provided an important stimulus for local bosses looking for wider, more powerful and more lucrative connec-tions. While politicians valued the dada's capacity to gather votes, the latter increasingly needed their connections with politicians in order to secure favours for their own clients and dependants. Their local prestige and influence could depend upon the efficacy of their connections. The insatiable appetite of politicians and political parties for cash, especially for their election campaigns, meant that their needs could only be met through the 'black' economy. In the 1930s, dadas collected subscriptions for Ganeshotsav or other festivals from local shopkeepers, who readily recognized that it was in their best interests to cough up. Thirty years later, Shiv Sainiks raised the income for their shakhas, to stand bail for their friends as well as to pay the costs of festivals and local events, not only from shopkeepers and banias but especially from liquor and matka operators during prohibition. In the 1970s, with the end of prohibition, smuggling gold as well as high-value consumer goods that otherwise attracted high import duties became a lucrative cash-fuelled business and thus an important source of informal capital accumulation. By the early 1980s, the heroin traffic from Afghanistan, stimulated by war, passed sub-stantially through Bombay. The complexity of these enterprises placed them beyond the reach of most dadas. However, the elaborate nexus of cash, violence and political power that developed around them impinged upon even the more modest dadas of Girangaon.

As tariffs were lowered, smuggling lost its value and even gold lost some of its lustre. The heroin trade quickly proved a high-risk specialism. Property development and construction became the focus of attention for what were now being described as 'mafia' networks. Catastrophic urban planning, archaic tenancy laws and land ceiling legislation served to push up property prices swiftly while the construction industry offered high returns within the informal economy. Now local bosses could claim generous subventions for their political campaigns. Property developers eyed the lands on which slums and squatter settlements had been built. Indeed, some settlements had over the years improved and reclaimed the land on which they stood and thus made them yet more valuable for builders. When these external pressures on slums mounted, it also cre-ated opportunities for profiteering and protection rackets within them.

Similarly, landlords sought the help of dadas and local power brokers to eject their tenants protected by law, while the latter sought favours from politicians and local toughs to protect them, sometimes at a considerable and continuing cost. Thus, when Sahdev Tawde drew a sharp distinction between the 'tough and violent' Krishna Desai and those 'like Arun Gawli or Ashwin Naik and those Mafia people', he drew attention to an important shift that had occurred in Girangaon. In the 1920s and 1930s, dadas were in some measure constrained by the demands and expectations of the neighbourhood. The nexus of cash, muscle and political power that had taken shape in the city by the 1970s and 1980s placed them beyond the reach and influence of those they had once, at least intermittently, served. No longer could the residents of Girangaon impose, to any great effect, the constraints and obligations of reciprocity upon their patrons. If the Shiv Sena had deployed some of the same techniques as the communists in establishing their presence in Girangaon, the social, cultural and political relationships of the neighbourhood had changed almost beyond recognition.

The general strike of 1982[47]

By the late 1970s, millworkers were only too aware that their wages, living standards and working conditions had slipped far behind the levels that prevailed in the new industries like engineering, chemicals and, especially, pharmaceuticals. Substantial wage increases had been made in these new sectors, especially in pharmaceuticals, in the previous two decades. The deterioration of conditions in the city's premier industry had been accompanied by the continued stifling of representation for the workers. The RMMS now lodged firmly as the representative union proved wholly immoveable under the existing legal provisions. Sindutai Marhane, then working in the Phoenix Mill, described a common predicament when she recalled:

I used to be influenced by the communists, but in the mill, we were forced to become members of the Rashtriya Mill Mazdoor Sangh. They are the representative union and we had to go to them for everything. So we had no choice . . . The RMMS would favour those who were close to them and ignore the demands of those who were not with them.

In fact, for those whose sympathies had not been captured by the RMMS, their only recourse was to 'become members of both unions' (Ch. 5, p. 8). Indeed 'the reason why all the workers were angry' in 1982,

---

[47] For an account of the strike, see Van Wersch, *The Bombay Textile Strike*.

explained Kisan Daji Salunke, who worked in the Spring Mill, was 'what
the RMMS was up to. That was the real anger. The union was being
forced down their throats whether they wanted them or not.' As the sole
representative union in the industry, the RMMS often appeared to act
with impunity. 'The RMMS oppressed workers,' declared Salunke, '–
they were goondas. They would think of different ways to cut back on
wages, they would collect union dues by force.' Consequently, in the
early 1980s, 'the workers wanted a leader who would help them get rid
of these people' (Ch. 5, p. 15).

The Shiv Sena had established its own union, the Girni Kamgar Sena,
in 1980 in a bid to deepen its base among the millworkers. In protest
against the deal struck between the Millowners' Association and the
RMMS over the annual bonus, the Girni Kamgar Sena staged a successful one-day strike in November 1981 and then threatened to launch 'an
indefinite strike' in two weeks if further wage increases were not granted.
When, at a meeting on Kamgar Maidan, Thackeray called for a postponement of the indefinite strike on the basis of assurances he claimed to have
received from the Chief Minister, A. R. Antulay, the workers smelt more
than a whiff of betrayal. They concluded that they had been marginalized and their interests had been disregarded in a deal struck between
the Congress and the Sena. They walked out of the Kamgar Maidan.
The communists were now rapidly becoming a distant memory. Their
future lay firmly behind them. Workers in the Standard Mill invited Datta
Samant to act as their spokesman. Samant's reputation had been built
upon numerous successes in the engineering industry, the great Premier
Automobiles strike of 1979 and the daring attack on the Shiv Sena in the
Godrej factory at Vikhroli. It is clear from these testimonies that Samant
was reluctant to take on the bonus dispute in the textile industry, even
if the Standard Mill workers had invited him to lead them. Rather, it
was the millworkers who 'forced the leadership [specifically Samant] to
declare a strike'.[48]

The general strike of 1982 was Girangaon's last stand. It was sustained
for at least a year. Indeed, it was never called off. By the time it collapsed,
the textile industry had begun to be dismantled. In many respects, the
strike harked back to the solidarities demonstrated in Girangaon in 1928–
29, when the workers had effectively closed down the industry for about
eighteen months. A striker from 1928, parachuted into Girangaon in
1982, would have recognized the same massive, enthusiastic groundswell
that drove the leadership forward in the initial stages of the dispute. He

---

[48] For instance, Jaiprakash Bhilare, General Secretary, Maharashtra Girni Kamgar Union,
Ch. 5, p. 24; Kisan Daji Salunke, Ch. 5, pp. 25–26; Lakshmibai Bhatkar, Ch. 5, p. 28.

or she would have observed the caution as well as the determination that marked the first phase of the strike, the discussions at the mill gates and the calculations about how complete the strike might prove. The 1982 strike was indeed organized around a structure of chawl, area and zonal committees that had perhaps first come into existence in 1928. Following the pattern of 1928, some unionists encouraged those workers, who were in a position to do so, to return to their villages. Conversely, since a large number of strikers came from the Deccan districts of Satara, Sangli and Pune, 'thousands of bags of grain would come daily into Bombay from these districts' for the strikers, according to Bhilare, the general secretary of Samant's Maharashtra Girni Kamgar Union. The grain was distributed to the workers and their families through the 'zonal centres' established by the union in Girangaon (Ch. 5, p. 32). Yeshwant Chavan of the Lal Nishan party recalled that 'we thought that since this was going to be a long drawn strike, we should get the support from the peasantry. We thought of this as politically and economically necessary' (Ch. 5, p. 43).

In the first few months, the strike appeared to be complete. It proved impossible for the RMMS, the millowners and the government to recruit replacements for the strikers. As the strike went on, however, more deter-mined attempts were made to start the mills once again. Certainly, in 1929, similar attempts to take workers through the pickets, often escorted by the police, had been elaborately organized. But they were dwarfed in scale by the initiatives taken in 1982, beginning with the attempt to resume production at the Century Mill. Now the millowners' strategy was to ferry large contingents of workers into the mill to live and work for a week or a fortnight at a time until they could safely be relieved and replaced by another batch to replace them. Frequently, there was 'hardly any work on the machines, and very little production'. The workers, having been driven into the mill under guard, would simply 'clean the machines and the departments' (Arondekar, Ch. 5, p. 51). As workers resisted such attempts at organized strike-breaking, so violence began to occur in Girangaon. Our parachutist from 1928–29 would have rec-ognized these patterns of violence, but dimly, because they had clearly become more elaborate. The protagonists were now armed with knives and swords in 1982, rather than with lathis and stones as they had occa-sionally been in 1929. Thus, in 1982, armed masked gangs attacked strikers in 1982 in the Digvijay, Kohinoor, Ruby and Podar Mills and an attempt was made to burn down the tents in which workers on picket-duty slept at night. Similarly, the RMMS believed that 'Datta Samant's people were capable of doing anything. They once beat up everyone in a whole locality – in Koliwada – because they were going to work in the mills.' The age of Keshav dada Borkar was steadily being overtaken by the age of Babu Reshim and Arun Gawli.

Necessarily, the longer the strike lasted the harder it became for workers to subsist. Some workers sought jobs in the city, in construction, as jobbing painters or as manual labourers. Some travelled to the power-loom towns like Bhiwandi and Ichalkaranji to find work. Children, it was said, took up 'small jobs' and 'mill workers' wives would go out to work as domestic workers here and there' (Sindutai Marhane, Ch. 5, p. 53). Dhondu Mohite recalled that his children started a batata wada stall (Ch. 5, p. 52). Several simply sold whatever they possessed. Kisan Salunke recalls having to sell 'all the vessels' and then to chop 'the lathis that belonged to my father' and that he had 'used for fighting during his communist days' to burn for fuel (Ch. 5, p. 51). Some began to drift back to work simply because as Arondekar put it starkly, 'they were starving' (Ch. 5, p. 51). The long general strikes of the 1920s and 1930s had entailed a similarly continuous crisis of subsistence for the workers.

For all their similarities, however, there were important differences between the strikes of 1928–29 and 1982. Most obviously, the 1982 strike occurred within a more complex and intricately woven political context. Democracy, political parties and their varying stakes at different levels of government impinged upon the strike and affected the negotiating position of the numerous parties to the dispute. Prakash Bhogle suggested, for instance, that the reason why the Shiv Sena did not press ahead with its threat to initiate a general strike in November 1981 was because some of its middle-ranking leaders were concerned that such action would raise the profile of the Girni Kamgar Sena and especially its secretary, Varadkar, and feared that they would be marginalized within the organization. Conversely, it was claimed that the RMMS put pressure on the Congress governments both at the state and at the centre not to allow a settlement with Datta Samant in case it undermined their own position within Girangaon. If Samant was able to present the strike as a triumph, he might have been able to attract sufficient support for the Maharashtra Girni Kamgar Union to dislodge the RMMS from its perch as the sole representative union. In addition, the eclipse of the RMMS would have adversely affected the Congress in several state assembly constituencies as well as damaging its prospects in the Lok Sabha elections. Another consideration for both the Congress and the Sena was the threat that a successful strike would greatly develop Datta Samant's influence in Bombay. 'I staunchly believe', Anant Kumbhar, who went on strike in 1982, declared, and he was probably not alone, 'that this strike [i.e. its settlement] was disrupted to stop the Doctor's popularity from growing' (Ch. 5, p. 67). Rival political parties thus had much to gain from driving the dispute into a stalemate. Certainly, the Congress, under Indira Gandhi's direction from the centre, appears to have stopped the Chief Minister in Maharashtra, after Antulay was ejected, from settling the strike. Nor would the Bombay millowners countenance making a deal with Samant for fear of leaving him entrenched within their industry. 'The millowners and the Congress government reached their own understanding,' as Arondekar, a retired timekeeper in the Swan Mills, put it. 'The Indira Gandhi government did not care about what happened to the workers. They let them starve into submission' (Ch. 5, p. 51).

It was the misfortune of the millworkers that they had became embroiled in this political stalemate. However, Arondekar's assessment also suggests that Datta Samant miscalculated. The astute leadership of a general strike on this scale required not only impeccable timing in initiating action but also in bringing it to an end. Perhaps, Samant calculated that he could adopt and maintain his own tough, unrelenting position because Delhi and the state government would eventually persuade the millowners to negotiate. He would certainly have been aware of the massive gains that would accrue to him from even a moderately favourable settlement, especially one effected through political intervention. For a successful conclusion to the strike would have greatly enhanced his political influence in the city, not only in Girangaon but also in relation to the millowners and within the long, dark corridors of the Mantralaya. Bombay's millworkers paid the price for his miscalculation.

In this light, the prolongation of the strike beyond the capacity of the workers to bear appears to have been a catastrophic mistake. Having embarked upon the strike with reluctance, the Maharashtra Girni Kamgar Union was unable to bring it to a stop. Perhaps, Datta Samant had given insufficient thought to a means of retreat or, to use a term that became fashionable among capitalists and officials as the industry collapsed, to his own 'exit strategy', once he had begun to lead a determined workforce in this massive strike. Perhaps, the difficulty lay with Datta Samant's style of leadership and its limitations. Datta Iswalkar's summation of Samant's leadership may throw some light on why a strike that began with such massive solidarity, enthusiasm and determination should have ended so disastrously:

He did not have his finger on the pulse of the people. He was a hero, but he did not know how to deal with the responsibility that people placed in him.

By contrast, Dange had shown repeatedly that he 'knew how far you could take the struggle' and 'when it was time to retreat' (Ch. 5, pp. 63–64). In retrospect, Samant failed to match the tactical acumen of the communist leadership of the Girni Kamgar Union in 1928 (perhaps even in 1934) even if he borrowed their name.

When the strike ended, and statistics were paraded to show the loss of mandays, production and revenues for the industry, it was remarkable that the closure of the industry in the leading centre of India's textile industry had resulted in no appreciable decline in the availability or output of cloth. Powerloom factories expanded rapidly. While minimizing fixed capital costs, the powerloom factories achieved more easily the flexibility in the composition of output and deployment of labour that the composite mills had long pursued with so much determination and even greater difficulty. By employing small numbers of workers, they often escaped the regulation of production conditions and employment practices that often, if too lightly, affected the formal sector. As the strike petered out, millowners found that they could spin yarn and outsource cloth production or even diversify into powerlooms themselves. It is one of the many tragic ironies of the 1982 strike that many workers had made ends meet during the dispute and thus sustained the strike by securing jobs in the powerloom industry. In this light, Samant's miscalculation in allowing the strike to continue indefinitely looks more like a failure to grasp the harsh realities of the economics of the cotton textile industry. Samant himself led the strike as a political figure, as a 'hero' of other struggles, but without any previous experience of the textile industry.

Looming over these economic realities, however, was a massive political, indeed cultural, fact. The Bombay millowners, like employers elsewhere in India, had been, from the outset and throughout the twentieth century, highly averse to the formation of trade unions and chronically anxious that any system of wage bargaining would inexorably lead to a situation in which labour would prove impossible to discipline. In the theory of industrial relations to which employers most readily subscribed, they appeared to be the most enlightened guardians of the workers' welfare. Yet, they had also consistently sought to squeeze the returns to labour. The employers' intolerance of and hostility to trade unions, their reluctance to negotiate with 'outsiders' and their tendency to threaten workers who spoke up in their own interest had contributed over time to a highly confrontational style of labour relations. Yet, to the millowners, the confrontational nature of industrial relations only seemed to demonstrate the validity of their theory of managing labour. In turn, it strengthened their resolve to exclude meddlesome outsiders and troublemakers and to refuse to deal with trade unions. The genesis, scale and conduct of the 1982 strike were integral to this dynamic of confrontation, both as cause and consequence.

The fierce and sustained resistance of the workers, and the complex task for the millowners of cutting their way through the multi-layered intricacies of trade union politics, led the latter increasingly to regard the composite mill as obsolete. For some, the long strike had imposed an insuperable financial burden and rendered the task of mobilizing capital to restart the mills virtually impossible. The millowners' perception of 'the labour problem' had from the earliest days of the industry exercised a severe constraint on their business strategies. Now these anxieties about maintaining labour discipline and about extracting acceptable levels of productivity at the lowest possible wages led them to dismantle the industry altogether. Faced with rising land prices, sustained industrial action, severe competitive pressure and a hostile fiscal regime, the millowners diversified, outsourced and withdrew from the industry. The real estate on which the mills stood appeared to be worth more than the industry could realize. In the powerloom industry, by contrast, the threat of labour was easier to contain, fixed costs were low and greater flexibility possible in responding to market fluctuations. As Vikas Kasliwal, Managing Director of S Kumars Suiting, owners of the Sreeram Mills, put it, entrepreneurs and managers 'all want to reduce employment'. They took it as axiomatic that

this labour is a headache, today they are demanding 'x', tomorrow they are demanding 'y'. If you want to modernize, they say 'no'. So the mindset became this – the less labour you have the better it is (Ch. 5, p. 3).

The 'labour problem' had remained the persistent difficulty for the millowners in transferring the burden of the industry's structural crises onto their workforce. What appeared to them as the insuperable burden of managing labour in the formal sector eventually led capital to retreat into the relatively unregulated powerloom industry, where small groups of workers, with fewer rights, less bargaining power and weaker political traditions, could be deployed with greater flexibility and at lesser cost as the imperatives of the market dictated. This then was at least in part the substantive meaning that globalization was to acquire in the new lexicon of the international political economy.

* * * * *

The powerful public presence that the working classes had established in Bombay by the early twentieth century had exerted a determining influence on the formation and reproduction of the city's distinctive urban character and civic tradition. Increasingly from the late 1960s onwards, the public presence and political influence of the working classes were progressively cut back. The marginalization of the working classes in the late twentieth century was accompanied by fundamental changes working their way through the city's political culture. By the late nineteenth century, as Bombay had developed into a major metropolitan and industrial centre, it had also witnessed the emergence of a distinctive cosmopolitan and eclectic political culture. The city was characterized by its diversity and hybridity, not wholly surprising in a city of migrants. Its public life was marked by its secularism, its equidistance from the particularisms of caste and religious community and often its transcendence of their differences.

The emergence of this political culture had owed something to the degree of autonomy from colonial domination that the city's elites had been able to assert since the earliest days of the East India Company settlement. British power established itself late in western India and expanded slowly. The Company's political weakness and the relative poverty of their merchants increased their dependence on Indian merchants and dubashes. As a result, Bombay's elites had been able to appropriate considerable influence and wealth. Commercial partnership lent itself to political collaboration. Bombay's mercantile elites acquired a grip on important and lucrative areas of the city's economy, including, and indeed especially, the cotton textile industry. By marked contrast with Calcutta and Madras, the city's elites swiftly acquired a significant share of local power. From the 1830s onwards, they were firmly entrenched in local government. They were frequently consulted by colonial officials. They gained ready access to, and moved easily within, the Governor's court. Necessarily, they focused their attention on the city, where political power and influence were open to them, and ignored the hinterland over which they had little control. From this secure and significant base, they extended their influence over provincial affairs and by the 1890s began to exercise the determining influence within the Indian National Congress. As they battled for power within the Municipal Corporation, where they gained, by the 1880s, greater representation on a relatively wide franchise, they took particular pride in public standards in the city. This civic pride was manifested in rhetoric, philanthropy and in a measure of commitment to the working of the institutions of urban government. Of course, their benevolence was often selective, their rhetoric was often disciplined by their parsimony and their best intentions were qualified by harsher calculations of particular interests. Nonetheless, this civic ideology served to ensure a certain minimum in standards of governance and in public expectations about the city's institutions. From their application, most of the city's residents gained something.

The opportunities opened up by Bombay's growth brought people into the city from the whole Presidency and, indeed, further afield. It ensured that no single social group, whether defined by caste, language or religion, dominated its commercial or political life. Conversely, as migrants streamed into the city, they had every reason to keep their eye on its opportunities rather than dream wistfully of their rural homes. Bombay's history ensured that it never really became a city of its hinterland. It was neither simply a Gujarati nor a Maharashtrian city, until the reorganization of the state took an awkward, if decisive, step towards its definition in 1960.

However, the development of this civic ideology should not obscure the fact that, as the city expanded, its poor lived in appalling conditions and often barely at levels of subsistence. Their exploitation can be measured in their low life expectancy, in the high rates of industrial accidents and the range of occupational diseases. Observers frequently noted in the early twentieth century how rare it was to see workers over the age of 45 employed in the cotton mills. However, the city's workers were by no means passive victims. They resisted the demands made upon them by the employers and the colonial state. Their ability to combine and strike work was observed from at least the 1880s. By the 1920s, in the face of the hostility of the employers and repression by the state, a powerful labour movement had developed in the city. From the late 1920s, witnessing the development of this labour movement, increasingly under communist direction, the city's ruling elites feared intermittently that Girangaon had become an insurrectionary centre. In the 1920s and 1930s, the city's workers had declared their political presence. The maintenance of the city's civic tradition and cross-communal political culture, even in the face of communal riots, would not have been possible without the stake which the working classes had claimed within its imaginary.

Nothing undermined the political culture of the city more seriously than the continuing failure of its cross-communal elite to accommodate the poor and manage labour more generously. This is reflected in part in their response to working class discontents. The Bombay millowners, like most Indian employers, refused to tolerate the presence of trade unions and, when they came to be established, they sought as far as possible to weaken and marginalize their role in the industry. As working class resistance gathered force, its public presence at times appeared menacing to the city's propertied elites, the employers and the state. Both before and after independence, working class resistance intermittently evoked severe repression. Colonial rule had given Indian mercantile and landed elites the means to discipline and control labour more effectively.

With independence, they sought to extend and tighten their control. At the same time, the political solidarities of the working classes, welded together at least partially through the struggles of the 1920s and 1930s, began to fragment under the pressure of trade union rivalries and political competition by the 1950s. As trade unions became the instruments of political parties, their quest for followers served to further fragment workers' organization, sometimes along the lines of caste, language and religion. Thus, the advent of democracy held out the promise of consolidating the political presence of the working class and the urban poor but in practice served to incorporate them into the political process on terms of such subordination that their political influence was considerably diluted.

While working class resistance had undermined existing methods of labour control, the employers and the state attempted to restructure the labour force and reorganize the framework of industrial relations. From the 1930s onwards, the textile industry differentiated with increasing clarity between 'permanent workers' and a sizeable 'informal sector' within the industry of dependent casual workers. The growing body of industrial legislation served to entrench this distinction and to extend it across the labour market. As these 'permanent' workers, whose employment rights were now better protected, drove up their wages or resisted efforts to alter work practices, employers and managers sought to assert their 'right to manage' against them. On the other hand, the informal sector continued to expand. Not only did workers here have few rights and poor returns, but employers, politicians and the state felt few obligations towards them. The closure of the textile industry, with the development of outsourcing to the power looms, and de-industrialization in the city in general, can be seen as the logical extension of this strategy of 'informalization'.

Casual workers and those employed in the so-called informal sector were often forced by their insecure conditions of work and low wages to depend even more fully on contractors and intermediaries, patrons and caste fellows, and assorted pedlars of influence, power and credit. By the 1960s, therefore, as the Shiv Sena emerged, the containment and repression of working class resistance had created the conditions for exacerbating caste and communal differences. These shifts in the structure of the labour force and the nature of the labour market, accelerating since the 1960s, coincided with fundamental changes in the city's politics and together they pressed in the same direction. In the 1930s, the communist Girni Kamgar Union had been an effective agent in industrial relations but it had also created a wider community of political sentiment around it in Girangaon. By the 1950s, the communists were still a significant force in the labour movement but they had begun to lose their position of dominance in Girangaon. The communists responded to the first signs of their decline by jumping aboard the Samyukta Maharashtra movement and hoped thereby to revive and extend their wider political appeal. However, the argument that working class culture was essentially Maharashtrian and that the workers' Bombay could only be safeguarded if it was integrated into the new state, served to reduce to a linguistic and communal base what had been a wider and culturally heterogeneous class movement. As a consequence, the communists surrendered ground to those who made the 'nativist' argument with more force and who felt free to carry its implications further. As the Shiva Sena emerged from the interstices of the Samyukta Maharashtra coalition, employers began to see the advantage of inviting it to break up the base of the militant unions of the Left. To a large extent, they succeeded. Trade union rivalries, with a sharpening political edge, fragmented the solidarities of the labour movement further and opened it up to greater violence.

In the aftermath of the 1982 strike, the public presence that the city's working classes had seized in the civic life of the city was increasingly nullified. Their claims to a stake in the city's social framework were swept aside. As the industry was dismantled, and the social organization of Girangaon began to disintegrate, workers sometimes sought protection in caste and communal affinities and the social connections built around them. With its active neighbourhood presence, its readiness to do favours for its clients, to find jobs for the boys, to confront authority and to terrorize the powerful on behalf of individual members, its spectacular displays of violence and its increasing access to state power, the Shiv Sena offered a kind of citizenship to workers, now seemingly disenfranchised and wholly subordinated, and created an arena in which they could at least fleetingly make a claim for dignity and equality.

At the same time, there was a more fundamental and, indeed, more general, process at work. It may be argued that the propensity of a democratic state to protect human rights and civic freedoms, including freedom from want, that is the civility of its practices of governance, will be determined largely by the attitude to the poor entertained by politically and socially dominant groups. De-industrialization, the diversification of investment and the stripping of the textile mills to capitalize on the value of land, was in part the outcome of political choices. They did not disclose a generous attitude towards labour or its stake in the city. Indeed, the formation of new nexus of cash, muscle and office by the 1980s, operating on a larger scale of wealth and power, was facilitated by the workings of democratic politics, but also suggested a certain degradation of governance. Local bosses were now no longer simply the arbiters of social exchange within their own domain. Their reach had extended deep into, and at times apparently hollowed out, parts of the structure of the state. While the civic traditions and political culture of Bombay until the 1960s, characterized by its apparent secularism and its transcendence of caste and communal difference, was inconceivable without the assertion of the public presence of the working classes, the degradation of governance was a necessary pre-condition for the pogrom against Muslims in Bombay in 1992–93 or indeed in Ahmedabad and Gujarat in 2002. The future of the city as a peaceful, habitable and successful metropolis will turn on the stake that its poorest residents, including the former mill-workers and their progeny among them, are allowed within its society. In this respect, as in many others, axioms that apply to Bombay city also apply to the workings of the nation as a whole.

Historians and the nation

On 19 December 2001, Mr Murli Manohar Joshi, the Human Resources Development (or Education) Minister in the BJP-led Government of India, speaking to the BJP youth wing, less than a week after the Lashkar-e-Toiba's attack on the parliament buildings in New Delhi, identified two types of terrorism: 'cross-border terrorism' perpetrated over two decades by Pakistan and by Kashmiri militant groups sponsored by its military intelligence, and the 'intellectual terrorism unleashed by the left', more specifically by 'leftist historians'. Their falsification of history had 'spread like a poison'. This 'intellectual terrorism' was, he asserted, 'more dangerous than cross-border terrorism'.[1] In exhorting the party's youth wing to counter both types of terrorism, the Human Resources Minister appeared to salute the influence of the historians with the demeanour of someone confident of his ability to destroy them.

The minister's statement followed several attempts to contain their supposed influence. Three months earlier, the Human Resources Minister had ordered about ten 'objectionable' passages to be deleted from four textbooks written for classes VI, VII and XI (that is for students aged 11, 12 and 16 respectively). These textbooks had originally been commissioned by the National Council for Education Research and Training in the 1970s and they had been written by leading historians – in the case of Romila Thapar, a scholar of the greatest distinction. The passages that gave offence largely related to 'ancient' and 'medieval' India, an elaboration of James Mill's periodization of India's history into the supposedly Hindu and Muslim periods that preceded its British apogee. Several passages referred to the practice of eating beef and to cow-killing in Vedic times; one discussed the contradiction between the archaeological and literary evidence for the historicity of the gods Rama and Krishna; two noted the effects of the hegemony of and 'indoctrination' by Brahmans in maintaining the caste system and specifically the hierarchy of the four varna orders. Two further passages from textbooks about the

---

[1] *The Indian Express*, 20 December 2001.

seventeenth and eighteenth centuries were deemed to have offended the sensibilities of particular communities. One passage noted that the caste cluster of warrior peasants called Jats founded its own state at Bharat-pur in Rajasthan and from there conducted 'plundering raids' in the surrounding region. In another, the historian Satish Chandra pointed out that the 'official explanation' for the execution of the Sikh Guru Tegh Bahadur by the Mughal court was that he had 'resorted to plunder and rapine'. Mr Murli Manohar Joshi, the Human Resources Minister, was then reported to have claimed in a newspaper article, apparently confusing rapine for rape, that Professor Satish Chandra had declared that Guru Tegh Bahadur had been executed for raping women.[2] Indeed, this may explain why the various Sikh organizations had threatened to take to the streets if the offending passages were not removed.[3] By the end of October 2001, the Central Board of Secondary Education had, following receipt of the government directive, informed all head teach-ers of schools affiliated to it that the National Council for Education Research and Teaching had 'deleted [the selected passages] with imme-diate effect' and directed them to ensure that they were neither 'taught' nor 'discussed' in class. But the Central Board is autonomous of the National Council and under no obligation to follow its orders. Within a month, not surprisingly perhaps, schoolteachers began to report that the ban had 'raised enthusiasm among the students to read the deleted passages'.[4]

This was not the first time that the state had adopted this role as the arbiter of historical interpretation. In 1977, when the BJP had, in its earlier incarnation as the Jana Sangh, been a member of the Janata coalition government, the textbook on Ancient India by R. S. Sharma had been withdrawn. It was restored to the curriculum once the Congress returned to power in 1980. Seven of the ten passages found objectionable in October 2001 came from Professor Sharma's textbook.

In a quite separate move in February 2000, the Indian Council of Historical Research withdrew from its publisher, Oxford Univer-sity Press, two volumes of documents which had formed part of its long-running project entitled 'Towards Freedom'. Significantly, it had been reported that since 1999 the Ministry of Human Resources had attempted to replace the old members of the ICHR and ICSSR with its own nominees.[5] The 'Towards Freedom' project had been conceived in 1972 as a counter to the 'Transfer of Power' documents from the

---

[2] Anjali Mody, *The Hindu*, 10 December 2001.   [3] *The Hindu*, 9 October 2001.
[4] *The Statesman*, 24 November 2001.   [5] *TOI*, 17 February 2000.

India Office in London, which were then being collected and edited by Nicholas Mansergh. Until 1988, the 'Towards Freedom' project was being conducted by the employees of the Indian Council of Historical Research. The aim of the project was to put together documents on the 'freedom struggle' for each year between 1937 and 1947. The first volume on the year 1937 appeared in 1985. In 1988, the second volume, which assembled documents pertaining to the year 1938, was withdrawn apparently because of what was deemed – this time by a committee of major historians – to be its deficient scholarship. A new committee of leading historians independent of the ICHR was charged with the task of completing the project under the supervision of Professor S. Gopal. Two volumes relating to 1938 and 1943–4 were published in about 1997. Two further volumes, one edited by K. N. Panikkar pertaining to 1940, and another dealing with 1946, edited by Sumit Sarkar, the most distinguished historian of India today, were withdrawn by the revamped ICHR in 2000. The fact that both Panikkar and Sarkar had been among the fiercest critics of Hindu nationalism is pertinent, even if it does not necessarily explain the decision to withdraw the volumes. The public outcry that followed forced the Council to explain its decision. The explanation was in part substantive and in part procedural. The Council claimed that it was the poor quality of the preceding volumes for 1938 and 1943–4 that had led them to the decision to scrutinize the volumes edited by Panikkar and Sarkar. The volumes on 1938 and 1943–4 had, they argued, reduced Gandhi to 'a mere footnote' and placed great emphasis on the Communist Party of India, despite the fact that it had played a 'traitorous role' in the freedom struggle. In fact, the volume on 1943–4 contained a whole chapter on Gandhi. In any case, the claim to rescue Gandhi from the footnotes of history becomes a little complicated, especially if we accept the close connections between the revamped ICHR and the BJP-led government. For Gandhi's assassin had been a member of the RSS, the most important component of the Sangh Parivar, and the cadre to which both the Prime Minister and the Human Resources Minister belong. Just as Gandhi had been assassinated for ostensibly betraying the nation, so now the Sangh Parivar trained their sights on historians whose betrayal lay seemingly in their interpretation of the past. The ICHR also argued that the volumes showed that the editors had been 'fabricating the past . . . for propaganda of a particular ideology' and, in particular, in order to 'sanitize' the role of the Left. There were also procedural objections: the claim that one of the published volumes was missing an index; that the documents had been arranged thematically when their remit was to present them chronologically; and that the volumes had not been submitted as required for the scrutiny of the Council. These points have been extensively debated since and it would seem that the last claim is false. The volumes edited by Sarkar and Panikkar have not appeared. For the moment it would seem that the remaining five volumes are unlikely to appear. Having spent Rs 4 crores over twenty-six years on the project, that is about £1 million at the rate of exchange in the 1970s, the Council might well reflect that it would have been better advised not to embark upon the task of creating an Indian Mansergh. Indian nationalism, this time in its Hindu colouring, had rendered impossible the attempt to document an Indian perspective on its independence and partition.

Necessarily, these official interventions in the writing of history, and the accompanying projects of educational and curricular reform, have major political implications. Indeed, the criticisms of the government's actions in relation to the textbooks and the 'Towards Freedom' project have been expressed in terms of both the violation of the right to free speech and democratic rights more generally and the political intentions of the BJP and the Sangh Parivar. But these events also have a bearing upon the status of history as a discipline, its modes of practice, both conceptual and sociological, and, indeed, the state of the historiography of India.

In particular, these government initiatives appeared to obliterate the distinction between the findings of historical research and public discourses about the past. 'If history is one-sided,' Vajpayee, the Prime Minister said, 'it should be corrected.' But it would be as well to ask how he could possibly know. Who indeed would be the judge of whether and when every 'side' of history had been brought into perfect balance? Who would prescribe the interpretative remedy that would bring history to this point of perfect equilibrium? In November 2001, one newspaper reported 'a policy decision' to have each textbook vetted by religious leaders before it was sent to the publisher. The notion that the balance of historical interpretation could be settled in the court of public opinion or by the judgements delivered by politicians and religious leaders rather assumed that history's claim to disciplinary logic or technical specialism could be jettisoned. Conversely, the scope for historians to defend their disciplinary conventions against everyday knowledge and the public discourse about the past depended precisely upon their ability to insist upon the specialism of their techniques. In a relatively open discipline, which may have an armoury of conventions but has refused to develop its own carapace of theory, which has drawn liberally from conceptual frameworks developed in cognate fields and whose findings often have large and subversive consequences for the contemporary social order, such claims to technical specialism or, more fundamentally, the relative autonomy of the historian's craft have been hard to sustain in public debate.

It is important to emphasize that the Hindu nationalist BJP, National Council for Education Research and Training, the Indian Council of Historical Research and the Ministry of Human Resource Development have now become increasingly and closely interconnected. The explanation that they offered for their censorship turned in part on the assertion that the historians themselves had been less than 'objective' and that they had sought to 'fabricate the past' for the sake of Leftist propaganda. They also felt compelled to delete passages from textbooks because 'people's sentiments would be hurt' or, as the BJP Chief Whip claimed, it would 'hurt Hindu sensibilities to teach small children that during the Vedic period, cattle sacrifice and beef eating were accepted practices'. Indeed, he asked, 'How can we allow school books to say that Ram was not a historical figure or that the battle of the Mahabharata never took place?'[6] He might have discovered the answer in the longevity of the textbooks. They had apparently been read for thirty years without causing great damage.

But there was a more positive, even aggressive, purpose. For Dinanath Batra, the General Secretary of Vidya Bharati, the education wing of the RSS, declared that they were fighting an 'ideological battle against the trijut (trinity) of Macaulay, Marx and the Madrasawadis'. Vidya Bharati advocated instead the 'Indianization, nationalization and spiritualization' of education.[7] Among its aims were to inculcate in schoolchildren 'indigenous knowledge' and 'India's contribution for mankind' and 'to reflect the national ethos adequately'.[8]

Many historians, including some of those whose books have suffered cuts, might accept the need to liberate our thinking about the past from the thraldom of Macaulay, Marx and the madrasas, and there are, of course, other sources of captivity. But not all would agree that its objectives should be those spelled out by Vidya Bharati and the NCERT. On the other hand, the historian-critics of government policy have not simply argued that they operate according to the professional imperatives of the discipline and that these cannot simply be cast aside by public opinion. They have also sought to emphasize the political purpose to their writing. Their claims have rested not only on the correctness of their history but

[6] *The Hindu*, 28 November 2001; Sahmat, p. 65.
[7] *Indian Express*, 22 November 2001.
[8] A. Jain, 'Indianising Education, De-Macaulayising Polity', *Manthan*, January–March 2001, 7–11.

also on the rectitude of their secular nationalism. Thus, Professor R. S. Sharma, whose textbook on Ancient India was thrice-banned, noted that 'Indian textbook writers should always bear in mind the basic values enshrined in our constitution while communicating their ideas to school students'. Of course, he observed, 'they should not ignore the [scholarly] consensus' except on 'minor details', when presumably the 'basic values' should have precedence.[9] In some respects, by operating on the same terrain as their censors, historians have made it much harder to define and defend the relative autonomy of their scholarly domain.

The writing of history in India has to a large extent developed in relation to the state. This has served to complicate the claim that the task should be left to the professionals. Histories, chronicles and genealogies compiled in the sixteenth and seventeenth centuries were often written with the patronage of the Mughal court and other kingdoms. The expansion of British power brought with it the tradition of the scholar-official. The scholar-officials conducted their inquiries within the framework of colonial knowledge, which their conclusions served to reinscribe. Representations of the pre-colonial past helped to legitimize colonial rule. Mighty tomes on the moral and material progress of India under colonial rule demonstrated the manifest virtues and the lofty purpose of empire. Of course, the British bureaucracy scrutinized the content of the curriculum in schools and colleges through the Director of Public Instruction while the Office of the Oriental Translator and the CID carefully examined historical and literary works, newspapers and pamphlets, poems and novels for their seditious content. The colonial state took a view about which historians were able to strike the right balance in their accounts of British rule. Generation after generation of school and college students brought up on the textbooks of G. T. Garratt, H. H. Dodwell, Vincent Smith or Edward Thompson suspected that there was another story waiting to be told outside the classroom and not necessarily retailed by professional historians. At the same time, Indian historians, often employed by the Education service, had begun by the early twentieth century to correct the authorized version. Frequently, they remained largely apolitical, in the tradition of Jadunath Sarkar, and concerned themselves with collating and interpreting 'facts'. Increasingly, however, more politically engaged and critical historians emerged from radical nationalists and the votaries of the Left while memories, biographies, fictions and sometimes histories in Indian languages conveyed to their public that there was a great gulf between the chroniclers of the Empire's moral progress and the social experience of its subjects. Some of the most elegant and intelligent

[9] R. S. Sharma, in *The Assault upon History*.

writing, like Nehru's *Discovery of India*, paid relatively little heed to the conventions of the discipline. The problems of assessing and interpreting evidence did not overtly concern him. The arguments and trends which he discerned in the past were largely shaped and rationalized by what was broadly his own political vision and outlook.

After independence, historical research became professionalized and, at the same time, drawn more fully into the orbit of the state. The number of colleges and universities began to multiply. The Council of Historical and Social Science Research and the UGC stimulated the study of the past and helped to consolidate the profession. Nation-building and development appeared to continue the freedom struggle by other means and histories of the latter helped to legitimize the former. The Congress, wearing the mantle of 'the freedom struggle', had again inherited the British Raj. Moreover, historians gravitated towards a nationalist interpretation. Some inverted the history of the 'rulers of India' by writing about the leaders of 'the freedom struggle'. Increasingly, others began to revive the nationalists' critique of the 1890s which had first set out to show how colonial rule impoverished India and still others deepened the study of the institutional underpinnings of a nationalist movement which seemed to expand steadily until by the 1940s it embraced the nation as a whole. Historical research along these lines appeared to have an immediate relevance for the project of economic development and the creation of a new democratic state. Of course, a certain awkwardness remained: partition could only be explained in terms of colonial machinations or political betrayal. More fundamentally, rival interpretations, even within the framework of this teleology, were fiercely disputed. The interpretative space to the right was occupied largely, and especially in Britain, by the celebration of imperial tutelage and trusteeship: the stability and order which the British had brought to India's pre-colonial anarchy and lawlessness or the successful modernization effected by the telegraph, the railway and the first stirrings of industrialization. Not surprisingly, an interpretative consensus formed on the Left. But the problem here was the absence of a distinctive or plausible theory. The Left had always been diffident about the applicability of class and had often succumbed to ideas about the exceptionalism of Indian society. The dead weight of Marx's orientalism about Asia provided no respite. Since the 1920s, the political practice of the communists allowed them to pass under the hegemony of the 'bourgeois nationalism' of the Congress which they were seeking to subsume. If they attempted to enter the Congress and direct it in the interests of the working classes, they were likely to be submerged by it. If they attempted to retain their political identity, they might simply be jettisoned. Independence did not liberate the communist party from its habit of taking its political bearings from the Congress. The more persistently they sought to define their position in relation to the Congress the more fully they passed under its hegemony. For historians, this predicament opened up the possibility of an ideological consensus, which extended from an unspecified liberalism to an untheorized Marxism and whose boundaries were demarcated by their anti-colonial stance and their common interest in the past of India's future.

The growing professionalization of the discipline combined with its intimate connections with the state to isolate practitioners from their public. First, the most sophisticated history was written in English. In Bengal, the most prominent historians who wrote in English made it a point to write at least occasionally in Bengali. History in other Indian languages was generally confined to chronicles of events or the lives of great men. In some languages, a historical literature began to emerge. But the old chasm remained just as wide between the production of histories, largely now organized around the 'freedom struggle' and in English, and of plays and poems, novels and memoirs, which reflected more closely upon the social identity and experience of their readers and appeared in Indian languages. Second, the professional historians were further isolated by some of the glaring failures of India's nation-building. For instance, although the tertiary sector in education grew quite rapidly after 1947, the primary and secondary sectors grew too slowly to accommodate needs. Of course, it began from a weak base. The British in India had been concerned primarily to mobilize resources for their imperial purposes, rather less to educate Indians. Fifty years after independence, India accounted for about a third of the illiterate people in the world. While it contains nearly 17 per cent of the world's population, its share of global expenditure on education is less than 1 per cent. In terms of India's own annual public expenditure, barely 3 per cent is invested in education. Conversely, as Krishna Kumar has recently shown,[10] history has been taught rather poorly and unimaginatively in schools. In particular, it has been made to serve the ideological needs of the state, rather than to open up any curiosity about the past. Pupils may thus take away a residue of assumptions and often prejudices which it conveys, but as the memories of their classroom study passes, history remains a rather arcane and distant form of knowledge.

This gulf between the historian and his or her public was further widened by the tendency towards interpretation and ideological

---

[10] Krishna Kumar, *Prejudice and Pride: School Histories of the Freedom Struggle in India and Pakistan* (New Delhi, 2001).

conformity among historians, especially the most prominent and sophisticated practitioners. Behind this conformity lay the use of official and
academic patronage by the Left, which it is often said was as overt as the
recent attempts by the BJP to pack the ICHR and ICSSR, even if there
is a difference in the higher quality of historians who were patronized
by the barons of the Left from those now available to the power brokers of the Hindu Right. Nonetheless, the ideological conformity of the
1970s and 1980s entailed a considerable interpretative cost; the political
and academic price of its shift towards 'Indianization and spiritualization' could indeed be devastating. One historian's description of her
own encounter with the discipline as a student might suggest how such
conformity could be created and maintained, and how dissent could be
suppressed within the academy. 'We did not care', she wrote, 'to read the
works' of those scholars who 'it used to be fashionable to routinely dis-
cuss [as] . . . "reactionary". A studious silence was also maintained about
scholarship that was contrary to the ideas of the powerful "Left" historians. None of us had any illusions that the history we were taught as part
of the official curriculum was tailored to a significant extent by larger
agendas. Those agendas were certainly more progressive than the ones
that one sees today but they spawned an exclusionary history . . . When I
began to research and write, I felt enormously handicapped because what
I had been taught was grossly inadequate and ridden with jargon.'[11] It
would be wholly misleading, however, to suppose that this pull towards
conformity in Indian historiography has been exclusive to the Indian
academy. On the contrary, it has been manifested in different ways in
Britain and the USA as well. The historiography of India has witnessed
lively debates with sufficient frequency to suggest that they share scholarly conventions. However, the subject has developed along quite often
separate lines in India, Britain and the USA. In the 1970s, ideology
rather than method appeared to encourage this pattern of conformity
and difference. Today, perhaps as a consequence of post-colonial theory, the driving force would seem to be primarily methodological. Consensus signified conformity within smaller, more fragmentary and more
dispersed networks. In place of major ideological divisions, the historiography divided in India and elsewhere into similar blocks held together
by shared problems and approaches but which communicated less with
each other.

   These exclusionary practices inscribed into Indian historiography
served to widen the gap and indeed to sharpen the contradictions
between popular discourses about the past and the discourse of the

---

[11] Nayanjot Lahiri, 'History and Realpolitik', *Hindustan Times*, 9 September 2001.

professional historians. Underlying this contradiction were the existence and development of a diverse, extensive, fiercely contested popular historical knowledge. This popular discourse about the past owed something to the old tradition of court chronicles, bakhars and genealogies. But it also came to be inextricably connected to the delineation of social identities. This definition of identity occurred in the nineteenth and twentieth centuries largely in relationship with the state. A plausible representation of the past influenced land-revenue systems and the colonial understanding of customary law. It could determine the distribution of land rights, shape inheritance, strengthen religious hierarchies and determine social precedence in the nineteenth century. The expansion and centralization of the state and the development of wider political arenas enabled particular castes and communities in one region to compare their fate with comparable groups elsewhere and sometimes to demand more within their localities. Fresh claims called for revisionist histories; so did the demands of defending one's position against the encroachments of rivals. As the British attempted to associate more Indians with their rule, so they sought to balance them. Since they assumed that Indian society was constituted by a multitude of interests defined by caste, race and religion, Indians sought to organize themselves along these lines. The attempt to count and classify Indians, according to caste and religion, in the Census, led particular groups to present their past in ways which would accord them a higher status, social precedence or political advantage. As the British sought to associate a wider range of their subjects with government, or to bring forward those who seemed backward in their quest for Western education, so literate elites defined themselves differently to gain preferential access to government employment, colleges and universities. There was a similar scramble by some groups to deploy the past, even to define new castes, to shape the delineation of constituencies to advance within the changing systems of nomination and election in order to legislative councils. Caste histories proliferated, sometimes to legitimize the status and definition of their identity, sometimes to rationalize their claims for advances or advantage. Low-caste and untouchable intellectuals produced histories which demonstrated the process of their subordination through force, conquest and plunder. In a sense, these accounts carried the resonance of a nationalist history which demanded that the British quit India, while they claimed the restoration of their status and some measure of political restitution. These histories were also retained within collective memories and oral traditions. We know too little about them. They were rarely expository in form or systematic. Nonetheless, they yielded the perspectives from which people evaluated and weighed up conflicting representations of their past.

Of course, these collective memories and oral traditions did not merely relate to caste and religion. Often they were stimulated by migrations, social conflicts and political movements. Oral traditions, for instance the history of workers' struggles and of Girangaon, the mill district in Bombay, remained powerful as the communist union which led them divided and weakened, and came under attack from the Shiv Sena, and they have more recently been revived as asset-stripping and property development by the millowners have begun to break up the old mill district. As identities shaped by caste and religion, caste and ethnicity, social conflicts and political struggles intersected and changed, they have produced overlapping and conflicting histories. Since 1947, the significance of caste and community as a principle of organization has if anything increased. The fact that these historical traditions have remained both diverse and divisive and at the same time vital to social being and identity has rendered their own critical perspectives on the past resilient, sometimes impervious to the discourse of the discipline. The problems of language, access to education, the pedagogical practices in the teaching of history and the ideological conformity and narrowness of historians have hardened the boundaries between the popular discourses about the past and the findings and teachings of the academy. Reflecting upon the textbook controversy and the withdrawal of his own volume in the 'Towards Freedom' series, Sumit Sarkar observed that there had been 'a collective failure on the part of our community of historians' to communicate with students at more elementary levels of the education system, and, as he put it, within 'the culture' in general. On the other hand, Vidya Bharati, the education wing of the RSS, runs at least as many schools as the Central Board of Secondary Education, in which the textbooks reflect its own construction of India's contribution to the world civilization, project its interpretation of 'the traditional ethos of Indian society' and promote its objects of 'Indianization and spiritualization'.

I have focused upon the production of histories in India because these controversies have had considerable significance and because the relationship between the historian and his or her public has been the most complex. It is not intended to suggest, as historiographical surveys, especially those conducted in the West, sometimes assume, that nationalism has weighed exclusively upon the historiography in India. Indeed, nationalism has played an important role in approaches to the subject in Britain. Of course, an important characteristic of this nationalism, its assumption of the pragmatic good sense and unswerving empiricism of British historians, has allowed it no significant scope. In the United States, too, the style and approaches to Indian history have often projected assumptions derived from a discourse about domestic society and its relationship to

Asia, and at others, they have reflected largely domestic preoccupations. The historiography of India, in other words, has been constituted by several intersecting nationalisms.

In Britain, the history of colonial India has largely been approached in terms of its relationship with the Empire. Although, of course, historians have increasingly studied aspects of Indian society, they have usually pursued their inquiries within the terms of the grand narratives of empire. By contrast, in India, research on the colonial period has been engaged with its contemporary society. British historians have as a result gained some immunity from anachronism but the tradition has also been both more dry and distant. Because they have conceived their problematics within the framework of empire, British historians have also been more readily comparative. In this sense, they may also have been influenced by the epistemological status of Indian history within the discipline as a whole. Whereas the history of Britain is assumed to be simply history, part of the discipline's mainstream, whole continents, certainly subcontinents far away, have often been lumped together in the nether regions of 'area studies'. Since work in Indian history in Britain has often been conducted as a part of imperial history, historiographical influences upon it have often overlapped with the latter.

This has been paradoxical in at least two senses. First, until at least 1914, India was not seen as part of what Seely called the 'organic' empire. Until the 1950s, when Gallagher and Robinson published their article on 'the imperialism of free trade', and indeed in many hands for some time after, imperial history was the projection of British power, capital, constitutions and ingenuity across the world. As such, it did not necessarily offer an invitation to the study of colonial subjects, their societies and their politics. Moreover, despite the provenance of its inquiries, and its interconnections with imperial history, British scholarship on India has, with a few exceptions, contributed least to the understanding of colonialization in Indian history and the evaluation of its effects upon and consequences for Indian society. Writing in 1975, John Rosselli, the 'not quite British historian' (as he described himself), noted 'the peculiar problem' of the British historians who were over 45 years old. There was among them, he noted, 'a certain unwillingness to admit the possibility that the British Empire in India might be seen as a largely negative achievement'.[12] Since then, the issue has in some measure subsided simply by not having often been engaged. In the 1980s, under the shadow of Thatcherism, it was possible perhaps to kick away some of the burden of guilt fostered over the preceding two decades upon those who had chosen

---

[12] John Rosselli, 'On Trying to Be an Indian Historian', *Belfagor*, LVI, 31 May 2001.

to wear it. But since then, problems about the significance of colonialism in Indian history have scarcely been fully explored.

Two broad approaches have shaped the historiography of India in Britain. One developed out of the evangelical mission and more broadly the celebration of Britain's achievements in India. It was manifested in volumes which focused primarily upon imperial policy, constitution making and the details of administration. This historiography remained resistant to notions of economic imperialism which appeared 'too unpatriotic' and perhaps disloyal to make much headway in British universities. By the 1920s and 1930s, this tradition gained some impetus from doctrines of trusteeship, 'indirect rule' and the multiracial Commonwealth. The history of British rule in India became a moral progress, a steady evolution towards the Commonwealth ideal. Its purpose was to educate Indians for self-government. Independence would mark the fulfilment of British rule. Necessarily it was impossible to predict even in the 1940s precisely when Indians would be ready to rule themselves. Nonetheless, this provided a Whig historiography which flourished until the 1970s.

The moral progress of empire could be set against and in opposition to the crass notion of economic imperialism. Higher imperial ethics provided a lofty standpoint from which the authoritarian excesses of colonial agents could be judged. Colonial rule was inherently benevolent and progressive, carrying the white man's burden while extending his mission, bringing civilization and enlightenment to areas of darkness. But colonial rulers were also liable to display crude racist attitudes, distort local circumstances for imperial ends or show an unwarranted confidence in their own rightness. Their arrogance and greed provoked nationalism, undermined the ideals of trusteeship and threatened the future of empire. Imperialism, according to its higher ideals, should be flexible, pliant and responsive to criticism. Such imperialism might develop subject peoples but it would also preserve and perpetuate empire. Where these sentiments generated harsh judgements upon colonial officials and facilitated moral outrage at the nature of colonialism, they appealed to and coincided with the critique developed by nationalists and Marxists. The moral residue of this inheritance is to be found in the work of historians of the Left who also focus exclusively upon the methods of colonialism and neglect the more consistently exploitative purposes of imperialism.

The second approach is derived from the rather harsher view of imperialism taken by Gallagher and Robinson. Their argument looked in two directions. Imperialism could be satisfactorily understood only in relation to Britain's global interests. Yet local crises, local circumstances and local systems of collaboration defined the limits and possibilities of imperial power. The point of departure for the Cambridge school was to establish how India fitted into Britain's changing imperial system and how rule in India was adjusted to ensure that it better served Britain's international interests. As greater emphasis was placed upon collaboration and upon Indian agency, colonialism receded into the background. Both in Cambridge and outside, continuities with the post-colonial past, the weaknesses of the colonial state, customary practice and the resilience of local power imparted to British rule the shape of an Indian Empire. Closer attention to the locality rendered more remote from the historians' vision the larger purposes of imperialism. As historians delved deeper into complexities of Indian society and opened up new areas of research into the history of peasant resistance and agrarian movements, famines and epidemics, forest resources and water use, crime and policing, gender and labour relations, caste reform and communal antagonism, so the older tendency which had already begun to neglect the analysis of imperialism was exacerbated. At the same time, the study of imperialism has begun to fascinate historians of Britain. But this research has thus far tended largely to allow itself the indulgence and the pomp of studying rulers without subjects, political and ideological movements conceptualized in relation to vast and distant areas, populated, if at all, with somnolent inhabitants.

In the United States, the major stimulus to the study of Indian history derived from anthropology. Here, it was more explicitly than elsewhere the exceptionalism of India, its seemingly unique characteristics, which determined its point of interest. Caste, village and tradition became the points around which the study of Indian society was organized. The uniqueness and mystery of Indian culture dominated research agendas in the United States in the 1970s. By the late 1980s, the reception of Subaltern Studies in its post-colonial phase owed something to its introduction by Edward Said and something to a wider preoccupation with race and the authentic representation of ethnic community and culture. In the following decade, the study of Indian history in the United States defined itself, and its agendas, according to a powerful post-colonial conformity.

The extent to which Orientalist habits were deeply entrenched in Western traditions of scholarship about India is suggested by the ways in which it developed its own patterns of interpretative conformity. It has seemed to be a widespread assumption in the Western academy that it would be possible to capture the true meaning of Indian society and distil its essence through a single concept, theory or method. This has resulted in an almost literal, certainly rigid insistence upon the reality described by social and analytical categories. This commitment to a single concept which would serve as an explanatory key also rendered the subject susceptible to the capricious swings of intellectual fashion. Thus, caste and village studies dominated the agenda in the 1950s; the circulation of elites in the 1960s; and anthropologists found the key in a theory of factions which Cambridge historians then adopted rather pragmatically in the 1970s. 'Land control', which emerged out of village studies and accounts of revenue policies, provided another major focus in the early 1970s and it led to an increasing concentration on dominant castes and rich peasants.

In the 1960s, the study of Indian history was divided by national traditions and disciplinary boundaries. As intersecting nationalities were brought into relation to each other, so the most interesting research was to be found on the borderlands between disciplines. Nationalist myths and tradition have continued to influence the research on India in each of its major countries of study. Interdisciplinarity, however, has served to fragment and divide the subject and in a curious way to impede dialogue. Whatever the differences in its problematics, its conceptual apparatus and its research methods, interdisciplinary work has by its very nature little reason to respect the boundaries between specialisms and has succumbed to the temptation to treat the whole field as potentially its province. While it has subscribed to the illusion that it has transcended whole specialisms and academic divisions of labour, the proliferation of conceptual frameworks which offer the probability of explaining the whole has reinscribed fresh lines of partition. Indian historiography has thus shown a greater tendency to fragment with its lines of division increasingly organized around a principle of method or theory. This intellectual fragmentation has often allowed theory to be substituted for rhetoric. In their selection of research problems, in their assessment of particular kinds of evidence and in their evaluation of the completeness and plausibility of arguments, historians have appeared in the face of this fragmentation to identify with or base their judgements upon the language, metaphors and emotions associated with particular theoretical and explanatory frameworks. In other works, analytical judgements have been founded upon rhetorical claims which appear sympathetic and a rhetorical common sense which appears more compelling. The effect has been to impede the dialogue and debate within the citadels of professional historians of India across the world at the very point at which similarly emotive responses to an 'authentic national ethos' threaten to obliterate the conventions and procedures of the discipline in India.

Urban history and urban anthropology in South Asia

History and anthropology have been intimately, if somewhat fractiously, intertwined in the investigation of urban themes: the former borrowing promiscuously and not always profitably from the latter; anthropologists, looking increasingly for empirical support and historical depth, have often recoiled in frustration at the historian's fact fetishism. It is no longer possible to examine developments in urban studies within one discipline without reference to the other.

The particular success of urban history in the 1960s was symptomatic of a general crisis in the subject, arising though only in part from the growing interest in and development of the social sciences. While conventional political, constitutional and diplomatic history appeared increasingly narrow in scope, economic history, which for a while had offered a plausible alternative, seemed to confine itself to the application of neoclassical economic theory to data from the past. Some historians began digging in the quarries of the social sciences, framing their research in terms of their languages and taking on board their conceptual apparatus though not necessarily their techniques. Where conventional historical practice appeared to circumscribe the scope of research, a greater openness to the insights derived from sociology and social anthropology opened up an impressive range of fresh questions and lines of historical enquiry. The result was the proliferation of sub-disciplines within the subject: social history, oral history, women's history, demographic history. Urban history ranked among them. A function of the rise of social history, integral to the diversification of the discipline and its practitioners' search for the glamour of theory and rigour.

The consequences have been double-edged: if the scope of historical research has widened, it has also created the possibility of the discipline contributing actively to the discourse of social theory in place of its former role as the provider of information and tester of hypotheses. On the other hand, in their search for rigour, historians have often gone shopping in the supermarkets of the social sciences emptying the shelves indiscriminately before weighing the cost in conceptual confusion and theoretical bankruptcy.

As it developed, urban history projected itself self-consciously, even insistently, as a multidisciplinary enterprise (Hershberg, 1978; Dyos, 1968), a 'field of knowledge, not a single discipline in the accepted sense, but a field in which many disciplines converge, or at any rate are drawn upon' (Dyos, 1982: 31). Historians in pursuit of urban phenomena drew upon or dipped into every manner of social science and even extended as far as geography. In the case of South Asia, developments in anthropology registered an immediate effect upon historical research. The work of some writers on urban South Asia, notably B. S. Cohn and Richard Fox, cannot readily be boxed into either discipline. Some anthropologists drew their material from past times and historical sources (Appadurai, 1981), even as historians found convenient concepts and explanatory frameworks in anthropology, used oral interviews and ventured into more recent periods (Spodek, 1980). Significant trends in anthropology (Fuller, 1986a), from the era of village studies through Dumont to Chicago's Orientalist quest for the mind of South Asia, have each influenced the assumptions and emphases of historians, in both urban studies and more general enquiries, though not in ways which have always or entirely satisfied either.

The first part of this essay will examine the 'problematic' of urban history both generally and in South Asia. Then I shall attempt to set out a schematic chronology of urbanization in India. Finally, I shall examine some of the issues of urbanism as they have impinged upon South Asian history or derived from anthropology.

I

Few branches of the discipline have proved as introspective, as prone to meditate upon their own integrity, assess their progress, track the directions of current research, or investigate their difficulties with concepts, methods and sources as urban history. Yet there are few fields of enquiry which have displayed less clarity about the underlying purpose and problematic of research, with the exception, perhaps, of 'popular culture'. To some extent, its lack of intellectual coherence arose from the fact that urban history constituted 'a focus for a variety of forms of knowledge, not a form of knowledge in itself' (Dyos, 1982). This incoherence remained inconsequential as long as urban historians were required to do no more than concern themselves with events and problems which involved urban places. But a closer definition was always liable to expose its weaknesses.

'The authentic measure of urban history', Dyos declared in the early 1970s, 'is the degree to which it is concerned directly and generically with cities themselves and not with the historical events and tendencies that have been purely incidental to them' (Dyos, 1982: 36). Since then, it would be difficult to deny, the best scholarship to concern itself with cities approached their subjects as if their location were purely incidental (Cannadine, 1982: 217–18). By the end of the 1970s, a sympathetic reviewer of the discipline in Britain, its locus of most active development, was led to admit that 'intellectually' urban history 'stood for very little' (Cannadine, 1982: 207).

The fundamental problem, perhaps, has been to distinguish between those relationships and events observed in towns which may be seen as generically urban and those which may be typified as only incidentally so. Almost every aspect of the city as a social and economic entity can be more readily seen as being constituted by its relationships with the wider world rather than as an autonomous development. Thus, Pocock in his seminal article (Pocock, 1960), having worn the distinction between an urban and a rural sociology to the point of obliteration, concluded that the urban merely manifested the essential features of Indian social life in their purest form. But the conclusion was to overlook the most far-reaching implication of his original insight: that cities cannot usefully be understood as generic social entities, autonomous of the wider social, economic and political structures in which they are embedded. Indeed, Pocock's conclusion to the contrary served in effect to restore the dichotomy between rural and urban sociology which it was the objective of the argument to break down.

If the distinction between what is generically and incidentally urban has appeared to be opaque and arbitrary, the fundamental dichotomy between the urban and the rural has proved no easier to sustain. Just as many small towns dotted across the Indian countryside display no recognizably 'urban' features, so several of the largest industrial cities manifest what may be perceived as rural characteristics. Conversely, the countryside may express the qualities of urbanism, whether in terms of economic activity or social attitudes. The rural–urban divide has been notoriously slippery. Indeed, the categories themselves have to some extent been constituted out of the assumption that rural society was stagnant and backward, forming the passive recipient of the active, dynamic influences of urbanism. Residual assumptions about the city as a generic entity are also likely to impede our understanding of rural society.

It is perhaps significant that 'classical' sociological theory, in the work of Marx, Weber and Durkheim, did not make the town the object of their analysis. The central problem of 'classical' sociology was the rise of capitalism and industrialization in the West. The town as a social form provided only a partial view of the underlying social processes it sought to analyse, even if it was a condition for their development. Subsequent attempts to formulate theories or typologies of towns as social and economic entities have continued to fail. Underlying this failure has been the difficulty of sustaining the town, assumed to be a generic social entity, as an independent variable or protagonist of social change. To deal with the problem of origins or account for historical change, most generalizing arguments and typologies based on the city as a generic form have had to move into the suburbs, the countryside or the wider world beyond (Abrams, 1978).

The lack of a firm conceptual base and an effective theoretical discourse have arisen from and aggravated the weaknesses of the urban as a social category. Not surprisingly, the result has resembled conceptual chaos. In 1966, Bedarida had found in French urban history only 'diversity . . . a series of scattered initiatives . . . at times encroaching on other . . . varieties of approaches. The concept of urban history itself remains confused: sometimes it is restricted to a narrow synonym of town planning, sometimes it is so enlarged as to mean social history at large, the city becoming the framework of the whole society' (Bedarida, 1968: 57). Seventeen years of hectic scholarly activity could only offer many of the same fundamental problems as 'a good agenda for the historians of the next decade' (Bedarida, 1983: 406). This problem was not peculiar to France but lay at the heart of the discipline of urban history.

Few fields of research have been as shrouded in the thickets of concepts capable of consuming the novice and wasting the initiated. This proliferation of terms and typologies has arisen from the quest for a more satisfactory characterization (and typology) of towns; but new concepts have not always engaged the old and all now simply stand alongside each other. A preliminary but scarcely exhaustive list is instructive: centres and networks; rurban settlements and hierarchies of central places; sacred and ceremonial cities; temple towns and Islamic centres; colonial port cities and inland 'port cities'; pre-industrial and industrial, pre-modern and modern towns; generative and parasitic cities; plebeian and patrician cities; open, closed and subject towns. Their proliferation reflects the lack of definition and the diversity of analytical and investigative purpose. All these types are identified, some exclusively, in South Asia, but most tendentiously they are often set against what is known as the 'Western city' and the typologies of urban South Asia sometimes derive their rationale by contrast with the latter.

The conceptual mêlée of urban studies is reflected in the different strategies pursued by historians working in different countries, in spite of Braudel's dictum that 'a town is a town wherever it is'. This diversity of approach and preoccupation has been shaped less by ideological and theoretical debate than by dominant perceptions of the past in those countries – especially the ways in which the particular histories of urbanization were perceived. In Britain, the focus of research was dictated by its image as the workship of the world and by the rapid urbanization of the nineteenth century (Waller, 1982; Dyos, 1968; Cannadine, 1982; Fraser and Sutcliffe, 1983). In North America, where urban history was perhaps more closely identified with and as social history than Britain, the preoccupation lay not with the consequences of industrialization but the patterns of economic opportunity and social mobility (Frisch, 1979; Handlin and Burchard, 1963; Thernstrom, 1964; Thernstrom and Sennett, 1969). Cities represented the new 'frontier', and urban history an arena in which ideas about the openness and fluidity of American society could be tested. Indeed, American historians studying urbanization elsewhere frequently found in social mobility and ethnicity their organizing principles of research (Crew, 1973–4; Sewell, 1976; Lockhard, 1978; Mohl, 1983). By contrast, in Western Europe, the significance of towns and urban growth was located since Marx in the transition from feudalism to capitalism. The focus of urban history has been upon the middle ages while the city in the phase of industrialization has until recently been relatively neglected (Bedarida, 1968; Reulecke and Huck, 1981; Bedarida, 1983). On the other hand, in Russia, where capitalism failed to emerge along the same lines, historians have been preoccupied with why cities lacked the social and institutional characteristics of the West and the bourgeoisie remained too weak to transform the economic and social order (Langer, 1979). Similarly, the assumption that towns were unimportant wherever the rise of capitalism or industrialization has not been seen to have occurred has inevitably handicapped the study of South Asian towns. Thus in one view, the purpose of urban history lies in its value 'as a strategy for illuminating historical understanding in a way especially apposite for modern complex societies' (Fraser and Sutcliffe, 1983: 1). More significantly, because capitalism and industrialism did not eventuate in South Asia along British and West European lines, historians have simply assumed the absence of indigenous conditions for capitalist growth and until recently overlooked the dynamism and sophistication of its economy and the adequacy of its social institutions for the development of capitalism (Perlin, 1983; Washbrook, 1981).

The study of towns has been motivated by two concerns. First, urbanization was taken as an index of economic development and social change, not only for its part in the dissolution of feudalism in the medieval West but also as a measure of modernization in the Third World today. The second concern in urban studies has related broadly to culture. This has been interpreted not simply in terms of the culture of its inhabitants but more generally the urban as a social space is also associated with a state of mind. Of course, perhaps the bravest attempt at developing a conceptual framework for the study of the city as a generic social entity, the Chicago school, was grounded on the assumption that the urban constituted 'a way of life' and a specific mode of consciousness. Its effects are still visible in the work of historians and anthropologists who either ignore or reject the Chicago approach. Taking the urban as a state of mind, some still find in the physical form of the city the representation of the culture as a whole; attribute to particular towns a distinctive, integrative culture; or assume that urban living imparts a specific set of values and attitudes in varying degrees to city dwellers. Thus, it becomes possible to measure the 'assimilation' of rural migrants in terms of their absorption of what are defined as urban characteristics (e.g. factory discipline). Clearly, assumptions about urbanization as a function of economic development pervade cultural studies of urban phenomena, while culturalist notions have penetrated the understanding of the economic functions and character of towns. Studies of both culture and the economy of towns have called for an investigation of occupational groups and labour markets, the urban poor and rural migrants, and their economic contexts. Similarly, if urbanization is understood as a function of economic development, its underlying social processes have often been conceived in cultural terms.

II

Although there has been an impressive body of research in South Asian history related to towns, it has rarely focused specifically upon them. Studies which have refracted most light upon towns and urbanization have usually been attempting to address quite different sets of issues, some as apparently removed from the subject as the politics of nationalism (Bayly, 1975; Ray, 1981; Dobbin, 1973; Masselos, 1974). This was fortuitous and not the result of any debate and eventual rejection of an understanding of the city as a generic entity. Contemporaneously with its development in the West, studies of urban India began to appear rather slowly in the late 1960s (Sinha, 1965; Gillion, 1968; Fox, 1970; Gould, 1965; Dobbin, 1973; Mukherjee, 1970; Bayly, 1971; Lynch, 1967; Rowe, 1973; Singer, 1972), before picking up momentum over the following decade (King, 1976; Lewandowski, 1977; Ballhatchet and Harrison, 1980; Gupta, 1981; Grewal and Banga, n.d. [1983?]; Oldenburg,

1984; Frykenberg, 1986; Kosambi, 1986; Caplan, 1987; Kumar, 1988; Freitag, 1989; Kanwar, 1990; Dossal, 1991; Banga, 1991). Some of these were collections of discrete essays, embodying no single approach, explanatory framework or line of argument in common, and often as variable in quality as the work of the individuals who participated in them.

Since much of what we know about South Asian urban history has come from work which dealt with towns incidentally, sometimes accidentally, it is not surprising that approaches to the study of towns have tended to reflect approaches to the investigation of social and economic changes in India more generally. Three broad strands of scholarship may be identified. First, there are those who have taken urbanization to be largely an adjunct of a larger process of modernization. This is reflected at one level in the assumption that cities formed nodal points of influence from which social, economic and cultural change was brought to their rural hinterlands. At another level, the underlying process of social change was supposed to be unilinear, pushing society inevitably in a single direction, until it assumed the shape of the modern 'West' or gave rise to a recognizable form of capitalism or industrialization. This diffusionist view alone could justify such categories as the pre-modern (Ballhatchet and Harrison, 1980) or pre-industrial city, or, following Hoselitz, the colonial city which was economically parasitic but culturally generative (Hoselitz, 1954), or the colonial port city from where Western culture was supposedly spread through its hinterlands and 'the grand colonial design' implemented (Murphey, 1969). In terms of social relationships within the urban environment, this approach tended to emphasize the breakdown of old institutions and traditional forms of social organization and the transformative effect of Western education and an emergent 'middle class'. The problem with this approach lay not only in the numerous inadequacies of modernization theory, but also in its portrayal of the history of urbanization. For the colonial period probably witnessed the regression, not the advance, of urbanization. The largest cities of the Mughal Empire alone contained about 12 per cent of its population; in 1881, barely 10 per cent lived in towns.

Thus, in another view, the history of the Indian economy and urbanization is conceived in terms of 'underdevelopment' or dependency theory. As colonial rule retarded Indian economic development, so the cities acted as syphons through which the rural surplus could be extracted, its produce processed, consumed and exported, or its profits repatriated to the metropolitan centre. Cities thus formed an important link in the mechanism by which the rural economy was steadily impoverished by the colonial state and the metropolitan interests which it served. The result was a dualism between a dynamic, industrializing modern sector and a passive, stagnant traditional sector, which paralleled the urban–rural divide (Ray, 1985). This dualism was also reproduced in the urban social structure, in this line of reasoning, by the growing influx of rural migrants, who could not be wholly absorbed within the modern sector and formed the pullulating mass of urban poor, crowding into the city slums, prone to criminal and violent behaviour, dysfunctional to the demands of modern industry or immune to the disciplines of class struggle. These were the inhabitants of the informal sector.

Both these lines of argument, producing mirror images of each other, accommodated the history of urbanization within the terms of a counterfactual debate about whether Britain modernized or impoverished the Indian economy. But in a third view, the distinguishing characteristic of the Indian town lay in its Indianness. The key to understanding Indian society lay in identifying factors which were culturally specific to it rather than investigating its character in terms of general social processes and then, if necessary, proceeding to explain the difference. While it is not intended to suggest that the latter approach is epistemologically more valid, the former has tended to consolidate the ethnocentricity of social science, assumed India to constitute a special case and thus served to marginalize Indian studies as a specialism within a broader field of knowledge.

Thus, an important body of research on urban South Asia has been concerned with the uniqueness of Indian towns. This uniqueness is established in three forms. First, the tendency to classify towns as if they reflect 'cultures' – Hindu, Islamic and 'colonial', which may or may not have religion – has helped to confirm the perception of their difference from so-called 'Western' cities and attributed to Indian urbanization an entirely different trajectory of development. Second, Pocock's notion of the inviolability of the rural–urban continuum suggested that urbanization was not the product of Westernization or modernization but Indianization and traditionalization. The city was the repository and the fullest expression of Indian cultural traditions and social forms. Anthropologists and historians alike have in varying degrees been attracted to and developed further arguments about the persistence or even reproduction of rural institutions, social organizations, mentalities and modes of behaviour in the urban setting (Lynch, 1967; Rowe, 1973; Gould, 1965; Arnold, 1980; Chakrabarty, 1983 and 1981; Joshi, 1985). Weber's depiction of the peculiarities of Indian merchants has suggested a third characteristic of Indian urbanization and urban society which set it apart from the supposedly normative pattern of Western Europe. In this view, caste restricted mercantile organizations and diminished their strength in protecting or advancing their interests in relation to the state. The existence of the caste system has nudged historians and anthropologists, far less perceptive than Weber, towards emphasizing the peculiarity and specificity of Indian social and cultural formations. At the same time, the absence of formal mercantile organizations, like the guilds of medieval European cities, through which merchants and artisans might advance their interests, led Weber, and others after him, to assume that they were consistently and effectively subordinated by the state. Yet as Bayly has shown (Bayly, 1978, 1983), not only were merchants able to organize and act across lines of caste but they were able to strengthen their position in the eighteenth century, at the precise moment when apparent political instability and the demands of the successor states, engendered by their 'military fiscalism' (Stein, 1985), should have ensured their collapse. Similar assumptions about the inability of the working classes in the twentieth century to organize or sustain industrial and political action, except for spasmodic protests and spontaneous outbreaks of violence, based upon their rural character and ascriptive mentalities (Arnold, 1981; Chakrabarty, 1981, 1983; Joshi, 1985), appear to be equally untenable. Reviewing the state of the art at the start of this decade, Spodek suggested that the 'future of Indian urban history' lay with the pursuit of 'questions . . . which do not arise in the West' and, indeed, which 'ask the degree to which the Indian city is different from the Western'. For this reason, 'scholars must continue their evaluation of Indian institutions in their indigenous context before making too-hasty comparisons with Western modes of urban–rural evolution'. Yet making such an evaluation in culturally specific terms inside the casing of 'an indigenous context', while striving for 'a definitive view of the culture of Indian urban life', with a conceptual apparatus built from the historical experience of Western Europe, has hindered rather than advanced our understanding of South Asian cities or their contexts.

Nor has the conceptual weakness and theoretical laxity of urban studies lessened the difficulties. In South Asia, as elsewhere, the proliferation of increasingly arcane terms in quest of a more satisfactory characterization and typology of towns has yielded diminishing returns. Many of these categories have been founded on ahistorical or tautological assumptions. Thus, the 'morphology' of towns is sometimes read from the 'world-view', variously and interchangeably defined in terms of religious faith (Hindu, Islamic), national or racial community (European) or indeed political dominance (colonial), of its builders, inhabitants or, more ambitiously, the whole civilization. The difficulty with the 'world-view' as an explanatory category is that it is sometimes difficult to see what it is, what it excluded and frequently what it explains. Almost any eventuality can be brought within its explanatory scope. If the urban form of Madurai was the creation of the Hindu world-view, we would in effect be invited to assume that it had remained intact and unchanging since Kautilya enunciated his principles of town planning in the Arthashastra. When the form of Madurai begins to change in the late nineteenth century, this is ascribed to the substitution of the Hindu world-view by the colonial or European, made possible by the substitution of a category based upon religion by one derived from conquest and rule, or indeed race and region.

Moreover, to sustain the notion of the 'ceremonial city' it becomes necessary to assume, because it cannot be demonstrated, that in terms of its functions '*artha* or material gain was subordinated under the overarching umbrella of *dharma*' (Lewandowski, 1977: 303). The reason for this assumption 'that the economic function of Madurai was to sustain the city as the centre of empire' may just as easily describe nineteenth- and twentieth-century London. Research on medieval South Indian temples, moreover, has tended perhaps to demonstrate the inseparable interdependence of and erode the distinctions between artha and dharma (Hall and Spencer, 1980; Stein, 1960). Similarly, the rebuilding of Madurai by Viswanatha Nayaka in the late sixteenth century was, we are told, undertaken 'allegedly . . . in strict accordance with the principles laid down in the Silpa sastras' (Lewandowski, 1977: 306). Thus the layout of the city can be readily identified with the Hindu world-view, except that is for one minor point: the Nayaks, despite their 'careful attempt to follow urban planning principles laid down in the shastras' for every aspect of the city, built their own palace in the part 'considered inauspicious' in the same texts. The explanation for this eccentric behaviour, we are told, is that 'the Nayak rulers, if they did use the sastras in planning the city, were much less concerned about the cosmological significance of the location of the palaces and adminstrative buildings than they were about maintaining the temple in the centre of the sacred *mandala*'. The explanation is implausible, for whatever the ultimate priorities of the Nayaks, it is scarcely credible that they should choose to make their own palaces the sole and extreme exception to shastric prescription. Nevertheless, it is clear that the circular, if remarkably self-sustaining, logic of Lewandowski's argument is only maintained at the expense of a growing and profound uncertainty that the town was planned according to the Manasara Shilpashastra at all. Finally, if the morphology of Madurai, 'laid out in the shape of a square with a series of concentric streets (squares within squares) culminating in the great temple of Minaksi', derived from a Hindu world-view, why did Varanasi extend along the line of the river?

Similar difficulties have dogged attempts to define the Islamic town or indeed the colonial port city. If the morphology of the Hindu city was determined by the site of the temple and the clusters of caste-based neighbourhoods spreading outwards from it according to hierarchy, the Islamic town was characterized by mohallas which housed and were presided over by nobles and their retainers and dependants. Shahjahanabad was built in 1639 by the eponymous Mughal Emperor, intended as the Dar-ul-khulafat, a monument to the greatness of his rule, and a tribute to the glory of Islam. Its site was chosen not only because it was redolent of the past glories of Muslim power in India, but also for its sanctity as a place of pilgrimage, the site of the tombs of saints, pirs and holy men. Yet the imperial capital was built according to 'a design from the ancient Hindu texts on architecture' (Blake, 1986: 157; Noe, 1986: 239; Blake, 1991). Indeed, from the same Manasara Shilpashastra, from which the Nayaks, the Telegu warrior-kings of the South, may or may not have planned Madurai according to the dictates of their Hindu world-view. Moreover, the cultural significance of the mohalla pattern can easily be exaggerated. It may not have differed radically from the great wadas of the Maratha and Peshwai rulers and their own chieftains and retainers in Pune and elsewhere in western India. Furthermore, this pattern of building had a strategic value. Since many pre-colonial towns were built as assertions of local power and legitimacy and the control over them could be similarly contested, the construction of mohallas and wadas and the settlement around them of trusted chieftains, were a means of securing the king against the enemies within and without the city. South Indian temples also played an important role as fortified centres of power and legitimacy (Stein, 1982).

The colonial city as a cultural construct remains an equally implausible category. In some cases, it arises out of a limited conception of colonialism as a cultural relationship which facilitates the investigation of its 'impact' upon the city, outside the context of its significance in the processes of social change within the whole economy (King, 1980). Moreover, the significant characteristic of the colonial city is its relationship with the 'other' cultural space embodied in the native town. The indigenous and colonial sectors of the city are 'areas of urban space which are perceived, structured and utilized according to value systems unique to the culture in question'. The form of each sector is 'governed by the *institutional system* of each culture', notably, in the case of the native town, caste which 'partially accounts for the physical-spatial form of the city' (King, 1980: 9). In this light, it is instructive to examine how the Black Town in Madras came to be constructed (Neild, 1979). The existing area had been laid out by Indian merchants 'in a neat grid pattern of streets'. This was believed to be a colonial or European use of space. Thus,

To balance the foreign influence of the street pattern, the first Black Town was provided with a centrally-located temple and market; and the various resident castes were allocated separate streets. The British attempted to minimize their interference in the internal affairs of the Black Town, leaving most disputes to be decided by caste heads or influential merchants. In spite of these concessions to local customs . . . the old Black Town . . . failed to achieve a strong identity of its own.

When this town was demolished in the mid-eighteenth century for strategic reasons, its replacement was 'divided into several caste-defined neighbourhoods, each with its separate temple and bazaar' (Neild, 1979: 233–4). The Company's notion of 'foreign influence' and 'local customs', its conception of the fitting arrangement of urban space for the Black Town and of the social organization of its inhabitants clearly served to shape social action, though its effects were clearly neither intended nor predicted. Powers of representation and arbitration vested in 'caste heads and influential merchants' would have moulded the cohesion of social groups around them, serving to confirm the preconceptions with which the colonial rulers began.

At another level, it is plain to see that just as the Islamic Padshahi city of Delhi was constructed according to prescriptions of ancient Hindu texts, so the Indian settlements were not simply physical manifestations of the native mind in colonial cities but also the expression of the perceptions of Company merchants and adventurers of the cultural principles by which natives should, or would, prefer to live.

It is not intended to suggest that the British were able to shape and define every aspect of Indian life from the inception of colonial rule, but to indicate the problem of deducing the form or character of towns or developing an urban taxonomy from the imputed culture of its creators, controllers or residents. Indeed, this factor of culture has often been called into existence by a scholarly claim of privileged access. Thus, colonial port cities are defined by their 'essentially uniform character' throughout South and East Asia. The criterion of this 'uniformity' is that,

A Westerner could feel, to some degree, at home in any of these cities, and could also feel that only a few superficial aspects changed as he moved from one to another of them, across national or colonial boundaries and from one major Asian culture area to another fundamentally different one (Murphey, 1969: 67).

It might be suggested, however, that where 'a Westerner' might 'feel at home' does not offer the most promising material from which to fashion the conceptual tools for the investigation of South Asian towns. It is almost as if the category of the colonial city has emerged from the matching of the fantasies of eighteenth-century Company merchants and twentieth-century social scientists.

The heuristic categories employed in South Asian urban studies and used to develop typologies of Indian towns have arisen from an assumption of their exceptional character, set against some normative pattern of urban development and urban life. Studies of the Hindu, Muslim and colonial cities, corresponding to a flawed periodization of South Asian political history, have rested on the assumption that essential features and traits of these 'cultures' were distilled or realized in the form and structure of the cities to which they gave rise and in the functions of the urban economy. Moreover, these urban studies have done little to interrogate the coherence of the basic social category out of which they attempted to elaborate a typology. Indeed, the most significant attempt to interrogate the coherence of urban phenomena lumped together as an autonomous social category resulted in its resurrection and if anything opened the way for the investigation of Indian towns as a special case (Pocock, 1960). To assume the 'exceptionalism' of the Indian case serves to abstract it from the general discourse of the social sciences. Not only can this distort our understanding of South Asian society, but it can also diminish the scope of social theory which makes so gigantic an exception to its general rules.

III

If the city cannot be taken to constitute a generic social entity, the study of urbanization and urbanism may perhaps best be subsumed under factors operating within society as a whole. It is only in the context of wider social processes that it may be possible to identify the specific role of towns in the changing structures of social and political relations, the significance of patterns of urbanization and, indeed, its distinctive cultural character; or the lack of all these. By focusing single-mindedly upon social forms, the city itself, the neighbourhood, caste, headmen or panchayats, rather than investigating their underlying social processes or their social meaning, it has been possible to conclude that rural ways were simply reproduced in the city. On the other hand, attaching significance to the changed meaning of rural social forms in urban contexts has suggested that these transformations justify studying the city as a social entity and have facilitated its abstraction from the wider social and political forces within and alongside which it operates. This question of change and continuity is perhaps most usefully investigated by understanding the city not as a generic social entity but as a relational category, constituted by and dependent upon its wider political economy.

Pre-colonial Asia, particularly South Asia, was distinguished from Tropical Africa, the Americas and Australasia by the degree of its urbanization, its complex market hierarchies, its long-distance trading connections and its relatively developed class of indigenous merchant capitalists. European travellers to Mughal India were readily impressed by the size and prosperity of its cities. Historians have had to rely heavily on these accounts for 'indigenous Indian sources tended to take the urban phenomenon for granted, and as hardly worthy of notice' (Hambly, 1982: 435). On the other hand, it would be misleading to understand the growth of towns or the nature of social relations within them as a direct reflection of the buoyancy and dynamism of the agrarian economy. The dispersed putting-out networks for artisanal production (Naqvi, 1968; Chaudhuri, 1974), periodic village markets and less frequent, if larger, fairs sustained active and extensive relationships of production and exchange in the countryside without recourse to urban centres (Bayly, 1983).

The flows of trade, power and piety interacted to influence the pattern of urbanization in medieval India. But they did not act independently of each other. Rulers chose their capitals for the religious sanctity of their sites, and the presence of their armies, retainers and courts attracted religious specialists and artisans and boosted the commercial activities of these cities. Commercial expansion helped to generate revenues for the ruler's treasury. Indeed, many of the towns which owed their development to the initiative of the local ruler were chosen for their commercial potential (Chaudhuri, 1978). Temples acted as fortifications for local rulers and their retainers, played a role in the collection and management of revenue and invested in artisanal production (Stein, 1982; Stein, 1960; Hall and Spencer, 1980; Appadurai, 1977). Within these complex interlacings of political and social organization, it is impossible to identify an independent urban variable.

The notion that the mobility of the court and its military adjuncts made nonsense of urbanization has been severely modified. Certainly, the great North Indian cities, Lahore, Delhi and Agra, survived and even prospered despite the periodic withdrawal of courts and military camps (Chandra, 1986). Yet even in the eighteenth century while this political flux led to the frequent movement of capital cities and town-building, most centres survived, if in a streamlined form, the migration of the ruler. Moreover, merchants and artisans were also able to adapt and reorganize at a deeper level, through kinship ties, ascetic sects and pilgrimage networks, all of which effected economic connections which extended beyond boundaries of political influence and survived their redefinition.

The resilience and survival of towns in the last analysis depended upon the character of their rural hinterlands and most were able to function at a more modest level as urban administrative and market centres unless they were destroyed by the collapse of the local agriculture. The reproduction of political power demanded and depended upon investment in the social economy. Shifts in the patronage of rulers and location of 'capitals' led to the redistribution of trade and resources through the North Indian economy. Indeed, since the patronage of shrines, temples and religious foundations was important to the maintenance of the legitimacy of rule, this redistribution applied as much to centres of trade as to places of worship or repositories of learning (Bayly, 1983).

Indeed, the political flux of the eighteenth century may have strengthened the coherence of merchant capital, as it organized to deal with changed conditions, by extending kinship connections, developing new and sophisticated methods of accounting, and adapting systems of insurance. It has also been argued that the 'military fiscalism' of the successor states – the commercial and institutional consequences of extracting increasing amounts of revenue to pay rising military costs – may have given intermediate groups closer command over capital in the eighteenth century and strengthened their social and political position (Stein, 1985). Of course, this fluidity also registered its costs in the poverty and squalor of Mughal towns which travellers frequently reported. The commercial expansion engendered by the dynastic building was likely to attract labourers, soldiers, artisans and religious specialists and leave them stranded when the court and camp moved elsewhere. The political and commercial fluidity which characterized states as well as towns can also be comprehended in terms of the highly fluid and mobile economy upon which it was built. It was characterized by a scarcity of labour and the availability of land. Peasants fled overtaxation; wandering cultivators had to be attracted to villages with the offer of favourable revenue rates; revenue farmers and mercantile elites were forced to invest in agrarian production. The political superstructure which was thrown across this base was forged by diverse sets of negotiated relationships between rulers, local magnates, temples, urban corporations and peasants. These relationships were not negotiated between equal agents but they were strongly reciprocal. Just as mercantile connections linking vast areas of the subcontinent held firm beneath the level of political change, so the state often consisted of a network of fortified centres and a carapace of social and political relationships which sustained them.

The deployment of concepts like the state or the city in an excessively formal usage flattened the contingent and the negotiable character of the social relationships out of which they were fashioned as well as the reciprocities which they entailed. One consequence was simply to diminish the role of cities or to assume that merchants were powerless in the face of the state since urban centres failed to develop their own political entities and self-regulating institutions, beyond the mohalla and the caste panchayat; the case of Ahmedabad, with its European-style guilds, appearing as the exception as always which confirmed the exceptionalism of India's pattern of social change (Gillion, 1968; Hambly, 1982: 446–8). Another effect of this formalism lies in the notion of the Islamic or Indo-Muslim city, and the attempt to relate the essential characteristics of Islamic culture to the form and function of the city. Even in the heyday of the Mughal Empire, its metropolitan centres were influenced by local traditions of town-building and architecture and shaped by localized social and political relationships. Delhi, Lucknow, Agra and Lahore, let alone its lesser centres, counted a minority of Muslims among their populaces. At the level of the city as well as the state, Mughal rule depended upon the accommodation and collaboration of its Hindu subjects. It could not always develop a purely Islamic legitimacy. It is, therefore, not only the 'enormous diversity of urban economies and urban cultures' in South Asia which makes it 'as imprudent to seek for a model Hindu city as it would for a model Indo-Islamic one', but also the fact that the best that might be claimed for such a paradigm is its 'partially Islamic character' (Hambly, 1982: 438–9).

The first century of colonial rule probably witnessed some degree of de-urbanization and certainly a redistribution of urban centres. In the eighteenth century, the decline of the great Mughal capitals had been accompanied by the diffusion of smaller towns across the subcontinent, possibly inhabited by an even higher proportion of the population at the end of the century than at the beginning (Bayly, 1983). Until the 1920s, the proportion of the urban population in South Asia barely rose above 10 per cent. The old court centres declined and those which survived could no longer support the same scale of urban economy. Madras did not recover its population levels of the 1780s until the 1850s (Washbrook, 1981). In 1901, after half a century of gradual growth, the population of Pune was half the level of the 1780s (Divekar, n.d. [1983?]). In North India, the expansion of commercial production and the export trade, as well as the exertions of the Bengal Army, played an important role in the growth of inland towns in the early nineteenth century. Yet these towns were mainly dependent on their commercial and revenue functions and did not develop as more diversified centres of artisanal production (Bayly, 1983). For the most part, the decline of court consumption, the effects of deindustrialization on artisanal communities, the gradual recovery of adminstrative functions from revenue farmers and the imposition of state monopolies on the most valuable areas of commerce, and the separation of temples from their commercial and productive functions, reduced the dynamism of mercantile capital and altered the fragile balance upon which urban economies rested.

On the other hand, the expansion of British power shifted the centre of urban growth from the Mughal heartland to their seaboard footholds at Calcutta, Madras and Bombay. By the 1820s, these Presidency capitals were the largest cities in the subcontinent, with the possible exception of Lucknow and Lahore. Their early growth was predicated largely on their administrative function and the rapid expansion of exports. In the early nineteenth century, operating in the wake of the Company's mercantilism, European traders came increasingly to dominate the business of these ports. But there was no uniformity in the relationship between Europeans and Indians in these 'colonial port cities'. In Calcutta, the oldest base of the Company's commercial and political activity was also its firmest, and here racial domination and exclusion were most overt. In Bombay, where the British penetration of the hinterland, dominated by their strongest rivals, had been slow and established late, business and politics were characterized by collaboration.

The major impetus behind urbanization in this period was provided by the growth of the bureaucracy, the diffusion of law courts and the spread of educational institutions through which the talented, ambitious and wealthy might seek advancement. Provincial capitals and the location of district headquarters provided an important stimulus to urban growth and their relocation could have a decisive effect on particular towns. This was as true of the smallest sadr towns of Bengal (Islam, 1980) as of larger provincial centres. The stagnation of Pune in the nineteenth century was not only a reflection of the impoverished and introverted Deccan economy over which it presided but a consequence of the removal of its former political and administrative functions to Bombay. Similarly, the transfer of the administrative capital of the Northwest Provinces from Lucknow to Allahabad ensured the decline of the most celebrated of Indian court centres (Oldenburg, 1984; Ganju, 1980).

All these factors worked most consistently in favour of the Presidency capitals in the nineteenth century. In the early nineteenth century, the British attempted to exert greater control over these cities. From the mid-eighteenth century onwards, in Calcutta and Madras, and in early nineteenth-century Bombay, the needs of defence and fortifications encouraged some measure of town planning and led to the separation of European enclaves and in effect the creation of native towns. Closer attention was paid to the policing of the native town but these efforts concentrated rather more on watching its boundaries albeit with a sleepy eye than keeping a tight rein on its back streets and by-lanes. The growth of the colonial bureaucracy in Madras undermined the political influence of the Indian dubash and in general Europeans assumed greater control of town government. Yet by the 1830s and 1840s, Indian commercial magnates were being appointed as Justices of the Peace, the effective municipal authority in Bombay (Dobbin, 1973). Further 'municipal' initiatives took the form of conveyancing and sanitary policies in Calcutta and Dacca. But these should not be seen as attempts to control and govern, so much as a spasmodic response to the persistent fear of epidemic diseases, especially after the outbreak of cholera in 1817 when it assumed the proportions of a general panic in Dacca (Ahmed, 1980: 138–9; Sinha, 1965). For the most part, the policy of the colonial state towards sanitation was to leave the cesspools and open drains well alone and simply avoid the native town. The fashion for suburban living in Madras arose from the belief that it was 'more healthful' for 'mortality rates in the Black Town and other urban and village localities . . . were alarmingly high'. The suburban compound, it is said, was considered 'essential for the health and survival of Europeans in the hostile tropical climate of South India' – though not, evidently, for the survival of Indians (Neild, 1979). These forms of urban living have sometimes been conceived in terms of the imperatives of European culture. Yet if we need to investigate the underlying culture of these circumstances, we should perhaps more usefully examine the discourse within which Europeans and Indian elites judged the mimimum standard of life or the tolerable risk of death which the poorer residents of the town might endure.

The notion that the early nineteenth century saw the rise of 'colonial urbanism' is probably misleading. In fact, to the extent that fresh initiatives were manifested in the Presidency capitals they were a response to external factors which had little to do with the urban arenas themselves: the pressures of war and political conflict; changing ideologies of imperialism which were by no means immediately given practical effect; and the heightening commercial rivalries in the context of the depression of the 1820s and 1830s. There is little that is specifically or exclusively urban about colonialism. Its effects upon towns were the consequence of its impact on the political and economic structure as a whole: the definition of new political arenas and the development of bureaucratic structures, the consequences of the considerable weight of the revenue demand and the increasing subordination of mercantile capital.

In the later nineteenth century, as the depression of the 1830s and 1840s began to lift, new factors came to bear upon urban growth.

Railways stimulated the commercial activity of some cities and obliterated others, and developed some towns as railheads and bulking centres. The expansion of cash-cropping and the export trade in primary produce, flourishing in the context of favourable exchange rates and rising prices, the continued growth of the colonial administration and the establishment or expansion of cantonments and garrisons, and the early beginnings of industrialization also contributed to the growth of towns. But the weight of these factors needs to be placed in perspective. The rate of urbanization between 1881 and 1921 was extremely sluggish. Moreover, it would be misleading to postulate a direct connection between industrialization and urbanization. Political advantage rather than comparative cost enabled the jute mills of Bengal to compete effectively with the handloom weavers (Morris, 1984; Chandavarkar, 1985), while in sugar, the khandsaris held out effectively against the millowners (Amin, 1984). In the prosperous tracts of the Punjab which registered high rates of economic growth, small-scale industries flourished without ever leading to the expansion of factory production. Many processing industries were more conveniently located in the countryside than in the towns. Finally, the agrarian structure was by no means transformed, but rather shored up and preserved, by the commercial expansion and buoyancy. This was to have important consequences for the subsequent pattern of town–country relations in the following decades.

The depression of the 1930s marks another turning point in the history of urbanization in South Asia. The characteristic feature of the depression in India was the withdrawal of credit from the countryside. This was partly a consequence of the tightening of the money supply as a result of deflationary policies of the state and the repatriation of capital by the British managing agencies, whose role had been crucial in the maintenance and reproduction of rural credit supplies. In addition, dramatically falling prices and the difficulties of recovering dues in the countryside, on the one hand, and the protection offered by tariffs in some industries and by the disruption of international trade, along with the flow of cheap labour, attracted capital increasingly to the towns (Tomlinson, 1979; Baker, 1984).

In the late nineteenth century, growing demographic and commercial pressures on the land had forced smallholders to seek work in the towns. Most migrants travelled short distances in search of work to nearby towns or neighbouring districts, where there was a demand for agricultural labour, and returned to their villages with their cash earnings to pay off their debts or to buy seed. A small proportion migrated seasonally or even annually to the large cities. During the depression, while capital migrated to the towns, many smallholders found their rural base was shrinking. Scarce credit and higher interest rates only made it more necessary to find wage employment in the cities. The demand for labour in large-scale industries scarcely increased in this period. However, the large cities offered more diversified economic opportunities (Baker, 1984; Chandavarkar, 1983). In the 1930s, the population of towns of over 100,000 increased by almost three-quarters while the total urban population increased by less than a third. In the following decade, the disruptions of food and other necessary supplies to the towns, inflation, wartime scarcities and famine forced the state to organize grain rationing and public-distribution systems to obviate the threat of large-scale discontent in the major towns. These welfare services made the largest towns even more attractive to migrants from the countryside (Baker, 1984). From the 1930s, onwards, the largest cities recorded the fastest growth rates, the smallest towns entered decline or stagnated. Since the 1930s, the populations of the largest cities have multiplied ten-fold. While the absolute increase of India's urban population since the 1960s has been staggering, most of this increase has been concentrated in cities of over 100,000 people (Census of India).

Clearly, the basis for urban and industrial growth of the 1930s was far from secure. The agrarian structure lacked the dynamism to meet the needs of expanding industry whether in terms of supply or demand. Until the 1930s, the fluctuations of the urban economy had led to the movement of labour between town and country. During the 1930s and increasingly in the following decades, expanding urban opportunities have drawn in the slack of the countryside and their tightening has left labour stranded in the towns. As their rural resources have shrunk, so migrants have found it more prudent to seek employment in the largest cities, where contraction in one area of the urban economy may still leave them the possibility of finding work in another. However, the increasing segmentation of the labour market and barriers to movement between them have narrowed and complicated their options (Holmstrom, 1984; Harriss, 1986). On the other hand, rural migrants to the cities should not be viewed simply as the starving refugees of the countryside fleeing to the abundant economic opportunites of the city. Most migrants to the cities still attempt to maintain their village connections and those who are most securely employed probably continue to be most likely to succeed while the loss of rural ties is most generally the result of distress. Moreover, the rate of urbanization remains slow: the rural population having grown twice as fast as the urban since 1941. Nevertheless, the rapid growth of India's largest cities is probably symptomatic of agrarian decline and rural deprivation rather than economic development.

IV

The predominant concern of urban anthropology appears to have been with a complex of issues around the ways of life and states of mind, the attitudes and social organization of peasants in cities: their attitudes to work, the communities they create, their social and political conflicts (Mangin, 1970; Southall, 1973; Hannerz, 1980). These questions, however hard they press, in the light of recent patterns of urbanization, have until recently been largely neglected by South Asian historians. The effect of this body of anthropological work has been to diversify and broaden the scope of issues which historians might address: kinship, 'sociability', neighbourhood and community relations, patterns of residence, the experience of migration, responses to new rhythms and discipline of work.

But in using this work, there have been two related sets of problems. First, the thrust of this literature, the framework within which it is conceived, has been related to the 'urbanization' of the peasant. It has been difficult to escape the progressivist and evolutionary assumptions of questions posed in this way or their implicit categories of modernization. What we seek to ask in effect is how far peasants were transformed into working classes, how far the urban environment and those who inhabit it are modernized, how far South Asia became like Western Europe or North America. Of course, historians and anthropologists have wrestled with modernization theory, but its implicit assumptions and categories, even if overtly rejected, have not easily been pinned to the mat. In some cases, the method of reasoning can be circular as can its categories: we decide what institutions and forms of behaviour are specifically 'rural' or 'traditional' and then look for them in the city.

The second difficulty arises from the emphasis not upon change but rather upon continuity. Pocock's influential essay stressed continuities between rural and urban social organization in opposition to the tendency to comprehend urbanization as a function of modernization or Westernization. Subsequently, urban anthropologists, setting out to test the 'continuity' hypothesis, worked from the same initial assumption that Indian cities were a special case, expressions of a timeless Indian mind with distinctively Indian patterns of behaviour and modes of consciousness (Rowe, 1973; Lynch, 1967). Since the exceptionalism of India was assumed, it did not have to be either demonstrated or more closely defined.

Underlying both sets of arguments was a central focus on the caste system. Since the caste system is most obviously specific and distinctive, cursory gestures in its direction have been sufficient to obviate the need to examine the subject in the light of general social processes and through the interrogation of conventional social theory. On the other hand, studies which interpret general or 'comparable' social processes as modernization have tended to use the breakdown or transformation of caste as the yardstick for measuring social change. From opposite perspectives, perhaps mirror-images of each other, both lines of approach have begged the question of how different conditions or sets of circumstances reconstitute and sustain or else modify old social forms within new contexts and inject into them changed social meanings. Indeed, caste has sometimes so dominated the study of rural migrants into urban and industrial contexts that it has obscured some of the most important questions. As Chris Fuller remarks, for instance, 'there is very little anthropological literature which looks in detail at the ways in which Indian urban dwellers . . . maintain material links to villages' (Fuller, 1986b). Yet this issue lies at the core of any assessment of migrant responses to the city, the nature of urban identities or, more generally, if one chose, the structural similarities and functional necessities of the city and the village.

Perhaps a useful starting point in the investigation of 'peasants in cities' is to consider its purpose. Most frequently, migration was part of a peasant strategy to maintain a base in the village. Peasants sought cash earnings to pay off their dues to the state or the moneylender or to meet the cost of investment in land or in dowries. These cash earnings were often obtained through field labour or petty industrial employment in neighbouring districts, but among those peasants who went to the towns, indeed at any level of rural society, there were few who were entirely new to them. As a formulation, 'peasants in cities' presupposes and then exaggerates the dichotomy.

Migration to the city involved a wide variety of forms of rural–urban links. The situation of long-distance migrants from the Chota Nagpur plateau and west Bihar to the Assam tea gardens, sometimes under conditions resembling coercion, with a different relationship between workplace and village, diverged from the situation of migrants to the major industrial centres. Even among the latter, there was no uniformity of pattern. Textile workers in Coimbatore lived in their villages and commuted daily to work; a sizeable proportion of Bombay's workers migrated long distances and returned to their villages once a year.

Few migrants went to the city in isolation; they usually moved within the framework of wider kinship, caste and village connections. It was more common for the male members of the peasant household, and then, too, only some of them, to go to the city in search of work, than for whole families to emigrate. It was intended, indeed expected, that workers would remit some of their earnings to their families at the village base. But this could not always be fulfilled: wages were low, conditions of employment poor and uncertain, and costs of food, housing and other necessaries relatively high. Usually, urban wage employment simply enabled peasant households to roll their debts and to maintain their position in the village. Cases of social mobility through industrial employment were rare. For the urban worker, village connections offered an insurance system, a social bulwark against the instability of the urban economy. The cost of the reproduction of the labour force was thus at least partially met in the countryside; but an abundance of cheap labour in the towns enabled employers to minimize their fixed costs, manipulate their labour supplies and production schedules to meet short-term fluctuations of demand and thus perpetuate the instability of the urban economy.

Frequently, employers complained that workers were insufficiently committed to the urban, industrial setting; that it was difficult to get them to work on time or to work hard enough; or that their rural connections and mentalities encouraged absenteeism. These complaints generally arose from the difficulties of enforcing labour discipline to their satisfaction and sometimes expressed frustration at their failure to get more work for less pay out of their labour force. On the other hand, because peasants had migrated to the city with the intention of preserving their rural base, they were, in one sense, highly committed to their workplace, and repeatedly showed both ability and determination to coordinate and sustain industrial action to defend their position at work. Of course, whether they could effect this consistently varied with the strength of their neighbourhood and village connections, their bargaining power at the workplace as well as contingent political circumstances. Even in the case of long-distance migrants to the largest industrial centres, to Bombay, Calcutta and Jamshedpur, these village connections were maintained over several generations, as workers migrated as early adults and returned to their villages in old age, so that it becomes very difficult to separate the urban from the rural in the social economy of working-class families.

To a large extent, the social organization of migrant workers was shaped by the chronic instability of urban growth in South Asia. Jobbers, for instance, have been seen as an institution specific to India (although the term was Lancastrian), primarily labour recruiters and contractors, and cultural mediators between British managers and illiterate, rural workers. But their disciplinary function was paramount: to control labour at the workplace and to expand and contract the labour supply according to need and above all to reconcile these twin imperatives. They have often been described as village headmen in the city and they have often been built up into awesome figures of social control. In fact, their power varied with the industry, indeed with the labour process, and sometimes it was not very impressive at all. To maintain their effectiveness as agents of discipline and control at work, they were forced to build up a range of connections in the neighbourhood. But the more widely dispersed their activities, the more vulnerable their overextended empires could become. Indeed, in Bombay, it was when their efficiency as agents of labour discipline was seen to decline in the 1930s that the millowners sought gradually to write their role out of existence. But this has been more often understood as an attempt to modernize management rather than the tightening of control.

The notion of urban village communities or rural cities is not only a tautology, as Chris Fuller points out, but it is also unhelpful, if not actively misleading, about the nature of working-class neighbourhoods in Indian cities. For the social relationships of the neighbourhood were not inherited from the countryside but were forged anew from materials created by the particular social, economic and political contexts of the cities. Clearly, caste played an important role in the formation of the labour force. Migration occurred within the framework of kinship. Jobbers recruited along lines of caste, kinship and village connections. These ties were important in organizing for urban survival: finding work, housing and credit. Not surprisingly, caste clusters formed around particular occupations and in neighbourhoods. Caste connections and claims were also used to restrict entry into certain occupations and thereby to protect skills and wages or to strengthen the position of kinsmen within the workforce.

But there is also considerable ambiguity about the role of caste. In Bombay, Maratha weavers refused to work with Harijans because they claimed that the yarn had sometimes to be sucked from the bobbin to the shuttle. But they did not feel so defiled by Muslim weavers who were firmly established in the weaving sheds; nor did their caste fellows in spinning, who commanded less bargaining power, feel polluted by their Harijan colleagues. When the government built public latrines in Chittagong, the residents of the town burnt them stating that they preferred to defile the streets rather than their caste purity, but underlying this was a more earthy resentment of the sanitation tax they felt was bound to follow (Islam, 1980). Similarly, Gould implies that rural migrants realized the instrumental value of caste and reinterpreted it accordingly (Gould, 1970), although he did not develop this point in his more detailed empirical study of Lucknow rickshawallas (Gould, 1965). Caste, kinship, village and regional identities came increasingly to be used interchangeably. Moreover, most city dwellers were drawn into broader forms of associations which diminished the coherence of caste, both in a relational and in a systematic form. On the other hand, the policies of employers frequently imparted meaning to caste associations by attempting to diversify the ethnic composition of their workforce in order to reduce its industrial strength. It was often among the most marginal groups in the urban economy, casually employed or socially disadvantaged, that competition for jobs and other resources was fierce and caste identities and conflicts often at their strongest.

Similarly, historians have been too easily impressed by the power and control of local magnates, neighbourhood leaders and caste elders (Bayly, 1971; Lynch, 1967) and by moments when modernization seemed to undermine caste authority (e.g. Lynch, 1967; Dobbin, 1973; Conlon, 1977; Leonard, 1978). Yet these represented not so much the subversion of caste identities or a challenge to caste authority, but efforts, invariably too little and too late, to exert power and social control which had not been very effective to begin with. Otherwise, we would have to conclude that caste was breaking down continuously in Bombay since the early nineteenth century.

'Urban village communities' in so far as they existed were also constituted by the exigencies of housing, credit and labour markets in the cities. For instance, the uncertainties of employment required workers to report at mill gates every morning in order to be hired, but the inadequacies and expense of transport encouraged them to live near to their place of work. Power and influence in the neighbourhood derived from access to or command over housing, credit and work or other vital resources. Jobbers were often selected for their influence in the neighbourhood and several of the managerial cadres were deeply involved in organizing and servicing the needs of workers within as well as without the workplace. Moreover, the social organization of the urban neighbourhood cannot simply be understood in terms of patronage or power relations which flow in one direction. There were several locations of power and influence in the neighbourhood, some of them deriving from patterns of association within them and all of them operating under constraints. Social and political balances were continually negotiated, contested and reproduced between them.

'Peasants in cities' have often been characterized as politically and socially passive. But Indian migrant workers have often shown their ability to effect large-scale industrial action for long periods with impressive frequency. Recently, the migrant character of the workforce has been deployed to explain their spasmodic violence or even their propensity for criminal activity (Arnold, 1981; Chakrabarty, 1981; Joshi, 1985). But in these characterizations, historians have often simply taken over the perceptions of contemporary civil servants, employers and policemen. Historians and anthropologists continue to vigorously pronounce 'the culture of poverty' dead; but 'the culture of poverty' lives relentlessly on.

* * * * *

If the expansion of social history since the 1960s has left a legacy, it has been to interrogate social theory from its own perspective, partly by opening up some of its assumptions and categories to empirical research. The practice of urban history has helped to expose the inadequacies of the notion that the city formed a generic social entity, the foundation of most general theories of urbanization and urbanism, and it has increasingly suggested that towns and social relations apparently 'within' them are more satisfactorily comprehended in terms of the larger contexts in which they are constituted. Perhaps one way forward for urban studies may lie in looking at general social processes which involve and impinge upon towns in order to develop a series of middle-order generalizations about them to identify their specifically 'urban' content. But such an enterprise is doomed to fail, in terms of South Asian studies, if it should be predicated upon some generalized notion of the uniqueness rather than the comparability of South Asian society.

BIBLIOGRAPHY

Abrams, P. 1984. 'Towns and Economic Growth: Some Theories and Problems' in *Towns in Societies: Essays in Economic History and Historical Sociology* ed. P. Abrams and E. A. Wrigley, pp. 9–34. Cambridge.

Ahmed, S. U. 1980. 'Urban Problems and Government Policies: A Case Study of the City of Dacca, 1810–1830' in *The City in South Asia* ed. Ballhatchet and Harrison.

Amin, S. 1984. *Sugarcane and Sugar in Gorakhpur.* Delhi.

Appadurai, A. 1977. 'Kings, Sects and Temples in South India, 1300–1750' *Indian Economic and Social History*, 14(1), 47–74. New Delhi.

1981. *Worship and Conflict under Colonial Rule: A South Indian Case.* Cambridge.

Arnold, D. 1980. 'Industrial Violence in Colonial India' *Comparative Studies in Society and History*, (22)2, 234–55.

Baker, C. J. 1984. *An Indian Rural Economy, 1880–1955: The Tamil Nad Countryside.* Delhi and Oxford.

Ballhatchet, K. and J. B. Harrison. 1980. *The City in South Asia: Pre-Modern and Modern.* London.

Banga, I. (ed.). 1991. *The City in Indian History.* Delhi.

Bayly, C. A. 1971. 'Local Control in Indian Towns' *Modern Asian Studies*, 5, 289–311.

1975. *The Local Roots of Indian Politics: Allahabad, 1880–1920.* Oxford.

1983. *Rulers, Townsmen and Bazars: North Indian Society in the Age of British Expansion, 1770–1870*. Cambridge.

Bedarida, F. 1968. 'The Growth of Urban History in France: Some Methodological Trends' in *The Study of Urban History* ed. H. J. Dyos. London.

1983. 'The French Approach to Urban History: An Assessment of Recent Methodological Trends' in *The Pursuit of Urban History* ed. Fraser and Sutcliffe.

Blake, S. P. 1986. 'Cityscape of an Imperial Capital: Shahjahanabad in 1739' in *Delhi Through the Ages* ed. Frykenberg.

1991. *Shahjahanabad: The Sovereign City in Mughal India, 1639–1739*. Cambridge.

Cannadine, D. 1982. 'Urban History in the United Kingdom: The "Dyos Phenomenon" and After' in *Exploring the Urban Past: Essays in Urban History by H. J. Dyos* ed. D. Cannadine and D. Reeder. Cambridge.

Caplan, L. 1987. *Class and Culture in Urban India: Fundamentalism in a Christian Community*. Oxford.

Census of India, 1881–1981. Reports and Tables. London, Calcutta and Delhi.

Chakrabarty, D. 1981. 'Communal Riots and Labour: Bengal's Jute Mill-Hands in the 1890s' *Past and Present*, 91, 140–69.

1983. 'On Deifying and Defying Authority: Managers and Workers in the Jute Mills of Bengal, circa. 1890–1940' *Past and Present*, 100, 124–46.

Chandavarkar, R. S. 1983. 'Labour and Society in Bombay, 1918–1940: Workplace, Neighbourhood and Social Organization' unpublished PhD thesis. Cambridge.

1985. 'Industrialization in India before 1947: Conventional Approaches and Alternative Perspectives' *Modern Asian Studies*, 19(3), 623–68.

Chandra, Satish. 1986. 'Cultural and Political Role of Delhi, 1675–1725' in *Delhi Through the Ages* ed. Frykenberg.

Chaudhuri, K. N. 1974. 'The Structure of the Indian Textile Industry in the Seventeenth and Eighteenth Centuries' *Indian Economic and Social History Review*, 11(2–3), 127–82.

1978. 'Some Reflections on Town and Country in Mughal India' *Modern Asian Studies*, 12(1), 77–96.

Conlon, F. F. 1977. *A Caste in a Changing World: The Chitrapur Saraswat Brahmins, 1700–1935*. Berkeley, Calif.

Crew, D. 1973–4. 'Definitions of Modernity: Social Mobility in a German Town, 1880–1901' *Journal of Social History*, 7, 51–72.

Divekar, V. D. n.d. [1983?]. 'Political Factors in the Rise and Decline of Cities in Pre-British India – with Special Reference to Pune' in *Studies in Urban History* ed. Grewal and Banga.

Dobbin, C. 1973. *Urban Leadership in Western India, Politics and Communities in Bombay City, 1840–1885*. Oxford.

Dossal, M. 1991. *Imperial Designs and Indian Realities: The Planning of Bombay City, 1845–75*. Delhi.

Dyos, H. J. 1968. 'Agenda for Urban Historians' in *The Study of Urban History* ed. H. J. Dyos. London.

1982. *Exploring the Urban Past: Essays in Urban History by H. J. Dyos* ed. D. Cannadine and D. Reeder. London.

Fox, R. (ed.). 1970. *Urban India: Society, Space and Image.* Duke University, Monograph and Occasional Papers Series, Number Ten.

Fraser, D. and A. Sutcliffe (eds.). 1983. *The Pursuit of Urban History.* London.

Freitag, S. B. (ed.). 1989. *Culture and Power in Banaras: Community, Performance and Environment, 1800–1980.* Delhi.

Frisch, M. 1979. 'American Urban History as an Example of Recent Historiography' *History and Theory,* 18(3), 350–77.

Frykenberg, R. (ed.). 1986. *Delhi Through the Ages: Urban History, Culture and Society.* Delhi.

Fuller, C. J. 1986a. 'Progress and Problems in the Anthropology of South Asia'. Paper presented to the ESRC Review Conference on Modern South Asian Studies, Cambridge, 4–5 July.

  1986b. 'A Selective Review of the Urban Anthropology of Urban India'. Paper presented to the South Asian Anthropologists Group Meeting, London, 19–20 September.

Ganju, M. 1980. 'The Muslims of Lucknow, 1919–1939' in *The City in South Asia* ed. Ballhatchet and Harrison.

Gillion, K. 1968. *Ahmedabad: A Study in Indian Urban History.* Berkeley, Calif.

Gould, H. A. 1965. 'Lucknow Rickshawallas: The Social Organization of an Occupational Category' *International Journal of Comparative Sociology,* 6(1), 24–47.

  1970. 'Some Preliminary Observations Concerning the Anthropology of Industrialization' in *Peasants in Cities* ed. Mangin.

Grewal, J. S. and I. Banga (eds.). n.d. [1983?]. *Studies in Urban History.* Amritsar.

Gupta, N. 1981. *Delhi Between Two Empires, 1803–1931.* Delhi.

Hall, K. and G. R. Spencer. 1980. 'The Economy of Kanchipuram: A Sacred Centre in Early South India' *Journal of Urban History,* 6(2), 127–51.

Hambly, G. R. 1982. 'Towns and Cities: Mughal India' in *The Cambridge Economic History of India,* vol. I, *c.1250–c.1750* ed. T. Raychaudhuri and I. Habib. Cambridge.

Handlin, O. and J. Burchard (eds.). 1963. *The Historian and the City.* Cambridge, Mass.

Hannerz, U. 1980. *Exploring the City.* New York.

Harriss, J. 1986. 'The Working Poor and the Labour Aristocracy in a South Indian City: A Descriptive and Analytical Account' *Modern Asian Studies,* 20(1).

Haynes, D. 1991. *Rhetoric and Ritual in Colonial India: The Shaping of a Public Culture in Surat City, 1852–1928.* Berkeley and Los Angeles.

Hershberg, T. 1978. 'The New Urban History: Toward an Interdisciplinary History of the City' *Journal of Urban History,* 5(1), 3–40.

Holmstrom, M. 1984. *Industry and Inequality: The Social Anthropology of Indian Labour.* Cambridge.

Hoselitz, B. 1954. 'Generative and Parasitic Cities' *Economic Development and Cultural Change,* 3, 278–94.

Islam, M. S. 1980. 'Life in the Mufassal Towns of Nineteenth Century Bengal' in *The City in South Asia* ed. Ballhatchet and Harrison.

Joshi, C. 1985. 'Bonds of Community, Ties of Religion: Kanpur Textile Workers in the Early Twentieth Century' *Indian Economic and Social History Review*, 22(3), 251–80.

Kanwar, P. 1990. *Imperial Simla: The Political Culture of the Raj*. Delhi.

King, A. D. 1976. *Colonial Urban Development: Culture, Social Power and Environment*. London.

    1980. 'Colonialism and the Development of the Modern Asian City: Some Theoretical Considerations' in *The City in South Asia* ed. Ballhatchet and Harrison.

Kosambi, M. 1986. *Bombay in Transition: The Growth and Social Ecology of a Colonial City, 1880–1980*. Stockholm.

Kumar, N. 1988. *The Artisans of Banaras: Popular Culture and Identity, 1880–1986*. Princeton, NJ.

Langer, L. N. 1979. 'The Historiography of the Pre-Industrial Russian City' *Journal of Urban History*, 5(2), 209–40.

Leonard, K. 1978. *Social History of an Indian Caste: The Kayasths of Hyderabad*. Berkeley and Los Angeles.

Lewandowski, S. 1977. 'Changing Form and Function in the Ceremonial and Colonial Port City in India: An Historical Analysis of Madurai and Madras' *Modern Asian Studies*, 11(2), 183–212.

Lynch, O. M. 1967. 'Rural Cities in India: Continuities and Discontinuities' in *India and Ceylon: Unity and Diversity* ed. P. Mason. Oxford.

Mangin, W. (ed.). 1970. *Peasants in Cities: Readings in the Anthropology of Urbanization*. Boston.

Masselos, J. C. 1974. *Towards Nationalism: Group Affiliations and the Politics of Public Associations*. Bombay.

Mohl, R. 1983. 'The New Urban History and its Alternatives: Some Reflections on Recent US Scholarship on the Twentieth Century City' *Urban History Yearbook*, 19–28.

Morris, M. D. 1984. 'Industrialization in South Asia, 1757–1947' in *The Cambridge Economic History of India*, vol. II, *c.1750–c.1970* ed. D. Kumar. Cambridge.

Mukherjee, S. N. 1970. 'Class, Caste and Politics in Calcutta, 1815–1838' in *Elites in South Asia* ed. E. Leach and S. N. Mukherjee. Cambridge.

Murphey, Rhoads. 1969. 'Traditionalism and Colonialism: Changing Urban Roles in Asia' *Journal of Asian Studies*, 29(1), 67–84.

Naqvi, H. K. 1968. *Urban Centres and Industries in Upper India, 1556–1803*. Bombay.

Neild, Susan M. 1979. 'Colonial Urbanism: The Development of Madras City in the Eighteenth and Nineteenth Centuries' *Modern Asian Studies*, 13(2), 217–46.

Noe, M. V. 1986. 'What Happened to Mughal Delhi: A Morphological Survey' in *Delhi Through the Ages* ed. Frykenberg.

Oldenburg, V. T. 1984. *The Making of Colonial Lucknow, 1856–1877*. Princeton, NJ.

Perlin, F. 1983. 'Proto-Industrialization and Pre-colonial South Asia' *Past and Present*, 98, 30–95.

Pocock, D. F. 1960. 'Sociologies: Urban and Rural' *Contributions to Indian Sociology*, 4, 63–81.

Ray, R. K. 1981. *The Urban Roots of Indian Nationalism*. Calcutta.

1985. *Social Conflict and Political Unrest in Bengal, 1875–1927*. Delhi.

Reulecke, J. and G. Huck, 1981. 'Urban History Research in Germany: Its Development and Present Condition' *Urban History Yearbook*.

Rowe, W. D. 1973. 'Caste, Kinship and Association in Urban India' in *Urban Anthropology* ed. Southall.

Sewell, W. 1976. 'Social Mobility in a Nineteenth-Century European City' *Journal of Interdisciplinary History*, 7, 217–33.

Singer, M. 1972. *When a Great Tradition Modernizes: An Anthropological Approach to Indian Civilization*. New York.

Sinha, P. 1965. *Nineteenth Century Bengal: Aspects of Social History*. Calcutta.

Southall, A. (ed.). 1973. *Urban Anthropology: Cross-Cultural Studies of Urbanization*. New York.

Spodek, H. 1980. 'Studying the History of Urbanization in India' *Journal of Urban History*, 6(3), 251–95.

Stein, B. 1960. 'The Economic Functions of a Medieval South Indian Temple' *Journal of Asian Studies*, 19(2), 163–76.

1982. 'Towns and Cities: The Far South' in *The Cambridge Economic History of India*, vol. I, *c.1250–c.1750* ed. I. Habib and T. Raychaudhuri. Cambridge.

1985. 'State Formation and Economy Reconsidered, Part One' *Modern Asian Studies*, 19(3), 387–413.

Thernstrom, S. 1964. *Poverty and Progress: Social Mobility in a Nineteenth Century City*. Cambridge, Mass.

Thernstrom, S. and R. Sennett (eds.). 1969. *Nineteenth-Century Cities: Essays in the New Urban History*. New Haven.

Tomlinson, B. R. 1979. *The Political Economy of the Raj, 1914–1947*. Cambridge.

Waller, P. J. 1982. *Town, City and Nation: England, 1800–1914*. London.

Washbrook, D. A. 1981. 'Law, State and Agrarian Society in Colonial India' *Modern Asian Studies*, 15(3), 649–721.

Aspects of the historiography of labour in India

The Labour in Asia research programme is, it seems to me, a particularly important initiative because it registers and aims to build on the growing scholarly interest and increasing activity in the 1990s in Indian and Asian labour studies. It is significant that the first volume to appear in the newly projected *Economic History of South-East Asia* is Elson's *The Death of the Peasantry*, and Amarjit Kaur's work on labour is, I understand, due shortly to follow. Among historians and social scientists of India, the working classes, broadly construed, have also commanded increasing attention, as several conferences (at least two here in Amsterdam) and perhaps, more substantially, the numerous books, articles and theses which have recently been published, testify. Recent conferences in Calcutta, Bombay and most recently Delhi have suggested a quite considerable depth of interest and output. In the University of Cambridge alone, not in this field known for its radicalism or its particular concern with the history of subordinated and oppressed groups, there have been a dozen or more doctoral theses written or in progress on various aspects of the working classes in India – from studies of communism to the political movements of the urban poor, gender relations and household formation, child labour and the spatial politics of neighbourhoods, mill townships and urban squatter settlements, labour movements and caste, ethnic and communal conflicts. We may trace the genealogy of this body of work on Indian labour to the pioneering work in English and European social history in the 1960s and 1970s. Yet paradoxically labour historians in Britain, Europe and even perhaps the USA perceive their subject to be in terminal decline. How this apparent decline of labour history in the West and its apparent resurgence in India and Asia more generally is to be assessed and explained must be a matter of concern at the start of a major programme of research on labour in Asia. For how these divergent trends are assessed could serve to influence future directions of research.

I will not pretend to offer such an assessment or explanation in this paper, but it is with this paradox in mind that I have been thinking about the subject which I have been asked to address: that is, the historiography of labour in India. Until recently, most books about Indian labour were contemporary, not historical, studies, which sometimes cast a backward glance, often with great insight, in order to understand the present more fully. Historians have only quite recently begun to address themselves to the history of labour and the working classes. Until the 1970s, historians of modern India, although there were some important exceptions, were predominantly concerned with the clash between imperialism and nationalism, British policy and Indian response. Social historians followed this pattern and focused upon what they described as 'Westernization' or 'modernization' and its resistance or acceptance by 'indigenous' and 'traditional' culture.

The tradition of writing about Indian labour – and in this I include contemporary and political accounts – has passed through several shifts in perspective and approach but each has indelibly marked the subject. There have been roughly three waves of writing about and interest in Indian labour. In the wake of the First World War, the colonial state deliberated, even if it did not actively pursue, the need to promote industrialization in India as a means of generating the resources which would enable it to continue to serve Britain's global, imperial system. In the 1950s and 1960s, the concern with modernization and development produced another period of interest in labour. Finally, in the 1980s and 1990s, the influence of social history is to be witnessed in the growth of specifically historical studies of the working classes. Between 1910 and the 1970s, this body of writing followed two main, if distinct, lines of enquiry. First, several writers delineated what in the 1920s came to be called 'the labour problem': the barriers to the adaptation of labour to the needs of modern industry. In other words, although there were many answers, sometimes even an ideological reluctance to offer one, none avoided the question: why was labour so inefficient? Already in the 1920s there emerged a discourse about Indian labour which has continued to influence the 'problematic' and the explanatory frameworks which scholars have employed in the subject to the present day. For instance, Sir Stanley Reed, former editor of the *Times of India*, and the chairman of two committees between 1917 and 1922 to examine the causes and means of settling industrial disputes in Bombay, elaborated 'the labour problem' in a foreword to Burnett-Hurst's classic (and sympathetic) study of wage earners in Bombay, published in 1925. Reed attributed the lack of 'efficiency and stability of the labour force', which explained why Bombay's cotton mills could not compete with Japan and Shanghai, to causes 'found deep down in the social conditions of the people'. As a result, labour was scarce, never developed a body of craft skills and, being largely 'agriculturists', displayed 'incessantly migratory habits'. They had 'a low standard of technical efficiency' and showed no sense of 'responsibility' towards their employers. Their migratory habits ensured the separation of the worker from his family, with grievous moral and social consequences. Raising wages offered no solution, he argued, because it would only lead to greater absenteeism, more expenditure, mainly on drink and prostitution, and increased exactions by money-lenders, jobbers and liquor-sellers. So he concluded 'the immediate problem of Indian industry is not so much the raising of wages ... as the extraction of higher service for the wages paid'. It should not be thought that Sir Stanley Reed was simply unsympathetic to the plight of the working classes. He reported that their 'living conditions' were 'deplorable' and stressed the need for measures to improve hygiene and housing, advocated 'welfare work and social reform', warned against the effects of industrial fatigue and 'the pressure of intensive labour' and called for enquiries into disease and nutrition. Indeed, Burnett-Hurst, who asked him to write the foreword, was closely associated in London with the Webbs. Significantly, others who took a more favourable view of labour, as well as some nationalists, deliberated within the same discursive framework. Moreover, 'the labour problem' identified in this discourse and its symptoms were replicated at the core of studies of 'adaptation', 'commitment' and 'stability' by functional sociologists and development economists of the 1950s and 1960s, among whom may be included the pioneering historical research of Morris D. Morris. For all his differences with these scholars, the problems he posed and the categories he employed owed something to this discourse and a great deal to the work of contemporaries like Charles Kerr, Wilbur Moore and Charles Myers. The influence of this discourse is also reflected in the emphasis which continues to be placed on 'labour supply', the jobber or sirdari systems of recruitment, the so-called 'peasant mentality' of workers and the identification of a distinct 'casual' stratum of the labour force which was said to move by preference restlessly from job to job and remained averse to the contracts, disciplines and obligations of modern society. An economic historian, Gregory Clark, recently sought to explain 'why the whole world is not developed' in terms of native indolence everywhere outside Britain in the nineteenth century. In collaboration with Susan Walcott, he has sought to return to the agenda of Reed and demonstrate that 'the inefficiency of labour', or its reluctance to work at an economic cost, rather than 'managerial failure', accounts for the failure of the Indian textile industry to compete with Japan in the 1920s and 1930s. The culturalist interpretation of Dipesh Chakrabarty's work on the Bengal jute mills, with its assertion of the 'pre-capitalist character' and 'peasant mentality' of the working classes, can also be seen to be marked by the discourse which formed around attempts to delineate 'the labour problem' in the 1920s.

The second main theme in the body of writing about Indian labour related to strikes and trade unions. These studies emanated originally from the small, if growing number of publicists and philanthropists who became actively involved in organizing and representing labour, and to a lesser extent in official commentaries concerned to contain its threat. Until 1918, commentaries about labour in India, produced largely by social investigators, both official and philanthropic, focused upon the physical and moral degradation of the urban poor, and considered the means by which their conditions might be alleviated. The flurry of strikes which followed the First World War stimulated a wave of writing about labour which, in the context of widespread public anxieties about urban poverty and overcrowding, the rise of nationalism and the threat of widespread unrest, disclosed a greater sensitivity to, and apprehension of, the possible political consequences of impoverishment and exploitation. As publicists and philanthropists were drawn into representing workers during industrial disputes, they turned their attention to the growth of strikes and trade unions. They meditated upon the nature and weaknesses of trade unions, the role and effect upon them of 'outsiders' (that is, organizers who were not themselves workers) and the proper place of political programmes and ideology in their activities. The focus of these accounts was largely institutional. Their underlying political agenda was largely in the 1920s and 1930s to persuade employers and colonial officials to accept and recognize trade unions, preferably their own, as bargaining agents. Some sought to establish themselves in the public sphere as spokesmen for labour to whom the government could turn for advice. N. M. Joshi's tract on *The Trade Union Movement in India*, written in 1927, B. Shiva Rao's measured treatise on *The Indian Industrial Worker*, published in 1939, and the several books by Joshi's biographer, V. B. Karnik, on strikes and the history of trade unions emanated from this tradition.

For all the attention which trade unions have received in this literature, the fact remains that few trade unions maintained a permanent presence on the shop floor or in the politics of the industry before 1947. The emphasis on the institutional history of trade unions thus left a vacuum at its core: these were often unions without members. Their actions and policies were merely a function of the initiatives of the workers and the repressive response of employers and the state to these initiatives. Since independence, trade unions have acquired a greater institutional permanence, but the more institutionalized unions have usually served a small, perhaps decreasing proportion of the labour force. Publicists who wrote about trade unions before 1947 could scarcely uncover the elaborate historical fictions which these institutions concealed. Their legacy has, in combination with the Leninist notion that trade unions reflected a stage of class-consciousness, allowed trade unions a more prominent place in the history of Indian labour, certainly before 1947, than they merit.

In the 1960s and 1970s, as scholars focused upon development and modernization and sometimes assumed too readily that the Indian labour force was located at 'an early stage of industrialization', and, implicitly, that it was evolving towards the 'advanced stage' manifested in 'the West', historians and sociologists analysed the development of trade unions as the outcome of the conflict between modern institutional forms of organization and the social control of supposedly 'traditional' leaders drawn from the ranks of jobbers, recruiting agents and labour contractors. In this way, the history of the working class was made interchangeable with the history of their leaders, trade unions and political parties. In the work of Richard Newman, Eamonn Murphy and E. A. Ramaswamy, the institutional approach was carried to a new level of sophistication. In 1981, I had attempted to argue, in the light of the evidence of large-scale and sustained strikes despite the absence of trade unions, that the industrial and political action of the working classes in Bombay could only be fully grasped in relation to the social organization of the neighbourhoods. Since workers' combinations were repressed in the workplace, they drew upon their linkages with the neighbourhood to organize and sustain strikes and political action. Trade unions remained for the most part ephemeral to the networks and alignments through which workers organized and acted in defence of their interests. Dipesh Chakrabarty, addressing a similar problem in the third volume of *Subaltern Studies* in 1984, explained the limitations of trade union organization in terms of the hierarchical culture and the relations of deference which labour leaders fostered and, presumably, workers accepted. It offered an engaging portrayal of the attitudes of bhadralok trade union leaders, but doubts must remain, and they have grown with the recent work of Samita Sen, Subho Basu and Ranajit Das Gupta, about whether the babu–coolie relationship existed more fully in the minds of the babu than the politics of the coolie. The relationship between workplace and neighbourhood and its role in the formation of the social identity of the working classes have more recently been explored by Chitra Joshi, at the 1995 Amsterdam conference, Vijay Prashad in his study of the sweepers of Delhi and Punjab, Leela Fernandes's recent ethnography of the Bengal jute mills and most fully in Subho Basu's analysis of the jute workers and mill townships of Bengal between 1880 and 1939. The increasing concern among historians to allow greater play in their narratives for the agency of work-ers and popular political culture has also, in the work of Chitra Joshi, Dilip Simeon and Vinay Bahl, allowed trade unions to recede further into the background.

Nonetheless, putting trade unions in their place is not enough. Strong assumptions exist in the comparative and theoretical literature about the nature of trade unions as an institutional form. These assumptions have often been belied by the evidence from the Indian case. The formation of trade unions does not offer a reliable guide to working-class conscious-ness. We need to consider, probably in a comparative framework, the circumstances in which employers and the state came to tolerate and accept their existence. How, when and why they came to be tolerated, and on what terms, may tell us more about the nature of the institution in each political context, and the character of the social relations and processes of state formation, of which they form a part.

In addition to the studies of trade unions, and by trade unionists, there was another tradition of writing about workers' politics, which coincided with the growing influence of the communists in the labour movement from the late 1920s onwards. The communists assumed the inherent rev-olutionary propensity of the working classes and understood their own role to be the realization of this potential. They also took it for granted that the working classes were primarily concerned with real and immediate material issues. By contrast, nationalism appeared to be an effete bour-geois ideology which was unlikely to sustain, even if it was able to muster, mass support. To the extent that the Congress gained a mass following, the communists set themselves the task of entering the anti-imperialist struggle and directing the working classes towards their revolution-ary goals. Accordingly, they examined specific working-class struggles to measure the level of revolutionary consciousness and increasingly resorted to nationalist betrayal as an explanation for revolutionary fail-ure. These debates among Indian communists, which in part originated in the theoretical preoccupations of the Comintern, exercised a power-ful influence upon the subsequent development of Indian nationalist and Marxist historiography. To a large extent, Marxist historiography, seeking to defend the progressive tendencies within the Congress, became until the 1980s almost indistinguishable from its nationalist variant. Although *Subaltern Studies* sets out to provide an alternative to this Marxist his-toriography, its own concerns in the early volumes were focused almost exclusively upon nationalism. The historiography of workers' politics, as it developed along these lines, also encouraged the substitution of party and ideology for the social history of the working classes. Not surpris-ingly, later historians, including some of the Subaltern school, sought to privilege working-class or popular 'culture' in reaction to the weight of this substitutionism and its analytical limitations.

As historians of Indian labour drew more extensively upon European and especially English social history in the 1980s, the assumption that the working classes had an inherent propensity towards unity came increasingly to be fortified. In European historiography, too, the purpose of studying the history of the labour movement was to investigate how its historic mission, the achievement of socialism, could be advanced or even realized and to track its progress or explain its setbacks. The assumption that the concentration of workers into larger masses, with the development of the factory industry, rendered their interests uniform has led to the quest for its manifest consequences in the emergence of class-consciousness and, implicitly, to the search for explanations for the gulf between political expectations based upon class and their real shortcomings in practice. In the recent resurgence of Indian labour history, the search for such explanations has continued: ranging from competing identities of caste, religion and gender, to the hierarchical culture of South Asia, to political betrayal and state repression. The case of the Bombay working class in the early twentieth century suggests, however, that sectionalism is integral to the process of class formation. We need to postpone the conclusion that the working classes had a singular propensity to unity and to explain instead, in view of the enormous impediments to combined action, how and why they could come together at all.

Of course, recent scholarship in Indian labour history has interrogated and modified the problematics and explanatory frameworks which it inherited. Nonetheless, it is significant that the successive waves of writing about labour have left a powerful residue of their preoccupations, their analytical categories and their general approaches upon those who have followed and upon recent work. At a more general level, the twin problems of labour-force formation and working-class politics continue to provide the organizing principles for the recent literature. It would be fair to say that the most common focus for recent research has been the emergence of class-consciousness. In other words, historians have for the most part examined the social and economic history of labour largely as the background to the development of workers' politics and the nature of their social and political consciousness. To assess where, and how far, the recent wave has taken us, it may be useful to examine this historiography in terms of the other three categories which the Labour in Asia research programme has outlined: labour process and production relations, labour mobility and gender. The problem of consciousness and identity has remained the predominant concern in the recent literature. The investigation of labour process and production relations, labour mobility and gender has often proceeded as part of what have often been perceived as the 'wider' problems of culture and consciousness.

Although the social history of Indian labour has concentrated so heavily upon the factory system, the labour process itself remains an area of neglect. Of course, some historians have depicted the exacting conditions in which men and women laboured and described the heavy physical toll which they paid. Some have portrayed the everyday conflicts, the countless small battles for advantage and concession, which workers waged on the shop floor. But we still know little about the labour process construed as a process of interaction between employers and workers, which shaped the interplay of technology and production relations. The daily substance of labour politics was often the attempt by workers to organize themselves around machinery and the struggles they waged to control its use. Conflicts of this kind shaped the use and development of technology and thus determined in part the course of industrialization. They could foster solidarities among workers but also promote rivalries. It need hardly be said that the labour process in this sense constitutes the very substance of industrial relations. For all the significance of trade unionism in the historiography, it is extraordinary that the labour process has remained – with the notable exception of Ian Kerr's study of railway building – a peculiar and glaring omission. How is it to be explained? Perhaps, while scouring the archive for evidence of consciousness, we have not stopped to delve into the messy, intricate, often confusing details of technology. Certainly assumptions about the culture and mentality of both workers and entrepreneurs in the literature have barred the historian's entry into the workplace. For instance, there is a widespread assumption that capitalists were fortune-hunters who brought to their investment the interest in short-term gain, which traders and speculators might display, rather than the visionary genius of industrialists. Similarly, workers, being primarily peasants, have often been supposed to be ignorant and superstitious about their machines. But this intellectual exclusion has long political roots. Trade unionists, certainly before 1947, and probably in large measure after independence, too, were not overly concerned with the labour process and technology. Those who engaged with this question were often excluded from the workplace by the employers. For they had often gained both the sympathy of the workers to learn about the labour process and the knowledge to become formidable negotiators. There is also the historian's constant complaint about the paucity and unevenness of sources. I was fortunate to have been able to use the transcripts of the negotiations which followed the 1928 general strike and the depositions before the Textile Labour Inquiry Committee in the late 1930s to attempt to reconstruct a history of the labour process in cotton textiles. But the scarcity of accessible business records remains a great impediment to such research. Certainly, in India, labour historians will also have to become business historians if they are to grasp securely the complex intricacies and changing character of the labour process, technology and industrial relations.

Similarly, the study of 'inter-sectoral linkages' has been neglected and it remains vital at two levels. First, we need to know far more about the history of the various trades, employments and occupations by which the vast majority of the working classes and urban poor struggled to survive. The notion of the 'informal sector' has been a product of legislation and the manipulations of employers to restrict their social obligation to labour to a small proportion of the workforce. It has allowed us to distinguish far too clearly between the working classes and the urban poor. It would be impossible to make such a clear distinction before 1947. The neglect of labour beyond the factory gates owes much to the paucity of sources. They are elusive and fragmentary, but as the general historiography of labour and of cities develops, we will be better placed to use them effectively. Nandini Gooptu's study of the urban poor in Allahabad, Lucknow, Kanpur and Banaras in the interwar period will help to remedy some of this neglect. Clearly, one response to the problem of sources is to identify a particular occupational, or even caste, group and put together sources not ordinarily used by labour historians. New sources remain to be brought systematically into use. For instance, insolvency petitions are likely to tell us a great deal about business practice in the informal sector, but they may also tell us something about the lives, trades and occupations of the labouring poor. Similarly, criminal records at the magistrate's courts of the Presidency capitals and the small causes courts have not been used. They will throw considerable light on labour, but organizing and making sense of them will constitute labour of heroic proportions. Historians also use the methods of ethnography but they may need to deploy them extensively to delve into the long past and changing vicissitudes of non-factory labour. In doing so, of course, historians have a model for studying non-factory labour in the work of Jan Breman. This is a task of some urgency. Nobody who observes the turbulent everyday politics of Indian towns – the physical and economic insecurity, and especially the erosion to the point of obliteration of civil and human rights for the urban poor – could doubt the significance of the problem and its enormous implications.

The question of labour mobility leads us most directly to the heart of inter-sectoral linkages. It also lies at the centre of one of the most powerful, recurring contradictions in the discourse, colonial and post-colonial, about labour in India, but also elsewhere: the notion that labour was immobilized by tradition, the caste system and the village community and therefore impossible to recruit without specially designed measures and institutions; and that it was incessantly restless, unstable and migratory, and, therefore, impossible to pin down, discipline and control. This discourse has sometimes enabled dominant classes and the state to legitimize repressive measures against the working classes. Moreover, the study of various forms and conditions of labour migration can also provide some insight into the common processes working through the Indian economy, since at least the early nineteenth century, which shaped the formation of the labour force in diverse sectors, regions and industries, normally treated as analytically and chronologically distinct and separate. These processes, which arose from and informed the changing character of class relations in rural India since the late eighteenth and early nineteenth centuries, helped to propel the migration of some 30 million people from the subcontinent to plantation colonies around the world between 1830 and 1930, and no doubt comparable numbers from China and Java.

In the investigation of labour mobility, Indian historians have the advantage of the very strong base of research in agrarian history which has been built up since the 1960s. Although agrarian relations have concerned historians rather less than agrarian policy or peasant nationalism, there have been several valuable studies by Neladri Bhattacharya, Ludden, Gyan Prakash and Jairus Banaji. Jan Breman's *Patronage and Exploitation* set his own fieldwork in a very strong historical perspective, while labour mobility and migration has been a central theme of his subsequent work. Studies of agrarian labour have been accompanied by a number of case studies of migration from particular districts. Prabhu Mohapatra's careful and compelling study of the Chota Nagpur region, one of the major regions of labour supply for industrial labour, from which workers migrated to the tea plantations of Assam, the coal mines of Bengal and Bihar and the overseas plantations as well, has been fortified by his own recent research on indenture and the social and cultural experience of those who were recruited to work in the plantation colonies. Among the most interesting studies of labour mobility, in my view, is Jacques Pouchepadass's analysis of 'the market for agricultural labour in North Bihar' in the late nineteenth and early twentieth centuries. It provides an illuminating analysis of production relations, but also a highly nuanced account of the various forms of contract which prevailed in the region. In his account the movement of people in search of wages in the countryside is closely related to and provides a context for understanding long-distance migration to urban and industrial labour.

Although labour historians have often dwelt upon the 'peasant mentality' of urban, industrial workers, the nature of the rural connections of urban workers remains in many contexts to be fully explored. The view from the sending districts, frequently influenced by official reports, tended to exaggerate the seasonality of migration to the large industrial centres. Source materials generated in the cities, often by employers and policemen, exaggerated the flow of remittances to the countryside and therefore the surplus income supposedly commanded by industrial workers. The former did not attempt to integrate their assumptions about seasonal migration with the rhythms of the 'urban' labour market. The latter did not seek to reconcile their picture of remittances with the poverty and insecurity of employment, which most migrants experienced in the cities, and the degree to which they sometimes drew on the social and material resources of the village. Only in an integrated view, which straddles town and country like the workers and their households, could we see, for instance, that migrant workers were so dependent on their urban earnings for the survival of their households that they were committed to their factories and more active in defence of their jobs and wage levels than the classically urban proletarians with no rural connections. The treatment of labour mobility and migration has become a growing strength of the recent historical literature.

Gender, like labour mobility, is likely to lead the labour historian's search beyond the usual boundaries of his subject to questions and debates which are central to the interpretation of social change in India over time. Of course, labour historians have tended to neglect women's work; to the extent that they have addressed the issue, they have tended to treat it as a rather distinct and separate question. However, one needs hardly to point out that gender was integral to the formation of the labour force and indispensable to its reproduction. It remains a significant influence upon the labour process, patterns of migration, and the relationship between workplace and neighbourhood, the nature of class-consciousness and identity formation as well as trade union and political organization. Samita Sen's research has ranged across this spectrum of issues and beyond to demonstrate how the construction of women as workers was intricately linked to constructions of gender relations more widely. The marginalization and devaluation of women's work in public discourse coincided, not surprisingly, with the increasing participation of women in the labour force and the growing dependence of small peasant households on the intensive self-exploitation of female labour. Leela Fernandes has pursued some of these themes in the contemporary context in the Calcutta jute mills. Sociologists and anthropologists have addressed the question of women's work more fully but the signs are encouraging that labour historians have begun to remedy their long-standing neglect of labour. This might, we could hope, extend to the closer investigation of masculinity, especially of work and neighbourhood cultures and its particular inflection of working-class identities.

I have already addressed some of the aspects of the treatment of the labour movement and of 'consciousness', the other two headings in the Labour in Asia prospectus, so I will not return to them. But it does seem to me that an area which labour historians must investigate is state formation. As historians of society they have often treated the state as if it lay outside their core concerns, but the changing character of the state has been a continuous influence on labour-force formation and labour politics. It would be useful to analyse it systematically from the disciplinary perspective of labour history by examining in particular patterns of policing, discourses of public order and social control, the legitimization of repressive action as well as the workings of the judiciary and the formulation and effects of legislation.

There are some important limitations and absences which the recent wave of labour history has shared. First, this work has focused almost exclusively on the period between 1850 and 1950. We need to set this research in the context of long-term tendencies and developments in the labour market and production relations more generally. Second, this wave has perhaps been far too vulnerable to changing fashions in the West. Conversely it may have been less open to the influence of contemporary developments and of the insights generated by their study. We have also remained averse to crossing the sacred divide of 1947. Indeed, it is notable that many official archives have for a variety of reasons been slow to make post-1947 records available to historians. Since India's public culture remains rather open and at certain points dissenting and anarchic, it is sometimes easier to obtain fairly confidential sources from living participants or their descendants than to read the most innocuous materials in conventional archives. Third, it has focused exclusively on 'industrial labour' and operated implicitly with a rather narrow, conventional notion of 'industry'. We lack studies of labour in small industries before 1947 or in what in short hand may, for the moment, be described as the casual trades, service economy and unorganized sector. The history of transnational migrations needs to be more fully integrated with the history of labour within the subcontinent. Similarly, the formation of the 'industrial' labour force can be fruitfully located in the context of the broadly similar processes by which diverse sets of wage-earners were recruited in different sections of the economy. Certainly, the narrow focus upon 'industry' arose from the assumption that industrialization shaped the nature of the labour force and the character of the social struggle and its political forms. Indeed, a number of teleological interpretations of labour history have been built upon this assumption. On closer scrutiny, it has proved both epistemologically and empirically a rather shaky foundation which in turn has probably contributed to the perceived 'crisis' of labour history in the West. Finally, the focus on 'consciousness' as a starting point and object of the enquiry has led historians to pass over much too quickly what they have seen perhaps as contributory questions about the political economy of labour. It may even have helped to create an 'interior' discourse which has perhaps held labour historians captive and prevented them from reaching into broader areas of investigation which make their subject central to the large themes in the recent history of society.

If there is a crisis of confidence in labour history today, its causes may be traced in part to its period of buoyancy in the 1970s. As the focus of research shifted towards the ambition to grasp conceptually the history of society, its practitioners at first took it for granted that class provided the organizing principle of social relations. There was something inherently parochial about this assumption of the universalism of class. Histories of labour in developing countries, at any rate outside the West, were placed on an evolutionary scale moving towards, perhaps, but not as yet within, the same field of comparison in which scholars might conceptualize society. In addition, agenda was characterized by a populist ambition to reconstruct the authentic social experience of ordinary men and women and their everyday lives and struggles. The 'new' social historians turned increasingly to cultural anthropology to grasp the symbolic forms, popular beliefs and cultural practices through which 'ordinary people' construed their experiences.

If European labour historians are now diffident about the place of their own subject, this is at least partly because of the emphasis on a proliferating range of identities in social and cultural history, which in a sense their own scholarly practices have stimulated. But there is no reason why class should inherently and consistently form the dominant, let alone the primary and exclusive, social identity. The historians' task should be to identify and explain how these various identities form and play upon each other. Rather than assuming that class-consciousness, or other identities, or the categories for describing them, flowed naturally from social being, it would perhaps be more fruitful to explore how they came to be constructed in public discourse in the first place. Class as much as any other identity was contingent upon specific historical circumstances; so were the shifting interests of those who comprised these collectivities. Moreover, for the historiography of labour in Asia, these developments have a positive side. The increasing sensitivity among historians of the Western working classes to the competing and conflicting identities of ethnicity and religion, kinship and gender, neighbourhood and nation has focused attention upon the very issues which had, in the conventional view, rendered Indian society exceptional in the first place and sometimes even demanded a culturally specific sociology for its proper analysis.

Despite the enormous theoretical carapace which has been built around the term 'culture', however, historians, especially historians of India, have deployed notions of culture in a rather under-theorized, often in an ahistorical, fashion. Indeed, Raymond Williams once observed that 'culture' was the single most difficult word in the English language, but historians and anthropologists have too often approached the term rather briskly to their own peril and at significant interpretative cost. While they eschewed social and economic explanation as unduly deterministic and rejected implicit or explicit notions of its prior role in daily life, they continued often to assume that objective conditions inscribed a certain unity and homogeneity to particular social groups, whether these conditions were defined by production relations, ascriptive or primordial categories, ethnicity or gender. As a result, they have assumed away too easily the problem of explaining how social groups formed, whether in a material or ideational sense. Conversely, having assumed the existence of given social groups and categories, they have tautologically analysed how their preconceptions, beliefs and symbolic forms eventuated towards a point of correspondence with the prior definition of their objective status.

The growing concern with the formation of diverse identities since the 1970s has rendered historians yet more receptive to notions of difference. One aim of the post-modern critique was to release the dispossessed from the universalizing categories of colonial discourse. By stressing fragmentation and plurality, and asserting difference, it sought to enable the suppressed narratives of the dispossessed to be heard and to subvert the dominant discourse which, in particular, had imposed a Eurocentric rationality upon non-Europeans and facilitated their colonization. However, the assertion of difference, with its accompanying search for the true voice of the dispossessed (and not least their authentic representative within the academy), has often led to the reification of subaltern groups and their portrayal in essentialist terms. As scholars attempted to assert and claim difference, they have tended to reaffirm assumptions about the culturally specific, unique and exceptional character of Indian society. As a result, they have sometimes been led to restore some of the fondest shibboleths of colonial ideologues – for instance, about the propensity of the working classes to violence, their susceptibility to rumour, the paternalism of the expatriate capitalists and the filial deference of their employees or the centrality of religion to their political consciousness. This replication of colonial discourse, which arose out of the historian's culturalism, occurred most explicitly when scholars, in pursuit of the fragment, neglected to attend sufficiently to its social and political context. The politics and epistemology of difference thus yielded a rather antiquated universalism of its own.

Postscript

A recurring concern of the essays is the history of labour but, as Jennifer Davis notes in her Introduction, Raj never saw himself as a labour historian. He viewed society, culture and politics in their widest terms and on the basis of a stunning breadth of reading, and he was never afraid to engage with contemporary issues in the course of exploring the past. However, his perspective was firmly rooted to a particular point, revealed in a phrase which occurs on several occasions in these essays: that a society is to be judged by how it treats its poorest and weakest members. It is hard to argue with that judgement.

The essays take up many discrete questions, but Raj delighted in debate and came back repeatedly to three sets of issues where he hoped that his interventions would be telling. The first of these concerned the status of universal social theories and, especially, the theory of 'modernization'. Raj entered academic life in the 1970s when the optimism which had attended the 'liberation' of the former European colonies was already beginning to dissipate. Naively, it had been supposed that, freed from their colonial shackles, they would rapidly 'develop' along the same course as the societies of their erstwhile masters – towards liberty, prosperity and democracy, which represented the ineluctable destiny of the whole of humankind. And, in so far as they did not, it was the result of failings within themselves, peculiarities which 'obstructed' or 'arrested' their passage to progress.

Raj would have none of it. He possessed the historian's innate suspicion of general theory, perhaps holding with Max Weber that the more universal a theory becomes necessarily the more vacuous it must be – since, by definition, it can hold no particular content. Also, he blanched at '-izations' of any kind, which implied determinism and teleology, foreknowledge of where history must end up. He demanded to be shown specificities of context, mechanisms of change, the logic of situations.[1]

---

[1] For the fullest statement of this position, see Rajnarayan Chandavarkar, 'Industrialization in India: Conventional Approaches and Alternative Perspectives', *Modern Asian Studies*, Special Issue, 19, 3, July 1985, 623–67.

What he found profoundly altered his understanding of the phenomena loosely grouped under the rubrics of modernity and modern history.

One of his findings, reflected widely in these essays and also many other parts of his work, was that colonialism was not a superficial experience, easily cast off with the sailing of the British from India's shores, but deeply affected the processes and institutions associated with India's modernity. India's economy and large parts of its initial 'modern' state were built to supply services to an external colonial power: they differed in critical ways from the processes of economic development and state-building which underlay the protean experience of modernity in 'the West'.[2] So much, perhaps, would now be familiar in our historiography, and provide a pillar of shared understanding with post-colonial theory today. But Raj's perception of the nature and significance of colonialism went much deeper. On the one hand, he did not only see it as an external phenomenon imposed upon India. Its key agencies included many Indians themselves, most notably in Bombay where local business elites dominated the city's development. Colonialism was as much about 'indigenous' class relations as it was about 'alien' rule.[3] And, on the other hand, he insisted that the logic of domination and exploitation, which it set up, continued and even deepened after the British left.[4] History was not reversible and Indian society – or at least Bombay society – remained 'post-colonial' in a rather different sense from that supposed by its eponymous theorists. Indeed, his view of the post-colonial situation was particularly bleak: independence had thrown off many of the political constraints on the colonial state, limiting its ability to effect brutality and exploitation for all that it might have desired to do so. But its national successor knew no such limits and permitted the locally wealthy and powerful a freer range to impose their will on the city and its peoples.[5]

Raj's understanding here reflected his much greater comfort with the idioms of 'capitalism' rather than of 'modernity', with Marx rather than with Weber. His penetrating analysis not only of the labour process in the Bombay cotton mills, but also that of capital accumulation in the Indian economy, led him to doubt that the shift from an extractive colonial state to a more developmentally efficient national successor necessarily

[2] See 'State and Society in Colonial India'.
[3] See 'Bombay's Perennial Modernities' and 'Peasants and Proletarians in Bombay City in the Late Nineteenth and Early Twentieth Centuries'.
[4] See 'From Neighbourhood to Nation: The Rise and Fall of the Left in Bombay's Girangaon in the Twentieth Century'.
[5] 'From Neighbourhood to Nation' and 'Urban History and Urban Anthropology in South Asia'.

benefited those without capital and obliged to sell their labour.[6] Else-where, too, his debt to Marx – albeit in the role of provocateur more than mentor – was no less great and inspired many of his sharpest insights. In particular, he sought to bring back labour as an active agent in its own history and that of society at large. His arguments concerning the way that, via politics, the labour process shapes the process of technological change – rather than vice versa – and that political resistance shapes polit-ical domination – also, rather than vice versa – added new dimensions to the analysis of Indian history, and not Indian history alone.[7]

For, in spite of his impatience with general theory, Raj's work con-stantly hinted at a more general theory – or vision – of its own. He was certainly not content to leave India, or the colonial world, just as the exception to a rule of modernity founded in the West. As Jennifer Davis notes, as the product of a Western education himself, he had a profound scepticism of the way in which that rule was formulated, and of a 'Whig' self-history celebrating freedoms and prosperities claimed for (but not delivered to) most of its citizens. This distinguished him from many historians of India, who were inclined to take such self-justificatory self-history on trust, against which to set their own models of Indian exceptionalism. Raj was as restless with the received history of the West as he was with that of India and, in looking constantly between the two, essayed – at least implicitly – a species of general theory himself. With Marx, he took capitalism to supply the link and to provide the basis of any universal history: capitalists, be they British or Indian, shared more in common than they did apart; and certainly more in common that either did with the labour, British or Indian, who worked for them.[8]

But capitalism's trajectory, while bringing different parts of the world into closer contact, had no preordained path or direction. It was beset by multiple contingencies, derived as much from social and political as formally economic conditions. Its struggle to sustain profitability took many different forms in many different places, and the forms adopted in one frequently had implications for those adopted in the others. Raj's 'capitalism' was not a static system, seeking to find equilibrium, but a labyrinthine set of interconnections – conflictual, shifting and con-stantly threatening to undermine themselves. Economic rationality was handmaiden to the counter-rationalities imposed by society and politics.

---

[6] For his fullest statement, see Rajnarayan Chandavarkar, *The Origins of Industrial Capital-ism in India: Business Strategies and the Working Classes in Bombay, 1900–1940*. Cambridge University Press, 1994.

[7] Chandavarkar, *The Origins of Industrial Capitalism in India*; also here, 'Peasants and Proletarians' and 'From Neighbourhood to Nation'.

[8] See 'Bombay's Perennial Modernities'.

The only way to understand capitalism was to grasp the particularities of different situational logics, open up its inner workings in specific places and at specific times – when the reasons behind discrete outcomes might become apparent. Raj's brand of theorizing never led to succinct paradigms or predictions of the future. But frequently it offered deeper insight into problems of otherwise daunting complexity.

In particular, it offered novel interpretations of the concepts of class and of 'urbanity'. Raj's suspicions of 'modernization' extended to its subtropes of 'proletarianization' and 'urbanization': both, no less, supposedly drawn from experience of 'the West', but in reality barely reflective even of its 'real' history. Such notions robbed the workers of Bombay, with their enduring rural connections and ethnicity-based 'neighbourhoods', of the status of a working class; and the 'rurban' sprawl of Bombay of the status of a 'city'. Raj set out to restore both to their proper dignity, revising – *inter alia* – large swathes of social theory as he went along. His arguments on the way that rural connections could strengthen, rather than weaken, class militancy and on how social connections forged in the neighbourhood could determine labour relations at the point of production are now standard parts of the repertoire of social historians in fields much beyond India.[9] Also, he bitterly resented attempts to reduce the Indian city – that is, his beloved Bombay – to the category of an overgrown village. He argued for the broadening of the concept of the 'urbs' to include a much greater range of social experience, emphasizing especially multiplicity of connections with the outside world and role in introducing innovations, pioneering what has come to be regarded as 'modernity'.[10] By these standards, Bombay's seemingly 'rurban' settlements masked one of the greatest cities in the colonial world; and by these means, Raj – albeit with supreme irony – ended up making his own contributions to the theory of modernity.

The second set of issues to which he constantly returned was the provenance of nationalism, towards which his attitudes were necessarily complex. While by no means depreciative of the achievements of the Indian National Congress in advancing the freedom struggle against colonial rule, his stance in the working-class neighbourhoods of Bombay necessarily made him sceptical about the quality of the freedom that it pursued.[11] His perspective was inclined to emphasize the compromises

[9] 'Peasants and Proletarians' and 'From Neighbourhood to Nation'.
[10] 'Bombay's Perennial Modernities'; 'Sewers'; 'Urban History and Urban Anthropology in South Asia'.
[11] For a fuller statement, see Rajnarayan Chandavarkar, 'Workers' Politics and the Mill Districts of Bombay between the Wars', *Modern Asian Studies*, Special Issue, 15, 3, July 1981, 603–47.

being made with capital in the context of Bombay and the extent to which the working classes were merely being offered the opportunity to swap one kind of oppression for another. It was his career-long goal to rewrite Indian political history from the viewpoint of 'the Left' and, especially, the communist- and trades union-led workers' movements and organizations based in Bombay – which acquired a 'heroic' status in an *oeuvre* otherwise notable for its distinct lack of heroes.[12] He never completed this task, but left a series of sketches towards its goal in various parts of his published work, some more of which are included in this collection.[13] Had he done so, half-a-century of Congress 'triumphalism', which served to suppress sight of alternative kinds of 'freedom struggle', might have ended even more quickly than it did – and with considerable benefit to contemporary Indian politics.

However, in his later years, Raj became more reconciled to the Congress version of Indian nationalism with its emphases on a (albeit flawed) secularism and an (albeit limited) inclusivity. This was because the rise – or rebirth – of Hindu nationalism in the 1980s brought a sharpened sense of menace greater still. Two of the essays collected here represent powerful engagements with the phenomenon of Hindu nationalism, which has forced many historians of India other than Raj to reassess their perspectives on the past.[14] Raj was particularly concerned with the extent to which religious nationalism threatened to destroy the multicultural, perhaps cosmopolitan, character of Bombay's society: which had survived even the traumas of Partition without fully segmenting but, following the 1993 Bombay riots, was moving towards effective 'ghettoization'. His essay on religion and nationalism explores the 'racialization' of religious sensibility during the colonial period and its hardening further under the pressures of post-colonial times. Having skirmished with the meaningfulness of 'modernity' in the past, he showed himself fully aware of its darkest implications in his later work. Also, he considered the impact of Hindu nationalism on understandings of India's history. Intervening in the public debates which arose in the late 1990s, after the Bharatiya Janata Party was elected to government, he turned his spotlight on the relationship between historiography and power, which he explored with sensitivity and acumen. History has often reflected the perspective of 'the victor', so it may be no surprise that the new victors in Indian politics should want a history of their own. But is such a shift not also

---

[12] See Rajnarayan Chandavarkar, 'From Communism to Social Democracy: The Rise and Resilience of Communist Parties in India, 1920–1995', *Science and Society*, 61, 1, 1997, 99–106.

[13] 'From Neighbourhood to Nation'.

[14] 'Historians and the Nation' and 'Religion and Nationalism in India'.

the occasion to begin asking questions about the purposes and necessity of this relationship at all?

And the third set of issues to which Raj repeatedly returned also concerns the character of historiography. As Jennifer Davis notes, he was himself a participant in the 'new' social history, which developed in Britain in the 1970s under the influence of E. P. Thompson and Gareth Stedman Jones. In consequence, he was somewhat bemused by the academic status subsequently accorded to 'Subaltern Studies'. Partly claiming the same sources of inspiration, but 'globalizing' its references to include European thinkers as widely disparate as Gramsci and Heidegger and 'indigenizing' them to represent itself as of Indian origination, Subaltern Studies was swept up on the post-colonial wave of the 1980s and 1990s to become an international phenomenon and to conquer the heights of the American academy – albeit more in departments of social science and cultural studies than history. At many levels, Raj shared the objectives of Subaltern Studies: to challenge 'elitist' constructions of history; to bring 'the people' back into account; to find alternative and 'popular' sources of evidence. However, he differed sharply in the way that he went about pursuing them.[15]

For him, Subaltern Studies tended merely to invert the evaluatory criteria of elitist and determinist historiography – in both its neo-Weberian and neo-Marxist forms – but not to question their methodology and empirical status. As a result, Subaltern Studies' representations were inclined to emphasize the same features as elitist historiography, but just with the moral judgements turned upside down. On several occasions in these essays, for example, Raj takes to task Dipesh Chakrabarty for his celebrated 'rethinking' of working-class history in which the concept of class is made to appear alien and the so-called 'working class' are viewed as displaced peasants, bringing to the factory the 'traditionalistic' mentalite of the village community.[16] Raj pointed out that this was precisely the same view of them as held by the colonial authorities: the principal difference being only that, whereas Chakrabarty appears to celebrate their resistance to 'modernity', the colonial authorities deprecated it. But, as Raj's own work and that of several of the students who studied with him went on to show, both views entirely missed the experience of working in the factories and living in the neighbourhoods of the city, which forged new bonds and, at least on occasions, created moments of class solidarity as strong and tenacious as any that could be found in

---

[15] See Rajnarayan Chandavarkar, '"The Making of the Working Class": E. P. Thompson and Indian History', *History Workshop Journal*, 43, Spring 1997, 177–96.

[16] Dipesh Chakrabarty, *Rethinking Working-Class History: Bengal, 1890–1940* (Princeton, 1989).

the 'real' history of the West.[17] Whether in its colonial or its Subaltern version, the formulation simply overlooked where 'the action' really was.

Equally, Raj seriously questioned the no less celebrated formulation of the 'politics of the governed' advanced by Partha Chatterjee.[18] Here it is argued that whereas Indian elites and 'middle classes' may now have been drawn into the liberal culture of 'civil society' – marked by laws, regulations and constraints – the subaltern orders continue to live in 'political society' where violence in the face of oppression is viewed as rational and legitimate. But, for Raj, this looked far too much like the conventional 'bourgeois' representation of the 'lower orders' as inherently 'dangerous' and undisciplined, while their 'betters' were assumed to be naturally virtuous. And he was scarcely mollified by Chatterjee's attempts to justify the violence of the subaltern as reaction to oppression. Rather, he pointed out that, in Indian conditions, a great deal of contemporary social violence – especially 'communal' violence – was authored by the elites themselves, whose 'civility' could not be assumed; while, indeed, the 'subaltern orders' frequently clung to laws and legal processes for their protection, long after these ceased to serve them adequately.[19] Lawfulness and lawlessness were not the prerogatives of any single class.

Elsewhere, too, Raj came to see Subaltern Studies as representing the 'marked category' for much of his later writing. He found its romantic conception of an 'otherness' – be it in the village community, the hill tribe or the 'religious' culture – which subaltern society was seen struggling to preserve against the encroachments of 'modernity', to be no less obfuscating than the socialist Utopias which Marxist communists also claimed to pursue, and to be something of the same order of concept. His 'working class' were in Bombay city precisely because their rural idyll had ceased to be idyllic: they could not survive in the village without the resources of the city. There was no going back. Moreover, eyes firmly set on romantic retreat, as on Utopian advance, were inclined to miss the importance of the events in hand. Raj's 'working-class politics' centred on the small day-to-day struggles for dignity, autonomy and a living wage, which were clearly the priority of his historical subjects, if not of their better-fed historians seeking to use them as reference points in academic debates about which they, themselves, could not have cared less.[20]

---

[17] See 'Aspects of the Historiography of Labour in India'; 'Peasants and Proletarians'; 'From Neighbourhood to Nation'; 'Urban History'.

[18] Partha Chatterjee, *The Politics of the Governed: Reflections on Popular Politics in Most of the World* (New York, 2004).

[19] 'Urban History'.

[20] 'From Neighbourhood to Nation'. See also, Chandavarkar, 'Workers' Politics and the Mill Districts' and his 'The Making of the Working Class'.

Also, as Jennifer Davis notes, he quaked at attempts to bring 'culture' back into history, especially when the underlying conception of that 'culture' was plainly ahistorical and structuralist – for all that it was usually authorized by reference to major post-structuralist thinkers, such as Michel Foucault. Raj had no time for conceptions of 'culture' which violated the universal 'reasonableness' of his historical subjects. He sought to persuade his readers by showing that he (and they) might have acted in just the same way had they been placed in the same context – a context whose precise character he spent years in the archives investigating and delineating. He was a historian's historian who gave ultimate respect to 'the facts' in so far as they could be known, and which he devoted much of his life to trying to know. His detailed knowledge of his subject was vast and he was inclined to show impatience with those who spoke on the basis of the reading of a single 'text' or critiqued the nature of archives which they had scarcely visited or spun theories without regard to evidence.

But he was also no mere empiricist. His history broadly reflected his own humanitarian and secular values where, again, his differences from, especially later, Subaltern Studies became apparent. He was at his sharpest where its conception of 'otherness' tended towards the identification of 'India' with an exclusive, upper-caste version of Hindu culture. While no doubt well-meant, such representations of the 'true' Indian Other gave hostages to fortune in an age of resurgent Hindu nationalism.[21] To our cost, Raj never completed a sustained analysis of this resurgence – its character and its implications. But he was increasingly drawn towards the problems of the present and, in occasional remarks and asides, gave hints that there was a powerful analysis waiting to be drawn out. In particular, his own, highly original understanding of the nature of Indian capitalism implied new ways of viewing a contemporary situation in which the seeming 'triumph' of Indian capitalism, and the final achievement of faster rates of economic growth, has been attended by the multiplication of social and cultural conflicts. But above all, Raj felt himself committed to his city of Bombay, its multiplicity of peoples, its plurality of cultures. The destruction wrought on its society by the onset of exclusivist ideologies of the Hindu nation was palpable, and the cause of the worst nightmares of his later years.[22]

Raj left no 'school' behind him – nor would have wanted to. His own intellect resisted conformity of any kind and his most memorable seminar performances came, usually, when he began to argue with himself. He

[21] 'Historians and the Nation'.
[22] 'Religion and Nationalism in India' and 'Bombay's Perennial Modernities'.

questioned everything, not least his own beliefs, and he held that the function of history was more to probe, investigate and revise than to conclude. But he did leave behind a number of colleagues and former students deeply affected by contact with his intellect, whose quality at times was dazzling, and inspired to carry on his mission wherever exactly it might lead. It is hoped that these essays, notes and fragments, left in the proverbial 'bottom-drawer' of his desk, will continue that mission, and inspiration.

Bibliography of the published works of Rajnarayan Chandavarkar

BOOKS

The Origins of Industrial Capitalism in India: Business Strategies and the Working Classes in Bombay, 1900–1940. Cambridge University Press, 1994.
Imperial Power and Popular Politics: Class, Resistance and the State in India, 1850–1950. Cambridge University Press, 1998.

CHAPTERS IN EDITED BOOKS

'"Strangers in the Land": India and the British since the Late Nineteenth Century', in C. A. Bayly (ed.), *The Raj: India and the British, 1600–1947.* London: National Portrait Gallery, 1990.
'Workers' Resistance and the Rationalization of Work in Bombay between the Wars', in D. Haynes and G. Prakash (eds.), *Contesting Power: Resistance and Everyday Social Relations in South Asia.* Oxford University Press and University of California Press, 1991.
'Plague Panic and Epidemic Politics in India, 1896–1914', in T. Ranger and P. Slack (eds.), *Epidemics and Ideas: Essays on the Historical Perceptions of Pestilence.* Cambridge University Press: Past and Present, 1992.
'Nationalism, Ethnicity and the Working Classes in India, 1870–1947', in Stefan Berger and Angel Smith (eds.), *Nationalism, Labour, and Ethnicity, 1870–1939.* Manchester University Press, 1999, pp. 242–69.
'Questions of Class: The General Strikes in Bombay, 1928–29', in Jonathan P. Parry, Jan Breman and Karin Kapadia (eds.), *The Worlds of Indian Industrial Labour.* New Delhi and London: Sage Publications, 1999, pp. 205–37. Published simultaneously in *Contributions to Indian Sociology*, 33, 1 and 2, 1999.
'"The Making of the Working Class": E. P. Thompson and Indian History', in V. Chaturvedi (ed.), *Mapping Subaltern Studies and the Postcolonial.* London: Verso, 2000, pp. 50–71. (Reprint of previously published article.)
'Imperialism and the European Empires', in J. Jackson (ed.), *The Short Oxford History of Europe, 1900–1945.* Oxford University Press, 2002.
'From Neighbourhood to Nation: The Rise and Fall of the Left in Bombay's Girangaon in the Twentieth Century', in Neera Adarkar and Meena Menon, *One Hundred Years, One Hundred Voices: The Millworkers of Girangaon: An Oral History.* Calcutta: Seagull, 2004.

ARTICLES IN JOURNALS

'Workers' Politics and the Mill Districts of Bombay between the Wars', *Modern Asian Studies*, special issue, 15, 3 (July 1981), 603–47. Also published in H. Alavi and J. Harriss (eds.), *The Sociology of Development in South Asia: Selected Readings* (London: Macmillan, 1989) and in translation in *Purusartha*, special issue (Paris, 1992).

'Industrialization in India: Conventional Approaches and Alternative Perspectives', *Modern Asian Studies*, special issue, 19, 3 (July 1985), 623–67. Also published in P. O'Brien (ed.), *Industrialization: Critical Perspectives* (London: Routledge, 1998) and in translation in R. Lardinois (ed.), *L'Inde: études de sciences sociales et anthropologie* (Paris, 1989).

'From Communism to Social Democracy: The Rise and Resilience of Communist Parties in India, 1920–1995', *Science and Society*, 61, 1 (1997), 99–106.

'"The Making of the Working Class": E. P. Thompson and Indian History', *History Workshop Journal*, 43 (Spring 1997), 177–96.

'Questions of Class: The General Strikes in Bombay, 1928–29', special issue of *Contributions to Indian Sociology*, 33, 1 and 2 (1999), 205–37.

'Customs of Governance: Colonialism and Democracy in Twentieth Century India', *Modern Asian Studies*, 41, 3 (2007).

REVIEW ARTICLES

'Midnight's Children Come to Power', *London Review of Books* (lead article), 30 March 1989.

'India for the English', *London Review of Books* (5 March 1990); reprinted in *The Times of India Review of Books*, 1, 1 (August/September 1990).

OTHER OUTPUT

'Tipoo's Tiger', film for the Victoria and Albert Museum, Nehru Gallery of Indian Art, 1990.

'Political Ties that Heal and Bind', *The Guardian*, 22 May 1991.

Index